A Celebration of Spirit & Art

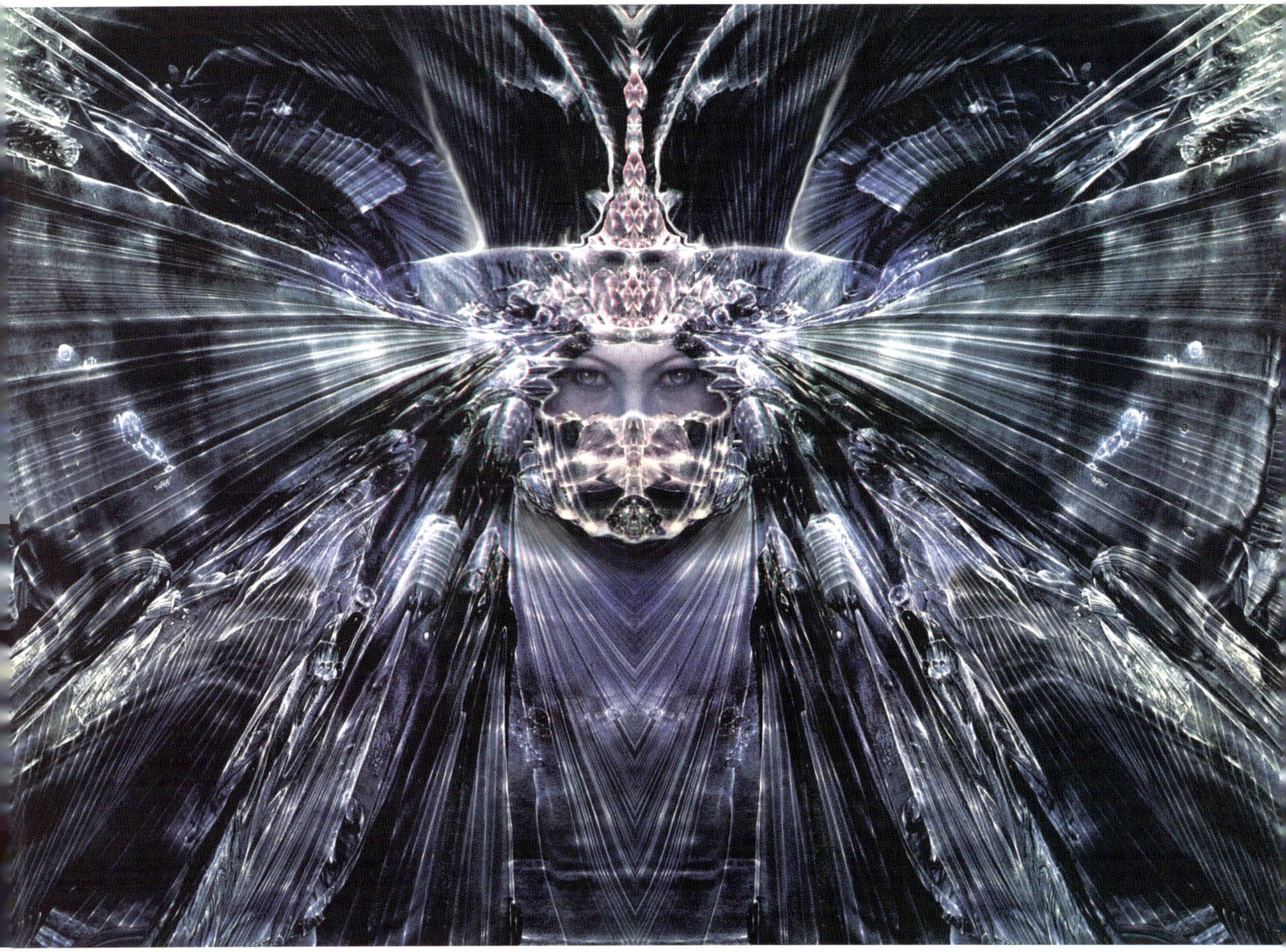

"Scheherazade," 40" x 20" oil on canvas by Robert Venosa, 1988

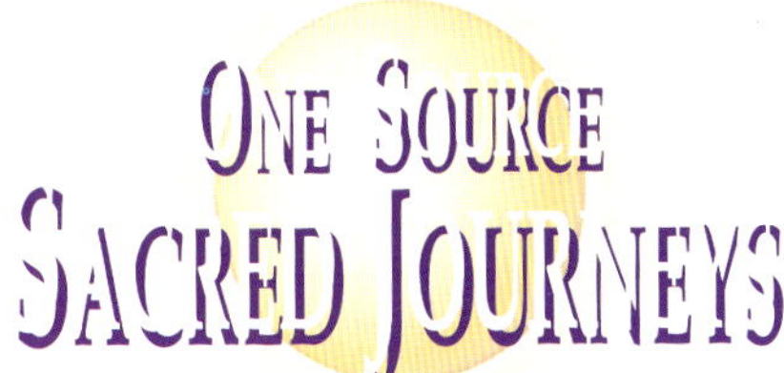

Markowitz Publishing, Paia, Hawaii

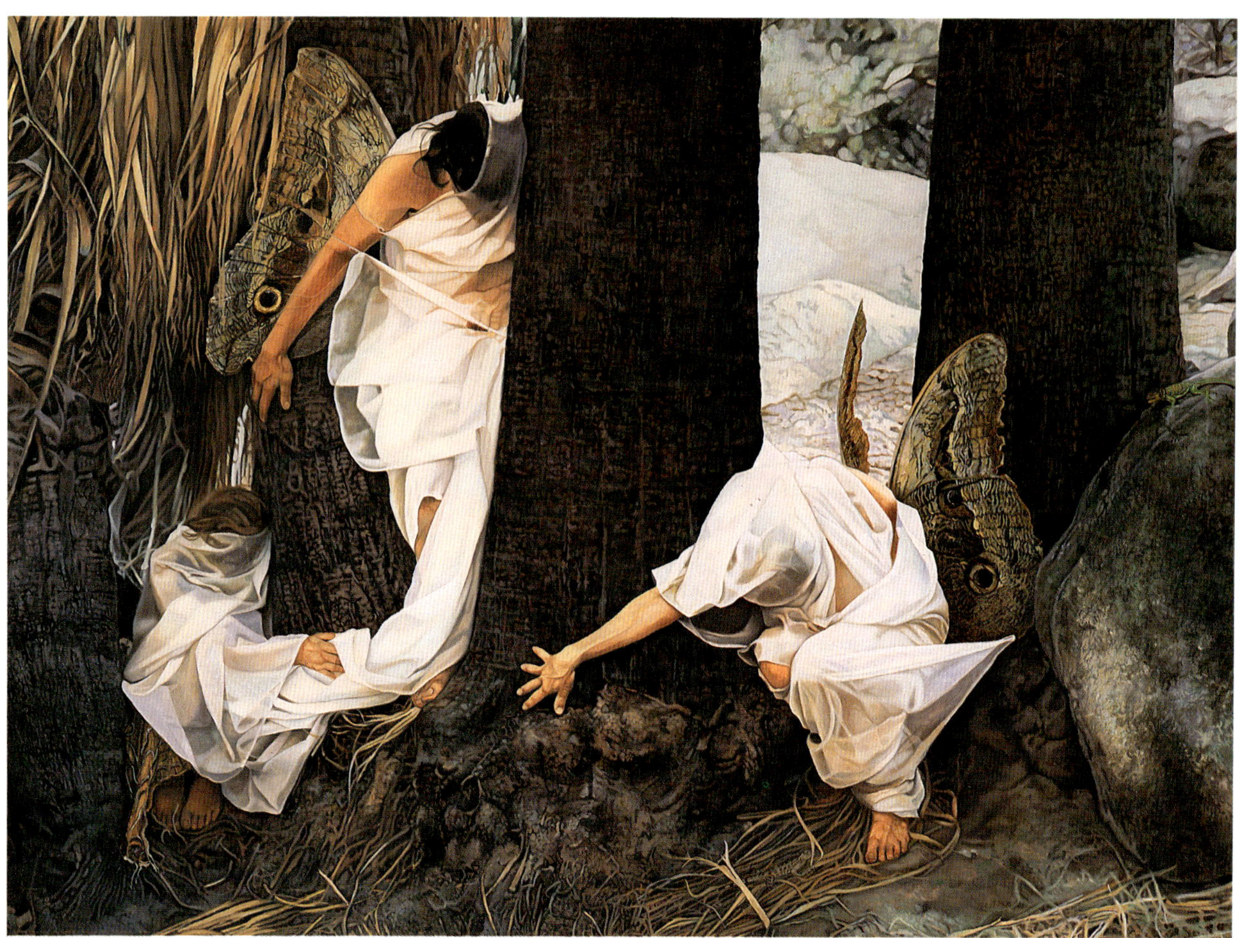

"Cocoons," 60" x 90" oil on canvas by Mariann Loveland, 1976

ONE SOURCE — SACRED JOURNEYS

Published by Markowitz Publishing, P.O. Box 1250, Paia, HI 96779.
Phone: 808 579-9737 Fax: 808 579-9387

Library of Congress Catalog Number 96-79541

ISBN 0-9655890-1-3

Printed in Hong Kong

First Edition

TABLE OF CONTENTS

PREFACE
By Ramon Kubicek Page 5

FORWARD

CONTEMPLATING THE ETERNAL IMAGE
By Ernst Fuchs Page 8

ART AND SPIRIT
A Holistic Worldview
by Mary Carroll Nelson Page 12

THE KISS OF THE MUSE
Artistic Inspiration and Transformation
by Philip M. Rubinov-Jacobson Page 14

THE NEW SPIRITUAL ART
Balancing the Inner World and Outer World of Expression
by K. Martin-Kuri Page 18

CONTRIBUTING ARTISTS

MARIANN LOVELAND Page 20

NANCY AZARA Page 22

BETH AMES SWARTZ Page 24

ROBERT VENOSA Page 26

TONY WALHOLM Page 28

PHILIP M. RUBINOV-JACOBSON Page 34

MARILYN SUNDERMAN Page 36

DEBORAH KOFF-CHAPIN Page 38

SANDRA REAMER Page 42

EL DIECKVOß Page 44

CHRISTIE FERTAL Page 46

K. MARTIN-KURI Page 48

CAROL AUST Page 50

KONSTANTIN KRILLOVICH IVANOV Page 51

TIM TIMMERMAN Page 52

MARK FREDRICKS Page 53

BENTZION Page 54

KAREN CHASTAIN-HAUGHEY Page 56

JEANNE PROM Page 58

JONATHAN WILTSHIRE Page 60

MELANIE MAUNG Page 62

LYNN ROTHAN Page 64

ANN ROTHAN Page 66

ALI MINER Page 68

LAURA WALKER Page 70

THIERRY CHATELAIN Page 72

BEN HOWATT Page 74

R. SUNDHARA BARRABLE Page 75

C BANGS Page 76

MARTINA HOFFMANN Page 77

MARILYN MARKOWITZ Page 78

KATHLEEN O'BRIEN Page 79

MARY CARROLL NELSON Page 80

MARCIA DIANE Page 81

JEAN FEAK FAHEY Page 82

JUDY HALL Page 84

MARY SAINT-MARIE/SHEOEKAH Page 85

CATHERINE WHITE-SWAN Page 86

BENNY H.V. ANDERSSON Page 87

ARTHUR DOUËT Page 88

GARY MARKOWITZ Page 90

LISA GORDON Page 92

OLGA SPIEGEL Page 94

INDEX

ARTISTS' BIOGRAPHIES & DIRECTORY Page 98

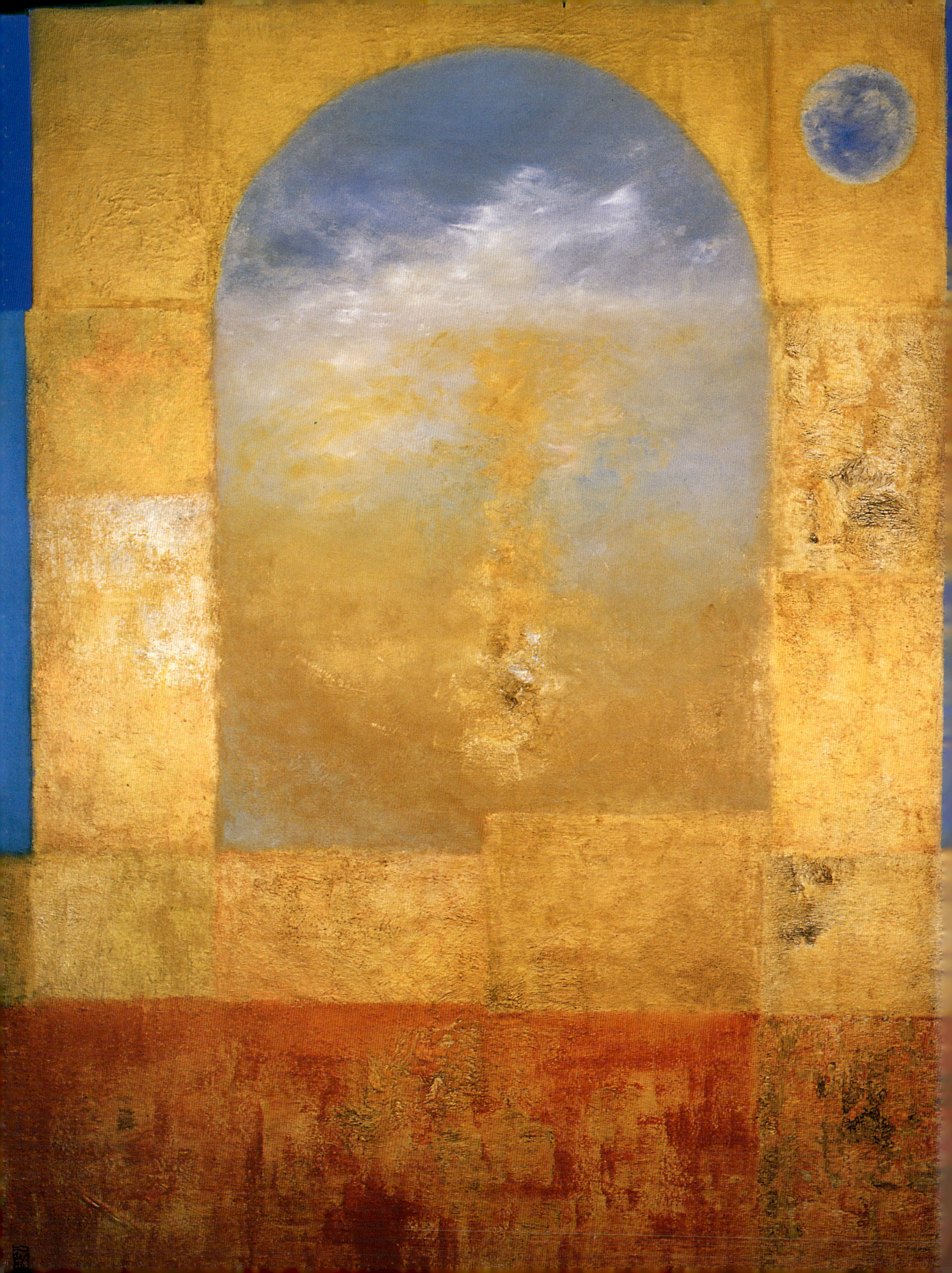

RAMON KUBICEK

PREFACE

In mainstream art, spirituality has had a troubled reputation. While everyone concedes the intuitive and emotional nature of art, anything further is a source of argument. Today mainstream art prefers to see spirituality as nothing more than a cultural conceit or a historical tendency toward romantic or religious themes. Yet a significant number of artists have resisted materialistic stereotyping and talk about their work as if it were a source of spiritual vision, wisdom, and healing.

The artists collected here represent a variety of styles and backgrounds, yet each artist's statement speaks of dedication to spirit, beauty, and revelation in similar ways. This is not a phenomenon in a void; aside from widespread cultural changes that are making it easier to see a unification of knowledge in the sciences and humanities closer to a spiritual interpretation of the universe, we have an art historical tradition of spiritually based work. In the twentieth century, such European artists as Beuys, Brancusi, Chagall, Kandinsky, Klee, Kupka, Malevich, Marc, Mondrian, Rouault, among others, worked with spiritual influence as part of their artistic approach. The same can be said of North American artists such as Dove, Graves, Lawren Harris, Hartley, O'Keeffe, Rothko, Tobey. The large 1986 L.A.C.M. exhibition, "The Spiritual in Art: Abstract Art 1890-1985," demonstrated how widespread has been artists' interest not only in spiritual systems like Zen, Yoga, and Shamanism but also in occult and mythic symbols.

The example of earlier twentieth century artists also shows that spiritual influence in art appears in the full range of possibilities from abstraction to full figuration. One stream of influence has been identified with a landscape tradition that responds to Nature as the manifestation of divine creative force, and this tradition includes the representational work of such artists as Albert Ryder as well as the more abstract work of Lawren Harris and the pure color fields of Mark Rothko. Another source of influences is the theosophical and metaphysical imagery emerging from the work of Kandinsky and Mondrian. Their work encouraged artists to borrow images from other cultures and to experiment with color and sound to create a psychophysical aesthetic which might inspire viewers more easily.

Both these traditions are present here, but by far the biggest influence for most of these artists seems to have been surrealism. Surrealism, created by the poet Andre Breton in 1924 and mainly associated with such artists as Dali, Ernst, Magritte, Tanguy, was influenced by Freud and by such practices as automatic writing and drawing. The world of dream was its preferred territory with the unexpected, the coincidental, and the bizarre the featured appearances. For all its strangeness and often compelling power, surrealism has been mainly agnostic and materialistic in its concerns, staying away from any subject of a spiritual nature. However, a small tradition of "veristic surrealism," interested in visionary subjects, has continued to the present day. Its principal exponent in the world may be Ernst Fuchs and his Vienna school of Fantastic Realism. With his technical facility, Fuchs has found commercial success, although as he suggests in his essay, not always critical success. Expert in Renaissance painting techniques, Fuchs has created work that is mainly illustrative and otherworldly. On occasion, his work seems close in spirit to the world of the decadents and symbolists at the turn of the century; elements of Pre-Raphaelite work and of an earlier Viennese generation of Klimt and his circle also appear at times. His work has attracted young painters from around the world to study with him, and some of his former students are represented here.

The subject matter alone might identify Fuchs and the other artists here as visionaries. Moving through

Opposite page: "Portal," 72" x 48" oil on canvas by Tony Walholm

the images we see mythic figures, angelic forms, creatures from some astral plane, geometric symbols of sublime or talismanic power. However, subject matter alone cannot create an experience. What is consistently true about the treatment in these works is that dream, with all its associations, is the significant impression. "Dream-like" or "eerie" settings are among the unfortunate cliches of some amateur work. What distinguishes this work, aside from technical considerations, is the willingness to surrender everyday logical constraints and familiar routines in order to embrace the unknown and the potentially ridiculous. Just as a true traveler does not know what he or she will find until it is found, in the authentic visionary work the mental voyage and the stretch of spirit merge with the creative process for the sake of discovery. But not only aesthetic discovery, for such is the basis of all art; here the experience is a discovery, configured through art, about oneself or about the world of spirit.

How can such an experience avoid being just narcissism or an expression of a mysticism so private no one can relate to it? The premises on which a shared artistic experience rest here are of two kinds. The first comes from personal conviction and preference. I see numerous exhibitions every year, and many of them show wit, technical accomplishment, and socially relevant themes. Some of these artists are proud of the fact they believe in nothing, and their work becomes a clever exercise of gamesmanship. Such, then, is their preference. Yet corresponding to our culture of gratuitous thrills and cynicism, we also have a culture dependent on the convictions of people who work for others and for change. Their preference is for belief in values beyond consumption and materialism. A spiritual art needs a corresponding belief in humanity and transcendence. The second premise is based on the fact that everyone dreams. Spiritual traditions everywhere and depth psychologists like Jung have asserted that dreams are not limited to a personal unconscious. The collective unconscious is the repository of humanity's myths, legends, and sacred symbols. Our dreams can touch this universal source and lead to experiences of delight, longing, and insight. Certainly, it is no secret that some use dreams as research and healing, following the ancient example of the Asklepian tradition in Egypt and Greece, where temples of "incubation" were sites of healing dreams. Today, workshops are given in the use of dreams for self-realization or in "lucid" dreaming, meant to develop deeper forms of awareness. Visionary artists, through their receptivity and ability to give form to intuitions, create art that reawakens a memory of illumination. Even if only for a moment, we are those transcendent beings it is our ultimate destiny to become.

Joseph Campbell called for the development of a planetary mythology to replace what he saw as the worn-out remnants of the major religions trying to be relevant in a rapidly changing world. Such a mythology cannot be a deliberate creation, but comes about as the consequence of all the creative, social and spiritual efforts of a society. Artists have a special place in such an enterprise, for they can be, as Campbell saw them, the contemporary shamans who nurture our visions. Such vision-building and keeping is at the moment still a neglected activity, because it is seen by too many, even in the art world, as frivolous or deluded. We have only to see the denigration of inspiration as a concept to be convinced of how much reclamation work we all have to do if we want vision. Inspiration is today a synonym for anything that gets us going creatively; in the mainstream art world, inspiration is seen as a nostalgic reflex trying to replace what most see is just a culturally conditioned process. The original meaning of the word refers to breath and spirit. In the spiritual view, we become enlivened through the act of breathing because what we breathe in is more than a composition of gases. All human beings, living and dead, share the same air, and so, in some mysterious fashion we become linked through the physical and mental process of digesting air and impressions to everyone who has ever walked the earth. We become linked to all the extraordinary moments of creation as well as to the moments of terrible suffering. This is not a fanciful metaphor but a connection with a basis in biological fact. The shaman and the visionary artist are the ones who remember such connections and also the means to achieve them.

Described in this way, the role of visionary artist seems to set an intimidatingly high standard. Most artists do not pretend to maintain any kind of superior insight. "Visionary" refers more to the expectation and goal of the artist rather than to any mode of being or realization. Artists working with spiritual intent whom I've met usually and genuinely see their artistic successes as the product of creative energy working through them rather than as the product of any virtue or talent. There is not even a specific mind-set common to all these artists, as we can see for ourselves when we look carefully at their work. The eclecticism here is proof of their individuality. But, as a preview, let us look briefly at some of these artists.

Nancy Azara is a New York sculptor who has been a leading figure in the feminist art movement as well as a healer. Her wood sculpture evokes an animistic universe, but rather than any social elements, it is the world of trees and the essence of wood that is dramatized. The sacredness of nature is the overwhelming experience. Azara's use of gold leaf and paint suggests some of the historical associations of wood, particularly in archaic cultures where the divine feminine was honored. Her "Hand Wall" connects us not only to touch, its enduring sensuousness and importance as a signifier of non-cerebral sources of knowledge and being, but also to all the cultures that have honored trees. Her "Spirit House" embodies the silence and mystery of shrines and refuges.

Ernst Fuchs' work here shows a highly detailed imagery with a rich sensuousness that might seem to belong to decadent fantasy. But the biblical imagery in "The Sign of Moses" (egg tempera and oil) and in "The Triumph of Christ" (pencil on canvas) point more to Bosch-like allegory, where exotic settings and religious symbols are used to evoke brooding mystery and the promise of revelation.

Deborah Koff-Chapin's Touch Drawings, selected from her "Soul Cards," reveal a series of faces and bodies in different stages of manifestation. The trance-like images derive their power from the process of expressive creation, which Koff-Chapin also teaches. This process is cognitive and healing as well as creative, allowing the practitioner to get in touch with personal issues and a journey of self-discovery. This process of spontaneous drawing is close to the surrealists' practice of automatic drawings and finding significant images through rubbings (frottage), but here allied to questions of emergence and personal growth.

Mary Carroll Nelson is a mixed media painter who describes herself as a layerist. Her use of different elements in a painting has led her to find other artists who work in the same way and to do research on the significance of layering. Layering is a process that recapitulates the different strata of cultural and personal history in the mind. The process of covering, uncovering, scraping and enhancing become intimately connected to the unconscious and can lead to a direct cognition. Her "Pleiadean Dimensions" (mixed media on masonite) brings together cosmic and nature imagery through the mediation of images of the divine feminine. Interestingly, this theme is being explored by a number of artists sensitive to the need for a new paradigm of cooperation and interconnectedness.

At first glance, Sandra Reamer's paintings "Cavern of the Warrior's Heart" (oil) and "Chthonic Spirits" (egg tempera and oil) are fairly typical but well done explorations of allover abstraction. Studied more closely, the different kinds of gesture and mark-making, from drip to a veritable alphabet of strokes, reveal her interests to be in a process of creation that is dynamically self-referential, visceral and synesthetic. The values that emerge are related to passion, struggle, and courage.

Philip Rubinov-Jacobson, a former student of Ernst Fuchs, brings the same technical mastery to his subjects as his mentor. His interest is in tapping the forces of transcendent spirit through creative expression. His imagery ranges from figurative studies (his muse series) to abstract explorations of inner worlds. His series on biblical prophets is here represented by "Aaron's Heart" (mixed media), a small piece whose intimacy fits its subject.

Beth Ames Swartz has been creating transformatlve art shown nationally for the last 30 years. Her recent "A Story for the Eleventh Hour" is a series symbolically depicting the terrible urgency of our combined ecological and social deterioration as well as showing our possible salvation through spiritual understanding, compassion, and loving practice. Works like "Shantih, Shantih, Shantih" (mixed media) and "The Return..." (mixed media) show her directness in presenting compelling images as well as the subtle and layered use of materials with multiple associations to personal and cultural history.

Robert Venosa's technically exact work is represented here by "Astral Circus" (oil on canvas). Its exhaustive detail with its etheric imagery, pulls the eye inward. The work recalls many of the techniques of such artists as Dali (for example, his "paranoic critical method"), allowing Venosa to create works that combine familiarity and strangeness. Ultimately, his work becomes an exploration of the inventive and combinatory powers of imagination itself.

Tony Walholm's abstract work shows a loving exploration of the surfaces and physical nuances of the created world. The images here are free of the forces of disharmony and dissolution, but rather show moments of beauty available to the willing eye. His "Vessel of the Three Realms" (oil on canvas) and "Satori Dances" (oil on canvas) invite us to merge with a subtly defined image whose real source of power is inward in the painting and in ourselves.

The range of these artists shows that art and spirituality as a co-evolving phenomenon in America is vital and growing. But unless such art gets a chance to be shown collectively, support will not emerge. For this reason alone, the publisher and curator of this collection, artist Gary Markowitz, should be commended for his vision and dedication in putting together this volume.

Ramon Kubicek has published essays on art as well as fiction and poetry. He has recently completed "Returning to the Source: Recent Transformative Art in North America" and "Art and Healing; A Practical Guide." Kubicek lives in Vancouver and teaches at the Emily Carr Institute of Art.

ERNST FUCHS

CONTEMPLATING THE ETERNAL IMAGE

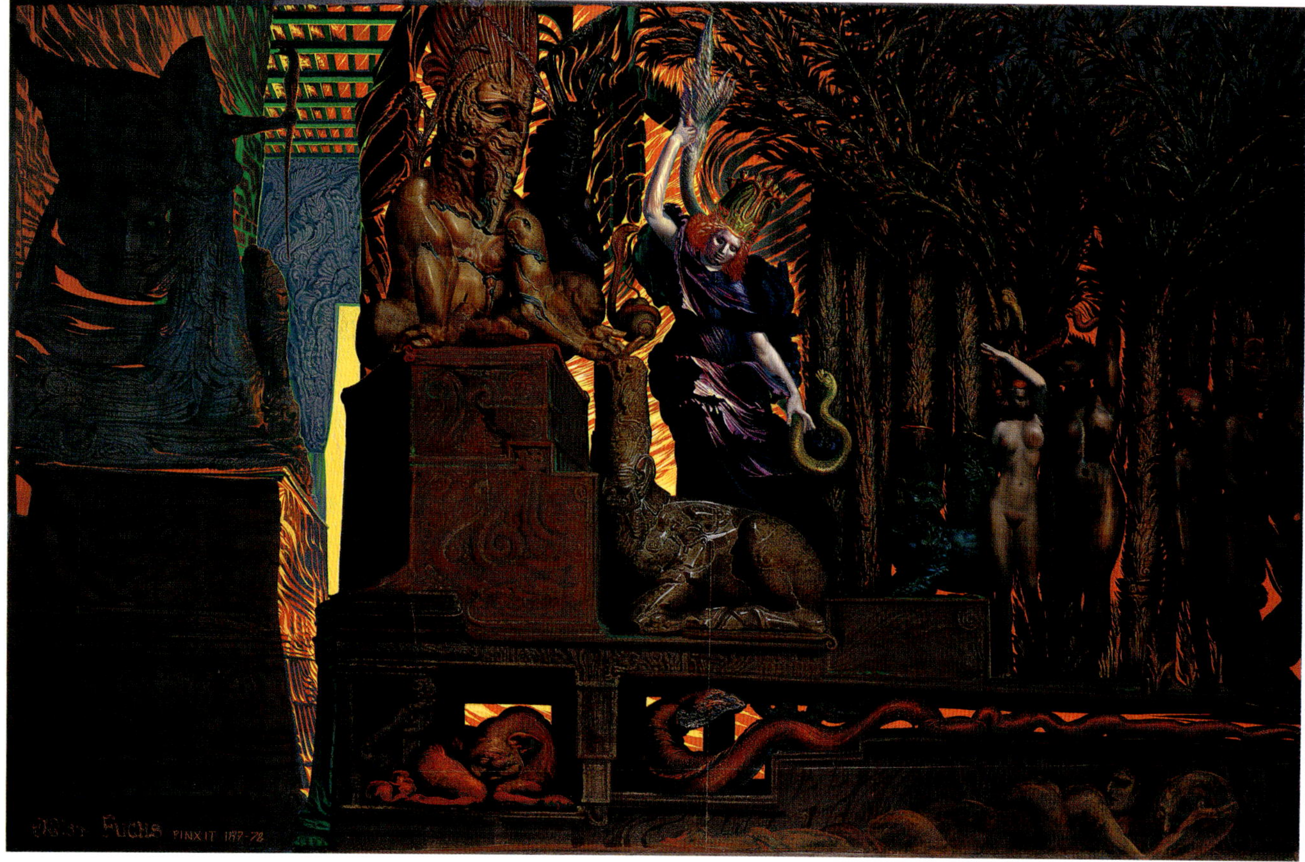

"Im Zeighen Des Moses — The Sign of Moses," 155cm x 195cm egg tempera and oil by Ernst Fuchs, circa 1973

Images are the language of the spirit, the messages from Heaven, manifesting themselves as they did in the tongues of the prophets. One should not argue that art has nothing in common with prophecy since, after all, the prophecy of the ancient people and art were identical. Prophecy expressed itself through the sisters, music and poetry, serving as forms of revelation. Tradition is the handing down of art. Although the word has been devalued today, this word "tradition" is the name for the fruitful root which turns art into a living chain connecting all people, from the first to the last. Tradition is another form of history, a history which was never written because it needs no writer. It is the metamorphosis of the art work in general and gives insight into the evolving spirit of humankind. In a certain sense, tradition can also be conceived of as value consciousness as it has manifested itself through the lives of all peoples, cultures and the eternal images they have created.

CONTINUED ON PAGE 10

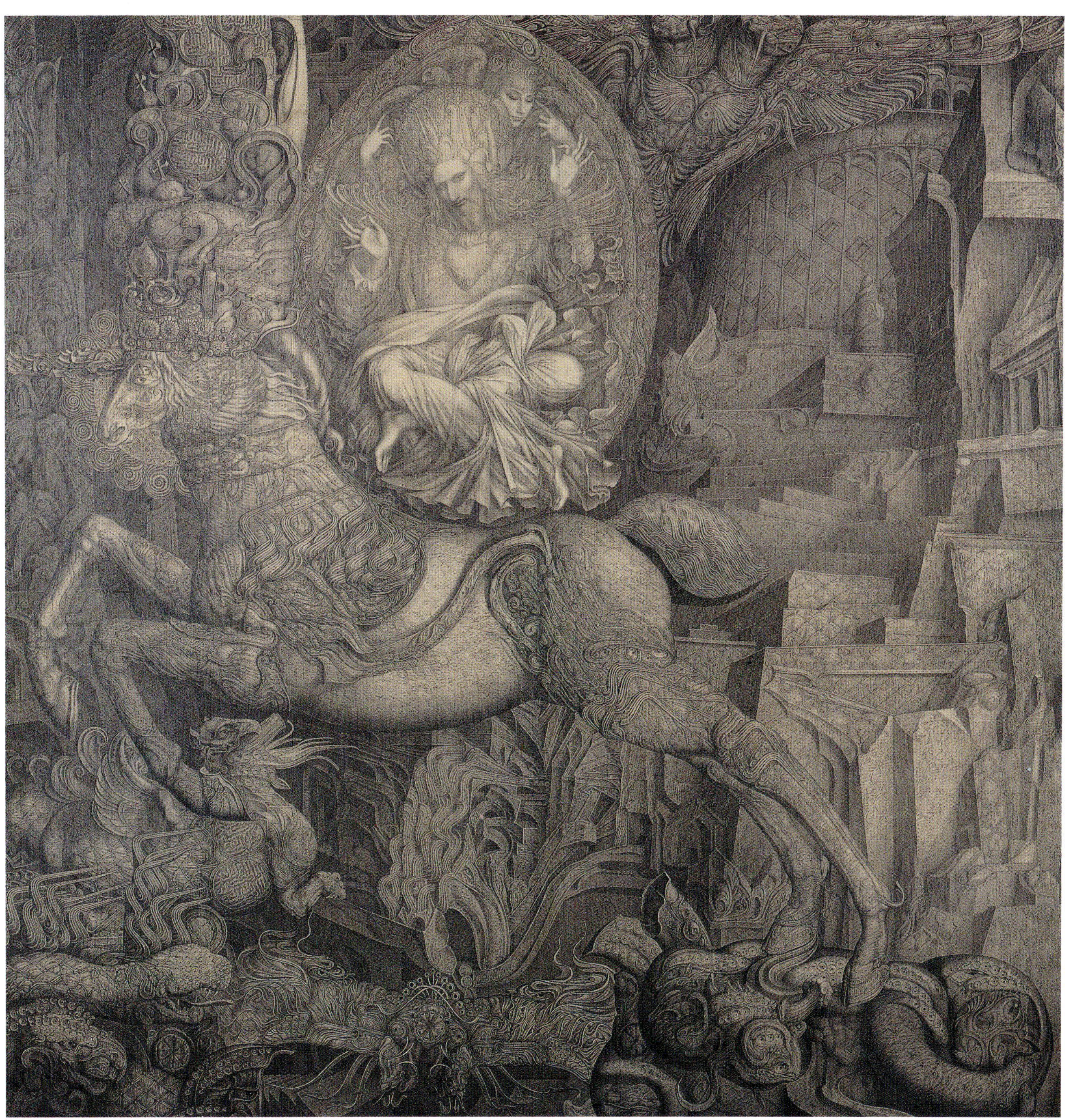

"Der Triumph Christi — The Triumph of Christ," 200cm x 200cm pencil on canvas by Ernst Fuchs, 1965

"ONE MIGHT SAY THAT THE SOUL PAINTS ONLY
WHAT THE DREAMER DREAMS."
— *ERNST FUCHS*

CONTEMPLATING THE ETERNAL IMAGE...

Images alone enable us to grasp the overabundance of the incomprehensible. By their means, that which cannot be articulated can be revealed. Language is itself a work of art; who can ever encompass it in all its possibilities? What an infinite variety of things gets itself started within the constellations of the spoken word, and yet not everything has been said or defined. As in the Talmud, commentary follows upon commentary, words upon words. In contrast, the image is always a definition and words cannot add to it or take away from it. They are at best a kind of key ring for keys that must be already in one's possession. How does one find those keys without resort to language, to logic? I call it contemplation. It gains access to meaning by intuition, and whoever is capable of dreaming with his or her eyes on an image can come close to its meaning.

Art is nearness to God, received without effort. This is the concise meaning and basis of a theology of art which is age old and has maintained again and again that jubilation erupts when God is near. Through that jubilation, the artist's nearness to God was brought through creative service without sweat or torment. Thus it springs, praise the poets of antiquity, effortlessly from the artist as a consistently sent success — "like Athena from the head of Zeus."

We must learn to understand the artist's continuous striving for "heaven" by first endeavoring to forget what an "enlightened" epoch with little insight has produced in terms of lame commentaries concerning the history and the myths of antiquity. If we succeed in doing so, then the coagulating wings of Icarus, the grasp of Helios itself, the prototypical existence of the artist, is before our eyes again as the creative flying power of the human mind which seizes all means and reaches all heights. Apollo, Dionysus, and all who — formed in myths, stone, and bronze — have reached our time, appear to me as truthful portraits of those great artists, those explorers of the ever-lasting super-human life. Their lives seem human in their appearance and yet their whole being, whether we consider their goodness, their wisdom, their fury or their joy (their being only an imme-

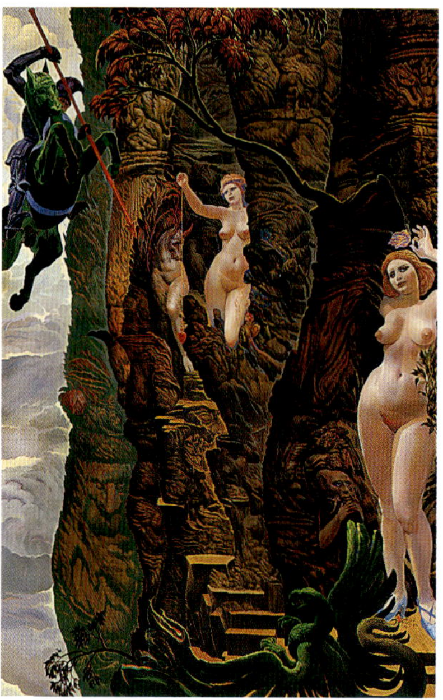

"Die Jagd Nach Dem Goldenen Herzen — Hunting for the Golden Heart," 3m20cm x 2m tempera and oil on canvas glued on board by Ernst Fuchs,

diate projection screen for our own, small being) is a kind of divine being pulsating with infinite creative thoughts and acts.

To create art is mythical activity, cultic action, even if the intellect comprehends nothing of it. This activity leads to an intuitive perception, even revelation. Through contemplating the image I realized that my concern with prophecy and myth from the beginning was highly relevant to the actualities of the day. In myths I never saw the past as such, but only as the source of the Now. What is religion, in the truest sense, if not the relationship of the now to its beginnings? Whatever was accomplished earlier in the artistic spaces of history before now, becomes the realm of what is known in psychology as the unconscious; it is the testimony of those who were here before us which is passed on and through us and to which we add.

The work of art has its source in the desire to create a means of transcending time, entering eternity. Because I have always been tormented by the fear of my end, of death, death may often be found in my paintings "in person." Again and again "Mr. Bones" turns up, wearing every kind of mask, and so he becomes a magus, a conjurer of life, capable of revealing even in the pit of decay and dissolution the ferment and transformation of new being. My work has broadened over the years and entered ever more deeply the realm of hermetic motifs -— an art made, in Oscar Wilde's sense, purely of art, in no way referring openly to the present and dedicated exclusively to the contemplation of the world of images in the Platonic sense. Its adherents are to be found only in the obscure groups of outsiders — most of them, like myself, not "contemporaries" in the banal, quotidian sense. Scattered through many countries they are members, as I understand it, of a secret lodge; the Masonic Order of Visionaries. Generation follows generation, as life is succeeded by death, death by life. And each passes on to the next the Great Question — the hope for salvation out of this finitude.

If art in our time enjoyed the respect that is its due and that it was accorded quite as a matter of course in previous epochs, we would not have quite so much trouble in justifying the meaning of existence as we have. As it is, however, people wilt away miserably like plants deprived of light, creatures without nourishment because they no longer realize that art resembles the original manna in the desert. Art alone enables everyone, even those who do not believe, to taste of the true values of life and to be reminded of the original template in which we all have our share of immortality. Art is the nourishment of the complete human being; it is the condition of our existence, the medium in which our lives are suspended, and since art knows no exhaustion, it is the medium of an eternal life, an inexhaustible life. For it is in art that the creative force expresses its inexhaustibility.

What moves me in a work of art is never really the work of human hands but that intimation of the best that is yet to come, of which the Creator allows us a glimpse now and then, using the artist as an intermediary. So it is not ordinary pictures that enter the realm of the timeless, but a special authenticity of imagery born of the visionary experience. Those artists who gain access to visionary states captivate us through their eternal imagery to fall under a spell of that reality. Yet, this highly individual phenomenon of visionary perception would have to remain a secret of the one graced with that special gift. Sharing it with those who have had no direct experience of it in a language, a vocabulary and syntax of imagery makes it comprehensible to all. The greatest of these artists are masters of a timeless, alchemistic art — stemming from traditions going back thousands of years and climbing the steepest summits of a restless present. They sense a reality more substantive than the "truth," and so draw us under the spell of the eternal image revealing some visitation or dream.

The past and the future are visions that the creative spirit, in its awareness of eternity, blend into the present. Thus the artist, in contemplation, creates both history and eternity. I maintain that the concepts of time and eternity are the stuff of poetry and that biography is a musical arrangement of the uproar made by our blood pulsating behind the listening walls of our eardrums. The certainty that what is past will reappear in the future gives the present its depth, sets it to work and makes it fruitful. It is precisely here that we find an essential element of creativity; the rediscovery of forgotten life. It is not too unusual for a vision of the future to coincide with the recognition that something believed dead or forever lost to us is very much alive because it can enter our awareness again. The work of art is simply a monument to the temporal within eternity. Art alone can confer and transmit to other ages an enduring validity of what is trapped in its own era. Only the spirit of the artist can capture what is ephemeral and ineffable, otherwise it is doomed to be forever lost to us.

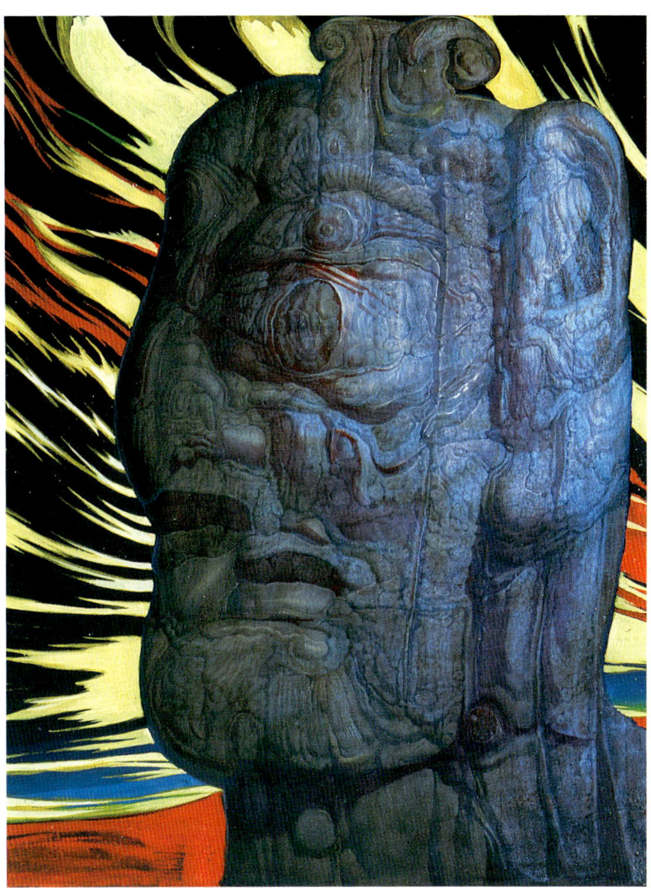

"Cherub Swischen Tag Und Nacht — Cherub Between Night and Day," 60cm x 74cm tempera and oil on canvas by Ernst Fuchs, 1974

Born in Vienna, Ernst Fuchs is a central figure in what has come to be known as the Viennese School of Fantastic Realism. From the beginning, his art has followed a surrealistic vein, and one of his most important mentors has been Salvador Dali. He is receiving widespread critical acclaim and has produced art as a painter, sculptor, printmaker, jeweler, architect, composer, singer, writer and poet. He lives in Vienna where he is busy attending to the establishment of a museum at his villa which will house works of his and other fantastic artists.

Perhaps Fuchs can best be described as a visionary — one who in Marhel Brion's words (a Member of the Academia Francaise) "sees beneath the surface of things; no obstacle can block the path of his perception; he is the discoverer of dizzying crystalline heights, the chronicler of unknown worlds. He is capable of conjuring treacherous Hell itself into submission, of keeping the supernatural and the natural in equipoise; like Moses he casts himself down at the threshold of Mystery, trembling indeed, yet sure of himself as seer and master."

MARY CARROLL NELSON

ART AND SPIRIT
A Holistic World View

We live at the end of a chaotic century, the last in the millennium. Buddhists and Hindus call this the Age of Kali, the time of destruction, but this is also a time of cleansing, when ideas that no longer fit the discoveries we have made are being swept away while new thoughts surge into consciousness. In art history, this is the most fertile period of creativity the world has ever known.

Art conventions lasted for centuries on end in the ancient Egyptian, Chinese and Mayan empires, effectively constraining all personal expression. By contrast, twentieth-century art can be documented by continuous changes of style as artists have ingested and responded to the major ideas circulating the planet.

Teilhard de Chardin posited a sphere of thought encircling the earth that he called the noosphere, which he likened to the geosphere, biosphere, and atmosphere. The noosphere he pictured for us is in motion, carrying thoughts from mind to mind like a wind of idea.

Through developments in communication, we are almost instantly aware of huge amounts of information compared with our forebears, even those who preceded us by only a century or two. The energy in the noosphere is rapidly accelerating.

Despite the seeming chaos brought about by retrograde impulses of fear-driven separation and hostility, another far more benign impulse is animating the noosphere — and this is the holistic movement. Holism is defined by John Briggs as "a harmony in which everything affects everything else."

Holistic and holism share the same Middle English root word, hal, as health, whole, hale and heal. It refers to being all of one unit, complete. In its essence, holism is about Oneness. It is a spiritual concept.

In our time, the spirit of holism is breaking down barriers between genders, ages, races, nations and political factions. Outbursts of cooperation and negotiation in place of confrontation, shared ideals, surmounting differences and instigations mark the progress of the holistic worldview that is ameliorating antagonisms.

Holism is having a deep effect on certain artists. Already accustomed to creating harmonies from disparate elements to form a work of art, some artists' antennae are picking up thoughts from the richly nourishing noosphere ahead of the rest. They are functioning as the scouts of society by expressing a holistic worldview with any means at their disposal.

In my work as artist, observer and writer in the mid-1970s, I became conscious of a postmodern, discernable movement that I termed Layering.

Layering is not a style. It is an approach to art based on an intention to express a holistic worldview. Such a worldview is the natural outcome of unifying ideas that have permeated the consciousness of literate people in this century. Layerists make similar references to Carl C. Jung's theory that a "collective unconscious" unites our minds at a subtle level. In *The Structure and Dynamics of the Psyche,* Jung pictured the human mind as stratified and implied that an archaeological exploration of the self will yield primordial archetypes. Einstein's theory of relativity and the theories of quantum physicists suggest that the essence of the universe can be expressed as energy. A sense of the universe as a dynamic related entity is widely shared among artists who practice layering.

Layerists, working independently, are attempting to symbolize multiple references to geology, archaeology, mythology, psychology, cosmology and eschatology. Layering is a generic term for creative processes in which each application of material maintains its integrity as a layer and all affect the final surface. The whole is far greater than the sum of the parts in a layered work of art. The layering process often plays a symbolic role in the artist's mind as a metaphor or

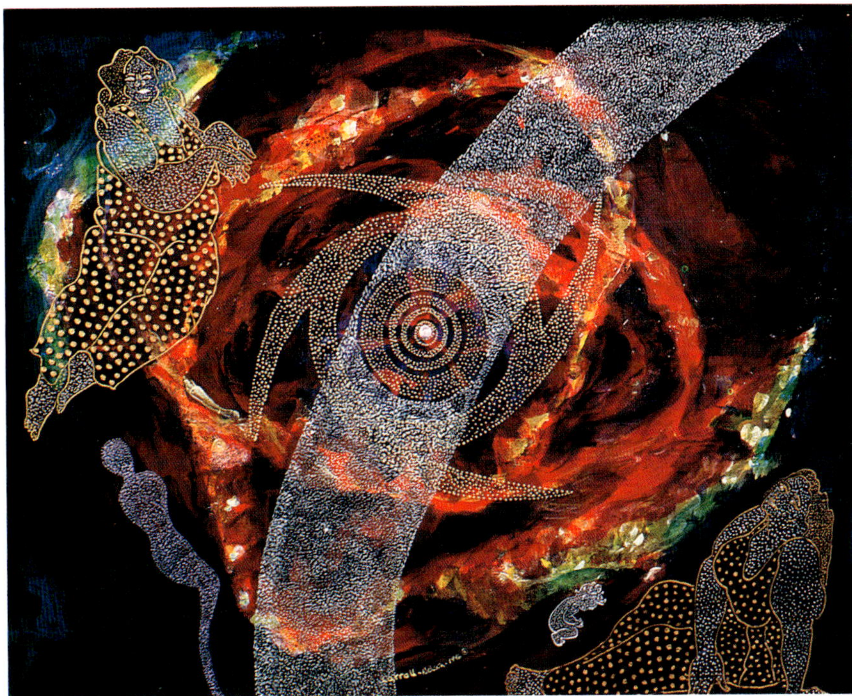

"The Seventh Transit," 16" x 20" mixed media by Mary Carroll Nelson, 1996

equivalent of a natural process, such as sedimentation, erosion, entropy, recession in space or time, simultaneity, synchronicity, or the cycle of birth, death and rebirth.

Layerists are sensitive to correspondences, analogues, and cross-references. The layers in their work are not always tangible. A layer might be merely a clue to an idea. Regardless of how it is used, the layer is an element in the work of art signifying connections made across time and space. It is the means to making a holistic work of art.

In effect, Layerists express a synchronistic perspective whereby many events or moments exist in one space, and many points in space exist in one moment of time. Layerists function as a nexus, the hub of a web linking them to all that is across time and space. When seen, especially in a group exhibition, their unifying art is recognizable as a carrier of spiritual intention.

Whether artists identify themselves as "layerists" or not, those artists today who are producing multi-referential, holistic art are creating from a similarly spiritual intention.

At the forward edge of thought in medicine, physics, and philosophy there is the repeated suggestion that we live in a multi-dimensional universe. With our five senses we are in touch with a mere fraction of all that is surrounding us. To become aware of other dimensions often requires a jolt, some event in personal experience that is deeply transforming to the psyche. The person who "wakes up" can, afterwards, sense the subtlety of this multi-dimensional universe. The artist who is awakened to multidimensionality is like a singer who has received voice training. The awakened artist senses an expanded range of vibration affecting the web of connections between self and stimuli. Once that awareness is expressed the artist takes on the role of signmaker or way-shower for the rest of society in much the same way a shaman takes on the cares of a village in order to bring about a healing.

Artists and shamanic sages share the capacity to express their new awareness. Artists do so by making a work of art, whereas shamans might develop a new method of teaching. Each of them absorbs from the multidimensional universe and responds creatively. Both are serving the same healing, holistic purpose.

A spiritual current flows through twentieth-century art. It was there in the earliest days of abstraction. While Einstein worked on his unifying theories, artists were fracturing forms and melding colors to suggest the elusive energies they felt around them.

Today's artists are the inheritors of technical discoveries in art materials and methods that give them endless means to express their spiritual awareness. Visually, contemporary work is a welter of variations in style and mediums. The kinship among spiritually inspired artists must be sensed. The spiritual intention that links their work is not as obvious as the surface appearance of abstract expressionism or surrealism, but it is there.

Those who find this volume in their hands have an opportunity to vicariously experience the consciousness-raising connections shared by this selection of spiritual artists. Through allowing the artists to show the way, the reader will discover in these images not only a healing tool but also a route to an expansion of awareness that the universe is much more inclusive and whole than we perceive in our everyday life.

The holistic message here is, "We are not alone. We are at one with all there is."

Mary Carroll Nelson is an artist, writer and founder of the Society of Layerists in Multi-Media from Albuquerque, New Mexico.

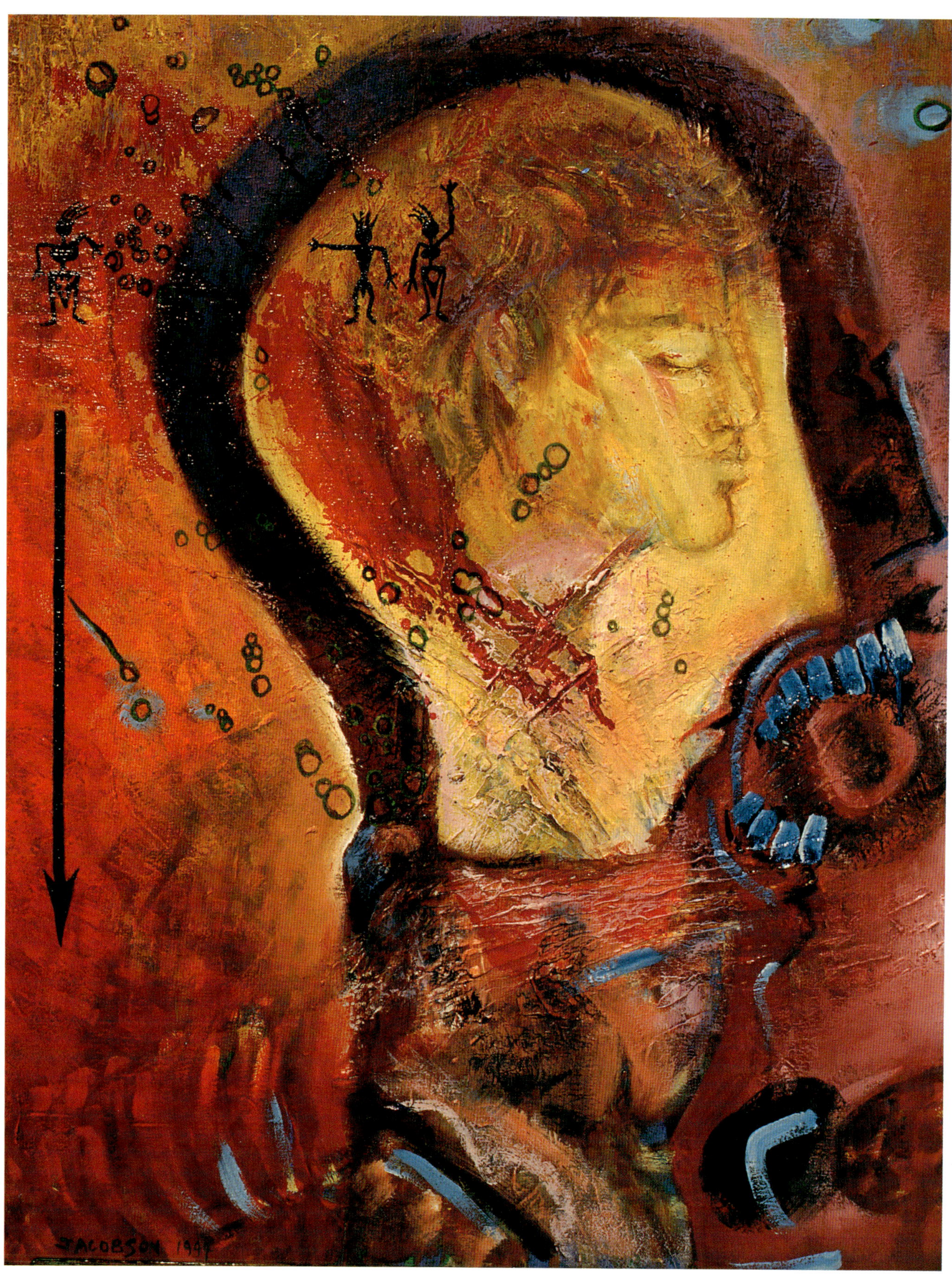
JACOBSON

PHILIP RUBINOV-JACOBSON

THE KISS OF THE MUSE
Artistic Inspiration and Transformation

Where does inspiration come from? How does it begin? Is it for everyone? Can anyone find it? Is the artist some special kind of person or is each person a special kind of artist? What is the source? When I am in a state of inspiration, something greater is moving through me. I recognize that I am the deep being called by the deeper, as well as the *call* itself. This mystery in which works of art are produced by the paradoxical combination of an act of the will and submission, is a result of bathing in the creative fire and madness of inspiration. Creativity is an ever expanding experience awaiting anyone willing to jump into the flames.

Many aspects of life may arise as sources of inspiration on many different levels: my wife and fellow artist, Sandra Reamer, is easily one of my great sources of inspiration, as well as being an intimate muse, but nature, the lover, the human form, the accidental, the spontaneous moment, the vision and ordinary objects can also contribute to the creative experience. For some artists it's an old barn on a side of a hill (Wyeth), the music of a particular composer (Kandinsky), the face of a lover (Knopff) or a color field evoking an emotional experience (Rothko). For others it may be scenes from the imagination or aesthetic heat rising off sexual currents.

Inspiration showers upon the invisible nature of man, that which is more vast than his comprehension and more measureless than his thoughts.

Inspiration gains momentum when we are brave enough to create — it is through courage that art is created. As my old mentor and friend, Ernst Fuchs, reminds us: "Art is nearness to God, it serves to unite. When inspired there is ease in creating, there is no effort." Inspiration cuts through the cultural trance suspending the prescribed goals and expectations of this conditioned cultural mindscape so that alternative realities and solutions may be perceived. What has inspired me the most is that which has been experienced beyond the imagination (or image-nation), a nation of vision without boundaries of concepts, rigid aesthetics and belief systems.

Artists relying on a particular paper, trick, technique, drug, political stand, habitual emotion, addiction or historical reference are not only limiting their potentials but replacing openness and skill with artistic crutches. Sometimes, inspiration comes only after imagination is completely and absolutely exhausted or simply ignored. When we surrender to our intuitive faculties we then open the doors to creative power.

"The Invisible Painting Between Three," 36" x 24" oil
by Philip Rubinov-Jacobson, 1994

THE KISS OF THE MUSE...

Imagination and mind must be transcended in order for inspiration to come, and yet consciousness must remain.

I have found that creative power and inspiration descends most often on the still mind. Such stillness is often achieved through a contemplative practice — meditation, painting, writing and other forms of art can be a natural spiritual process. The time just prior to sleep can also be an active creative period as is the time when we are just awakening. Between sleep and awakening the mind is surrendering. We are folding in toward the place where all things are born, where we are rejuvenated; the place where we finally relinquish all control. As we become free of the duality of mind, this and that, I and you, we begin to plug into a cosmic socket in which all sorts of information, scenes, sounds and smells are received on the journey. Art is a sacred path and intuition its gateway. Inspiration is the kundalini-shakti, the power that consumes the artist. When moved by this force, the artist is no longer a person with free will or personal aim but becomes the instrument of the creative-power. The inspired artist becomes a psychic navigator for humankind.

Like other artists, I have awakened in the middle of the night and run to the studio to paint or sculpt, draw or write in a mindless and frenzied state of ecstasy, seized upon, called. Inspiration is infinite in its form of arrival. Sometimes it comes to me as a blinding flash of light across the mind and then an overwhelming urge to paint. I get up and begin in a semi-trance like state and I have no idea what I will paint. I'm not even there. In another episode I may feel utterly electric, instinctual, even animalistic. Or, when I paint my model and muse, the poet Nancy Levin, time is transcended and all cultural encasements are dissolved as we push flesh to heaven. Other times inspiration flows like a warm and peaceful oil across my mind. I enter this place of timelessness, something else is at work. I am but a warm and peaceful pulse of love. I am the stroke of the brush. The process of both the painter and the writer involves a cloistered existence. Even the creative product of the painter does not require the artist at the exhibition, 'showing' or 'event,' nor the writer to be present during book sales. In his monk like solitude he develops an intimate relationship with Inspiration. When alone, one receives the Kiss of the Muse. Inspiration showers upon the invisible nature of man, that which is more vast than his comprehension and more measureless than his thoughts. Like a subtle essence permeating all space and all substance, inspiration is everywhere. It penetrates the innermost parts of our being. This inspirational energy is the force of transformation. Inspiration revises our self-image, from seeing ourselves as passive victims to being active agents of transformation. This is the single most important factor in changing the human condition.

Inspiration comes when you do not deny the child inside. Artists' conversations are peppered with uncanny observations that come from people who have remained in awe of their world and often have unique, central and child-like perceptions. And too, like a child, the artist is always searching, is optimistic and remains convinced that anything is possible. Children can will themselves to do anything or can surrender and be open to receive anything — artists retain this quality. The artist is only that child who did not allow or otherwise escaped the oppression on their creative individuality by various educational, economic, religious and political pressures. This inner artist child is ever waiting to be reclaimed by those who have been creatively wounded.

Facing and moving through fear is an act of courage. The arts require the courage to create and to act. The hero and the coward are both afraid. The only difference between them is that the hero acts even in a state of fear, he moves through it and the other does nothing. Each creative act is the food of intuition and leads to higher inspiration. This creative courage, evoking both audacity and self-worth at first, is followed by a dissolution of self and an immersion into the Absolute, generating an ease, flow and unity with higher forces. In yogic terms, the individual soul connects to the supreme soul. A strength evolves or is received by a higher order. One no longer feels alone in the creative act, but more of a co-creator. To look at art in terms of purpose instead of style: to ascertain where one is, how one got there, how now to proceed and to what end becomes central to the artist as mystic. Most artists spend their time making normal art, in the sense of administering to the existing paradigm. Many of them are unhappy with the situation as it exists, but fail to step out of the old mold. They do not see themselves as catalysts of change, whose ideas and judgments will actually create the future. We have no future except what we can envision, and what we envision will draw us toward itself.

So many artists are painting so many things — sacred art versus contemporary art, objective versus non-objective, fantastic versus abstract, each believing his or her style to be the purest and truest. This is no more true than one religion or spiritual path claiming a copyright on God or enlightenment over another. Something is obviously lacking in such an approach: humor, openness and breadth of vision.

When inspiration descends or arises in its fullness, it is sometimes like being in the throes of passion. I cannot help but associate inspiration and the creative process to love, a movement of love. The force of life pounds through my veins. When making love, as each of us disappears in climax we transcend the limited illusory state of ego-identification. At the moment of sexual climax we no longer remember our name, our profession, our debts or our successes. If we can picture our individual self as a beautiful drop of water and the absolute as the ocean, then we have merged at that climactic moment. The individualized soul has been swallowed by the supreme soul. The little i has immersed itself in the capital I. The artist must learn to evolve in a relationship with inspiration as he does with a lover. In love we must learn to surrender at times, an act of vulnerability, of bravery, and it is the same way with inspiration. Making love and making art is very much the same. We dance between asserting and allowing — we are co-creators. The creative process is a form of unconditional love. It is the heart's nature to want to circulate love freely back and forth, without putting limiting conditions on that exchange. Love, in its deepest essence, knows nothing of conditions and is quite unreasonable. Unconditional love has its reasons which reason cannot know and so it is with inspiration — it is larger than the person in whom it inhabits. It is mysterious, an attractive lover we learn to surrender to and eventually become seduced by. Through this, we give to ourselves the unconditional love we most hunger for which is followed by an inevitable fire of inspiration and continually increases creative powers. God has become all things and no one thing. All emotions, thoughts and non-thought, can be a vehicle for communication and reveal some hidden truth through artistic expression.

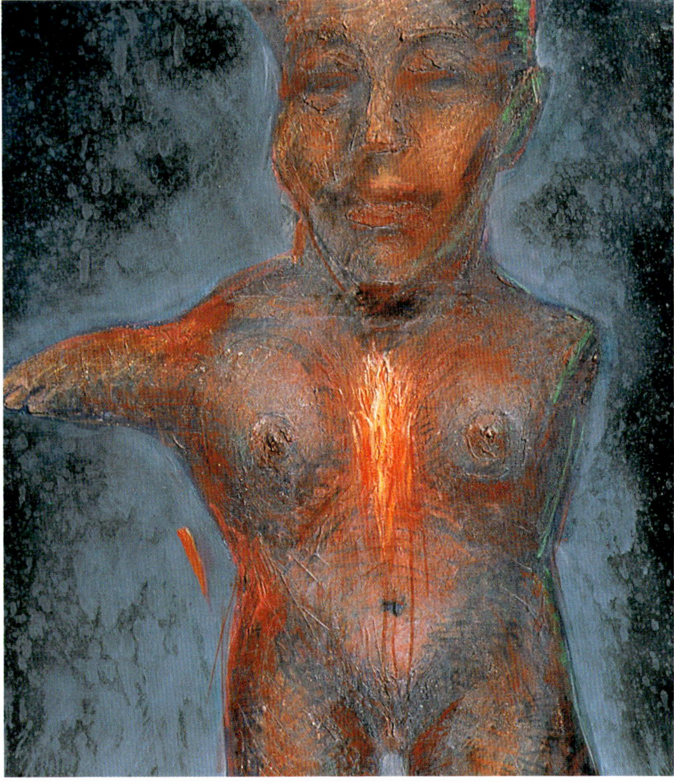

"Heartfire," 48" x 36" mixed media by Philip Rubinov-Jacobson, 1988

Artistic inspiration is like a radiant fire or a sharp sword that cuts through our frozen identities. It is a spiritually radical journey that is not Buddhist, Muslim, Hindu, Christian or Jewish that carries the surrendered lover over the ocean of ignorance to reveal some piece of truth or sublime feeling. Where there is truth there must also be love and where there is love there must also be beauty. True beauty uproots the heart of whosoever sees it and snaps all the fibers that fixed it to its ancient soil and carries it away. This breaking through to the heart is the transmuting force in the alchemy of art awakening us from a spiritual amnesia. This is the transformative power of art and this is what these artists have to offer us.

Philip M. Rubinov-Jacobson is an artist, writer, teacher and the Dean of Continuing Education at The Naropa Institute, Boulder, Colorado.

K. MARTIN-KURI

THE NEW SPIRITUAL ART

Balancing the Inner World and Outer World of Expression

Throughout the past centuries there have been many artists whose interest was to portray spiritual themes and spiritual perceptions. Their efforts to express Divine subjects in styles, image, colors and form have led to various art movements that reflect each era.

As we approach the twenty-first century we are experiencing a surging interest in the images of angels. Often this involves a renewed appreciation of Renaissance art with frequent replication of the style of that era. Such images of spiritual beings are quite linear and provide explicit definition of form. The viewer easily interprets the image of an angel, saint, or a biblical figure.

Towards the latter part of the twentieth century a new impulse started that I have worked extensively to develop for the last thirty years. Rather than the artist portraying spiritual personages or events, or one's own inner spiritual experience as, for example, in certain abstract art forms as was done earlier this century, there is now a merger happening between the two paths as reflected in a new type of spiritual art. The way of the inner and the expression of the outer are coming closer together to reveal Divine mysteries.

There is need for an objective artform that expands beyond the individual artist and can relay the truth of the spiritual world. It should also present such truths in beauty and with an atmosphere that awakens goodness. It is difficult to do this because of the precision required to balance the inner world and the outer world of expression. I spent many years exploring the field of color and light as well as extensive spiritual research to see if this was possible. I studied Goethe's work on color, the impulses of Rudolf Steiner, and many offerings that link the realm of art to the spiritual dimension.

I finally discovered the solution for creating this new type of art. I realized I had to allow God to penetrate through the artform in actual light. This radiance could not be created by any specific brush technique or pigment. Instead, I found it could be released through the process *as a response to the way I paint in prayer.* If we can expand our focus to the balance point between the inner and the outer world, we find ourselves at the threshold of miracles. The Divine can meet us there through our art.

There is an importance in our recognizing a new development in spiritual art. It will enable us to receive the impulses from heaven and perhaps pay attention to what the heavens are trying to say to humanity especially at this time in world history. There are consistent themes related to our remembering the loving care of the Creator and the caution that it is time to realign our priorities. Yet there is an even greater happening that we should be alert to and that is the need for the Godhead to infuse the world with more of His Light. This can be done through artwork, and through other artforms if the artist, or transmitter of that light, operates from the highest level of conscious selflessness. Art of the future must only be created out of the purest motives of selflessness without a quest for self-pleasure or only as an outlet of self-expression. Art has a higher calling to become a sacred vessel in which the Light of God can be held and shared. Then the glory of God can be expressed in the manifest world.

What this means is that the very material of the artwork must become consecrated. This can be achieved by approaching the easel or work table as if it was a sacred altar on which the process of transmutation of substance can occur if proper preparation and precision in color and form are used in combination with purity of intention. Then the act

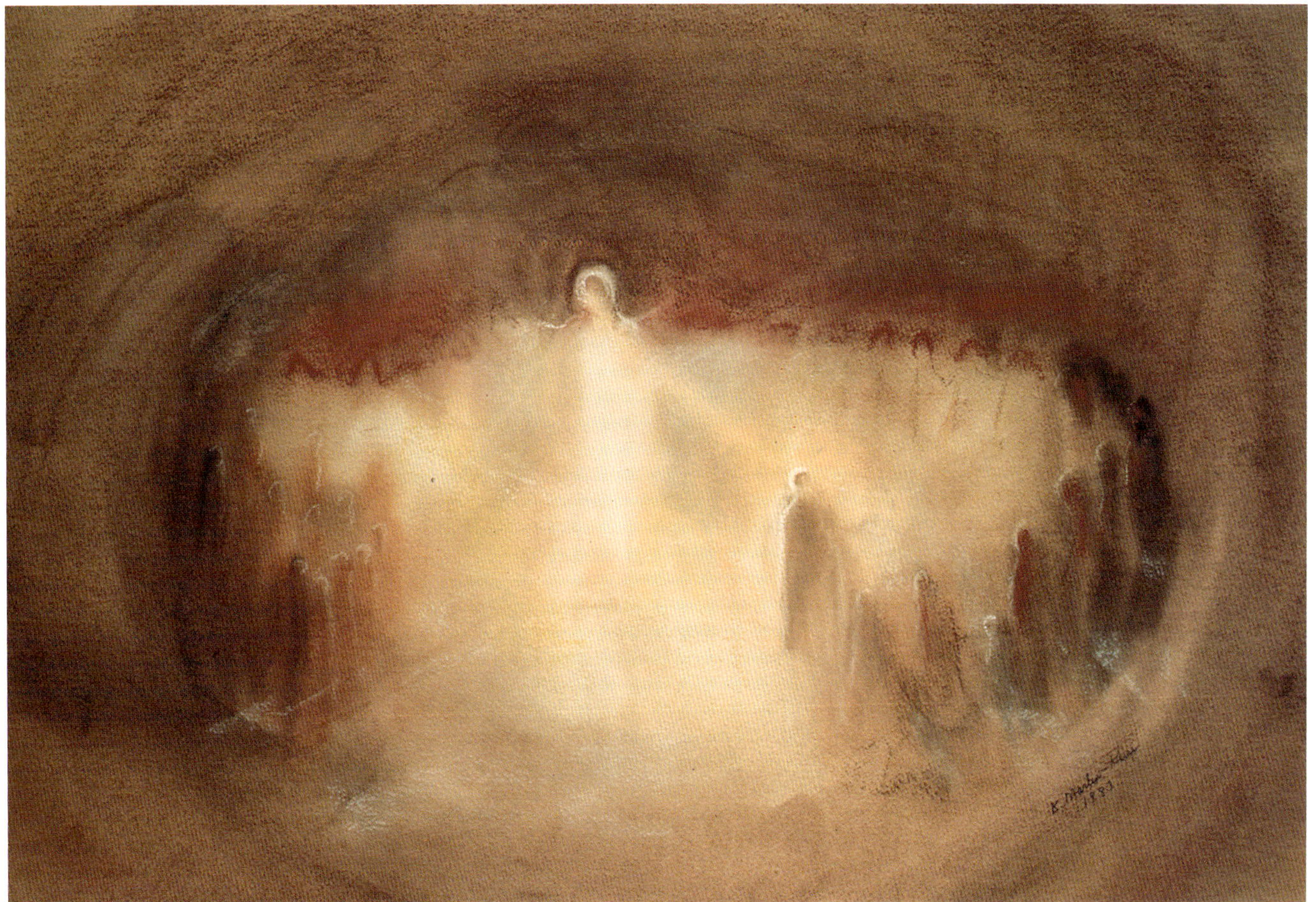

"Blessing of the Brother," 16" x 22" watercolor and chalk pastel by K. Martin-Kuri, 1982

of creating art becomes a sacrament as I believe it was intended.

In past centuries art which was considered to be sacred was kept in churches, temples, or public areas. Even today, an amazing amount of exquisite sacred art is not available for general public viewing (with the exception of those pieces in museums). Frequently I have wandered into a small church in a country town either in Europe, or here in the United States, and discovered breathtaking creations. They belong in those locations where they are connected with prayer.

A new tendency is arising among the populace during the last thirty years to seek sacred art for their own homes or offices. This marks a change in consciousness where the separation from the spiritual life and the mundane is becoming thinner at long last. Persons of the Catholic faith often had artwork portraying images of importance and comfort in their home, but for this to extend to other religions and even non-religious persons is a new trend. This has led to the acceptance of spiritual themes in art galleries, journals and even public places like airports and hotel lobbies. What is going on?

I think there is a demand in our civilization for visual reminders in our homes and work places that we are not forgotten in the midst of the chaos and frenzy of life. It is refreshing to be rushing down a public corridor and find a painting or mural that is filled with hope and also radiant with serenity. We are finally making a transition from artwork for political and social statement to art as a spiritual balm on the wounds of our civilization.

As we begin to integrate sacred art in our daily lives, and view it as a necessity with as much importance as proper nutrition we begin to feed the soul of our civilization. Our Creator is seeking to do this if we artists can allow this nourishing Light to be offered through the conscious surrender of our work for the Divine Good. We are living in a time of immense conflicts and darkness. This requires a lot of focus on our part to remain centered and balanced between the inner world and the outer expression. However, if we maintain this focus, the Creator will be the real artist of our time revealing the new Light from heaven.

K. Martin-Kuri is an artist, writer and author of A Message for the Millennium (Ballantine 1996), counselor, speaker and founder of 28 Angels in Free Union, Virginia.

MARIANN LOVELAND

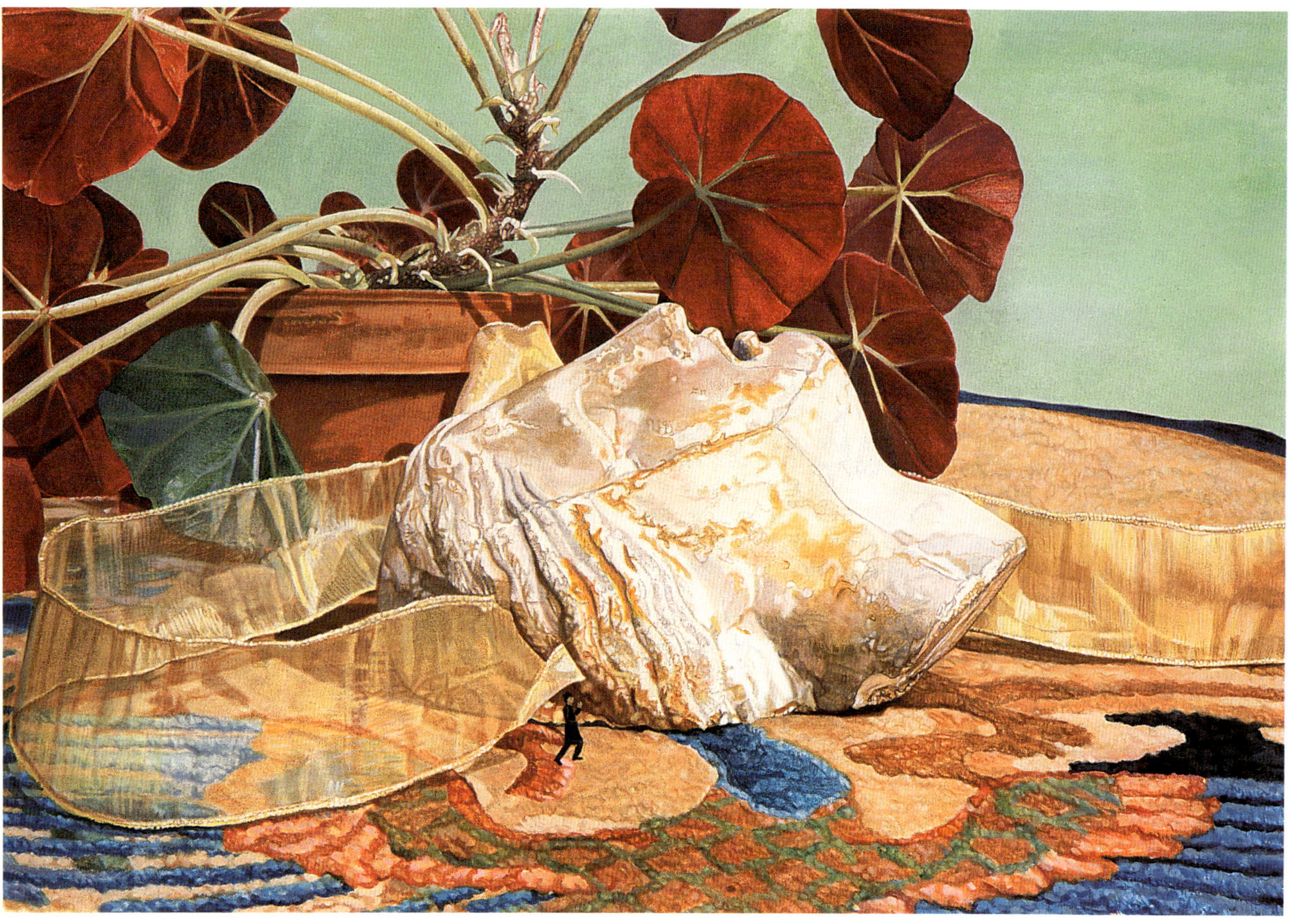

"Voice of the Muse," 24" x 36" oil on canvas, 1996

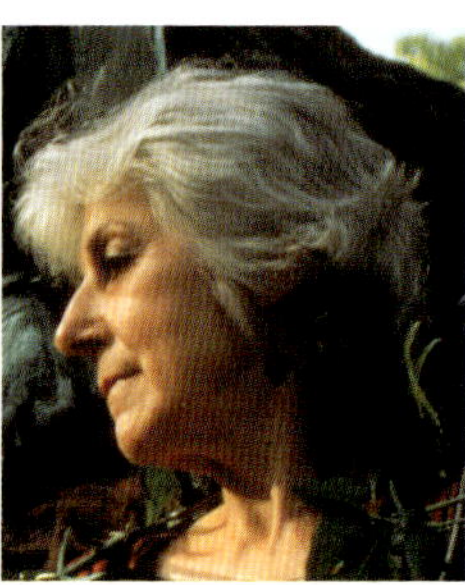

"... RESTRICTIONS UNRAVEL WITHIN MY WORLD OF ART."
— *MARIANN LOVELAND*

The shape shifting traces inherent in my reassembled images coalesce and evolve as archetypal symbols — metaphors of human experience. Even though the reality of life is constantly evolving and transitional, these templates of understanding through which one may glimpse meaning act as a stabilized matrix of consciousness that sustains an ideal. Although perception is limited by physical constraints that govern it — those provisional rules and organizing powers that hold life together in measurable dimensions — such restrictions unravel within my world of art.

In this pliable universe I suspend the laws of nature penetrating the surface layer of reality beneath the mirage of thought forms to explore paradoxical continents where the walls between worlds grow thin.

Mariann Loveland
444 North Aurora Street
Ithaca, NY 14850
Tel: (607) 272-1842

Opposite page: "Initiation," 60" x 48" oil on canvas, 1995

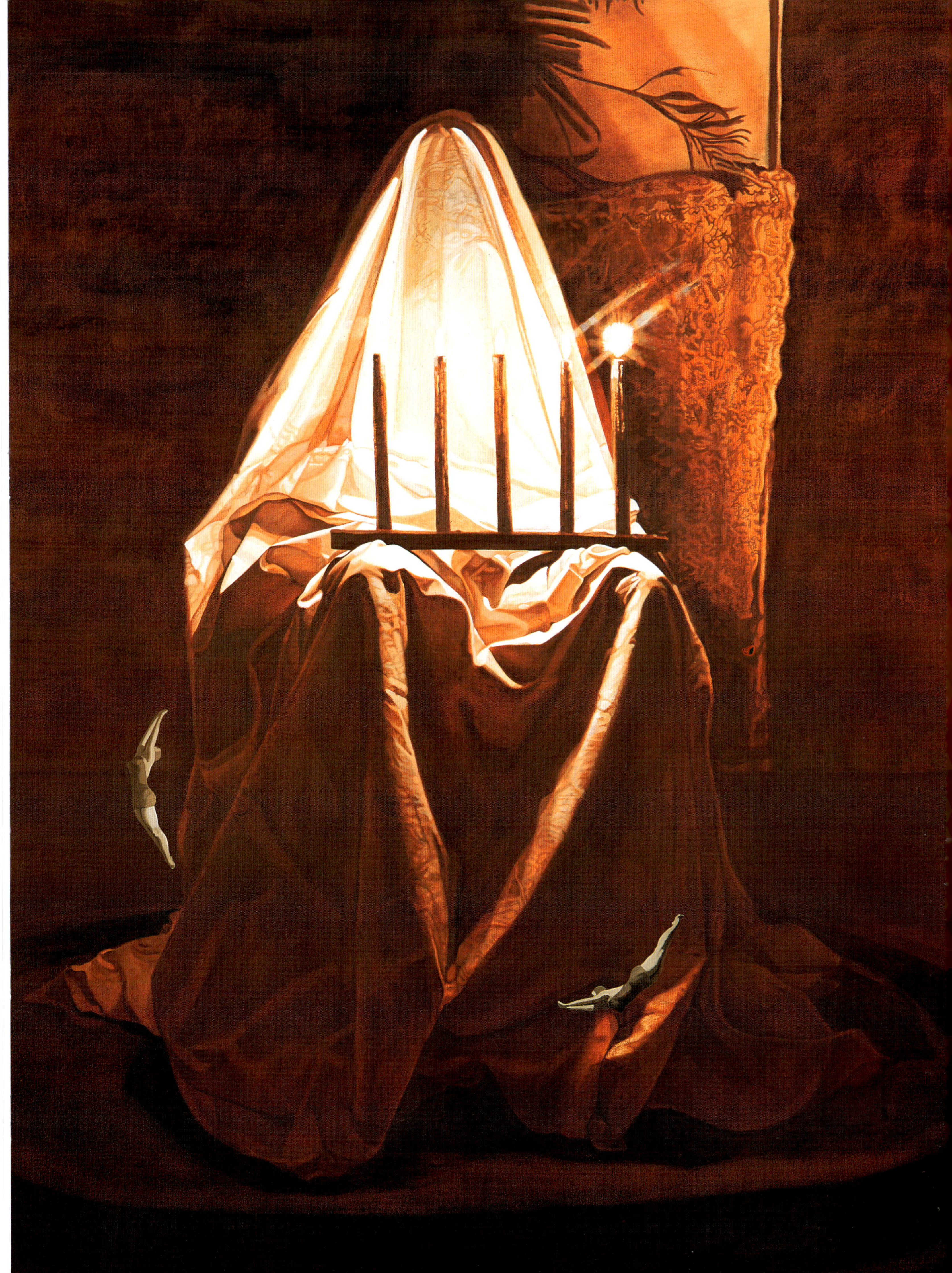

ROBERT VENOSA

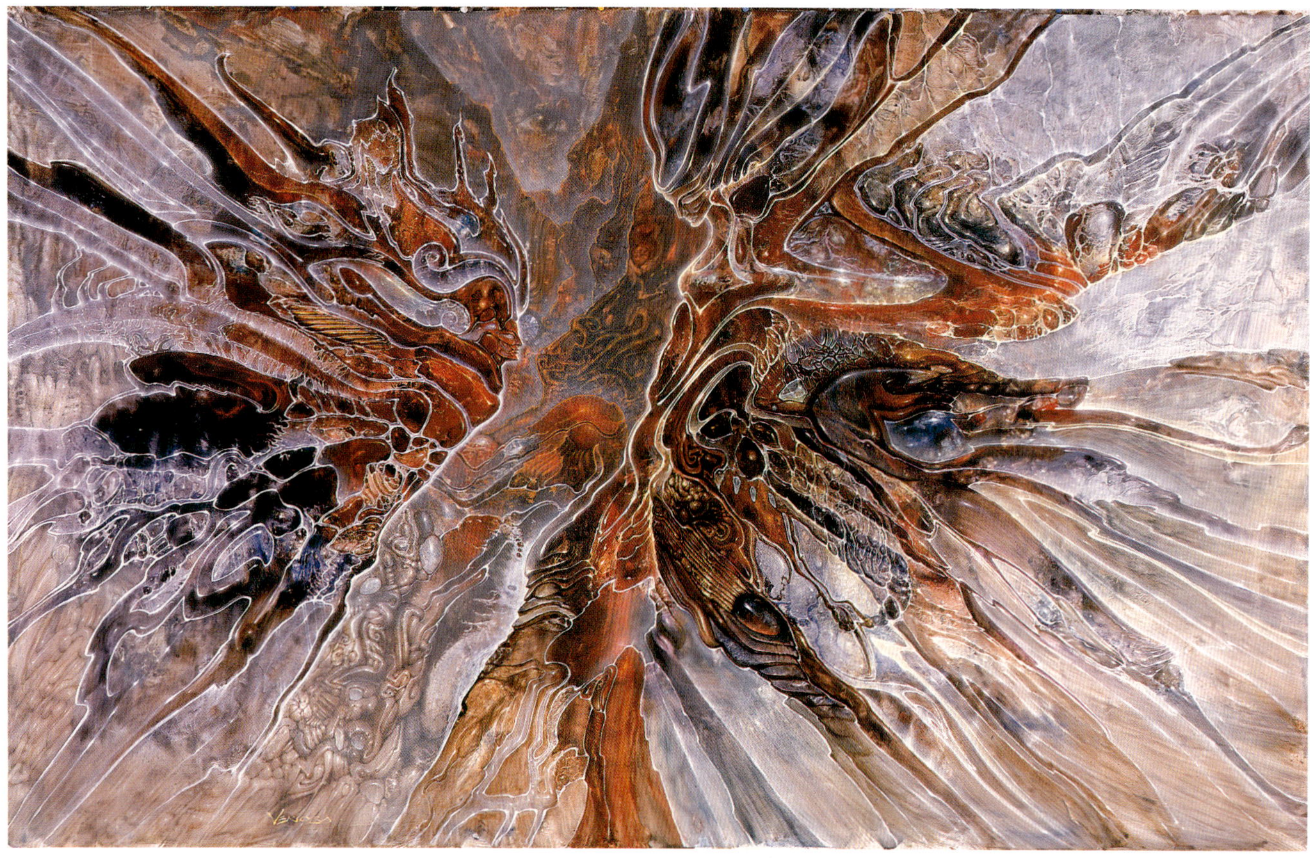

"Dos Angeles," 96" x 60," oil on canvas, 1995

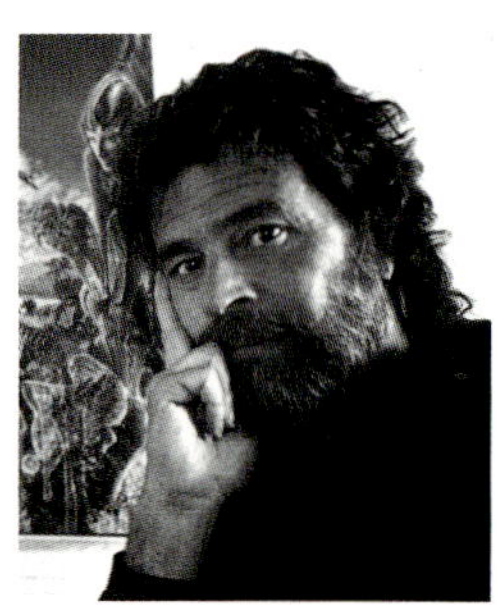

"THE PAINTBRUSH IS THE KEY THAT ALLOWS ENTRY INTO THE DIVINE MYSTERIES."
— *ROBERT VENOSA*

A work of art is no more than a flow of creative energy searching for form and manifestation through manipulation by the artist; its value/meaning is determined by the observer whose energy level and spirit capacity corresponds to that contained in the observed work. Many look at art, but few actually see it.

If we admit to an experience/thought-accumulating subconscious, then to be consistent we must also allow for a superconscious and the higher latitude of thought and creative potential it contains. Both are channels of time: the subconscious to the past, the superconscious to the future, and both contain the wish for expression. The artist, if he/she desires to be an architect of spirit-mind form, must ascend from the realm of subconscious symbolic representation and open up to superconscious guidance and experimentation.

During a recent exhibit of my work, more than one observer mentioned that the paintings opened up channels of vague otherworldly recognition, along with the feel of energy of a spiritual nature. If the true purpose of art is to foreshadow a higher state of reality, then the work of spirit-guided artists may not be as abstract or irrational as many of us are inclined to believe.

Robert Venosa
1430 High Street
Boulder, CO 80304
Tel/Fax: (303) 440-8905
email: venosa@csd.net

Opposite page: "Astral Circus," 36" x 46" oil on canvas, 1978

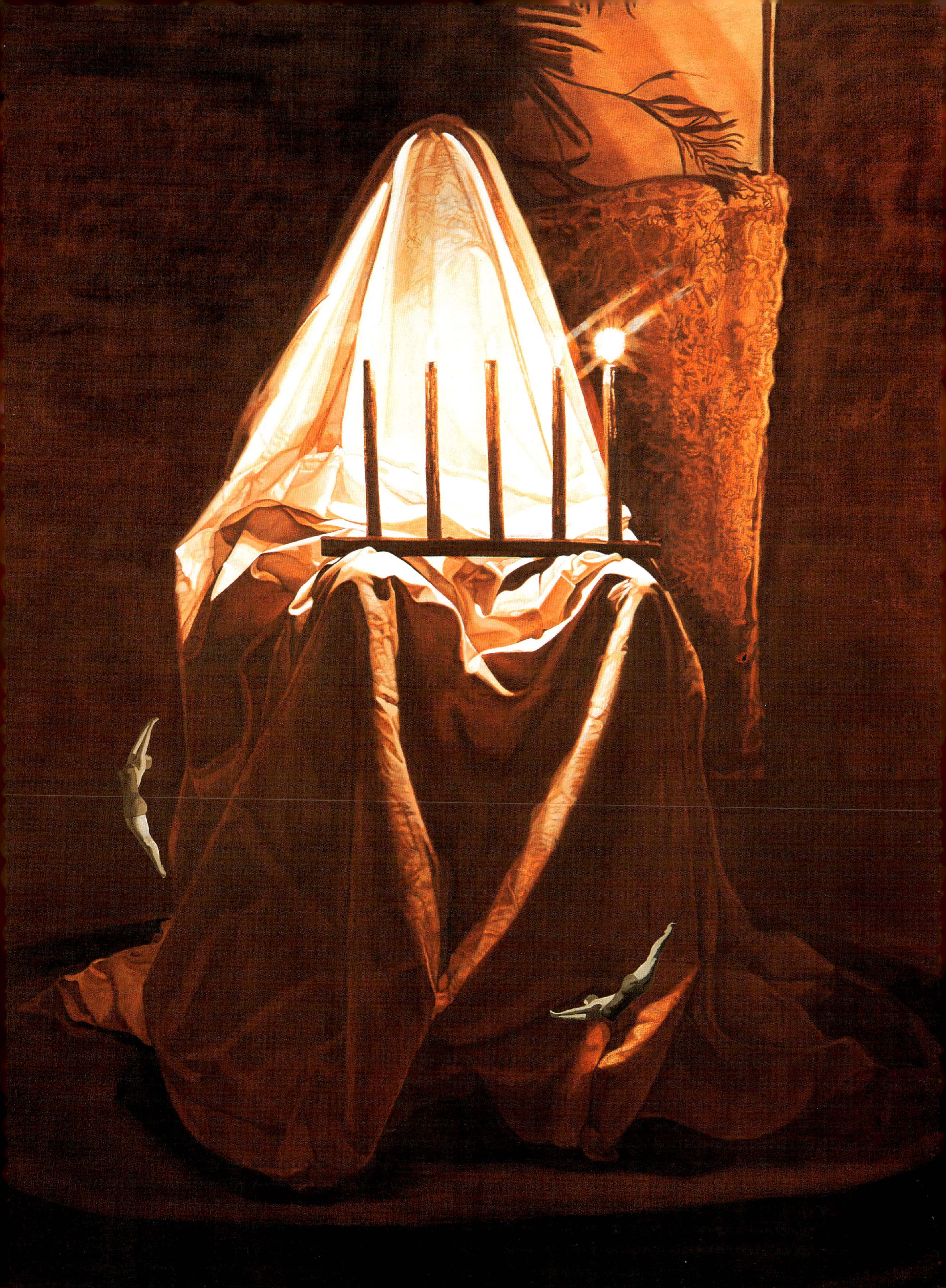

"WHEN I CARVE THE TREE I ENGAGE WITH THE HISTORY OF THE LIFE WITHIN IT."

— *NANCY AZARA*

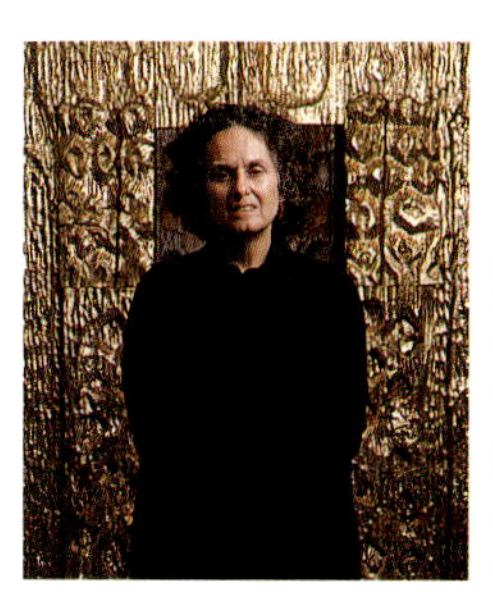

Photo: © by Jamie McEwen

NANCY AZARA

My sculpture is made of wood carved from trees. The carved wood is found on the streets of New York City, the beaches of the Dominican Republic, the shores of Northern Minnesota, and other places. It is often assembled, several pieces put together to make the whole. It is painted, colored, often with handmade paint and gold leaf which dresses and clothes the wood, so to speak, so that the actual forms begin to develop the presence of being and of garments.

Some of the wood that comes from the streets of New York is battered and unattractive, but when I begin to carve into it, the wood's beauty is revealed. Using raw material from different places allows the trees to offer different meanings to my work. Tree and human have a long connection to each other. They (the trees) have been traditionally used as a metaphor for the human self, frequently for women. When I carve the tree I engage with the history of the life within it. I listen to it, so that it participates with me in the experience of becoming a sculpture. I am carving an object that was once animate and has that presence embodied within. When I carve into it, I release the quality. I speak with it. The carving resuscitates the life that's been held in stasis. The tree becoming sculpture represents a way for me to parallel and illustrate our history as human and our voice as women. It echoes a memory of what went before and as I carve it, it changes into a newer, stronger, more timely, more relevant presence. In this way, my art is about discovering and reclaiming both the spirit of the tree and my own spirit.

There is a similar kind of silence that is found in sculpture as there is in a garden. The silence which is in *The Spirit House of the Mother* takes you the viewer to an inner place of vastness and quiet, where I want you to become both an echo of yourself, the presence of the echo and the silence around the echo. I want to have *The Spirit House* speak to you about the darkness, to bring light to it, to mix understanding and dialogue, yours, mine. I hope to bring spirit to you and because of this, to have you open and envision your heart in the experience of it.

Photo: © by Christopher Burke

"Hand Wall," 73" x 37" x 5" carved and painted wood with gold leaf, 1996

Text from the book *Feminist Foremothers,* published by The Haworth Press, Inc., Binghamton, NY ©1995

Nancy Azara
91 Franklin Street
New York City, NY 10013
Tel: (212) 925-5777

NANCY AZARA

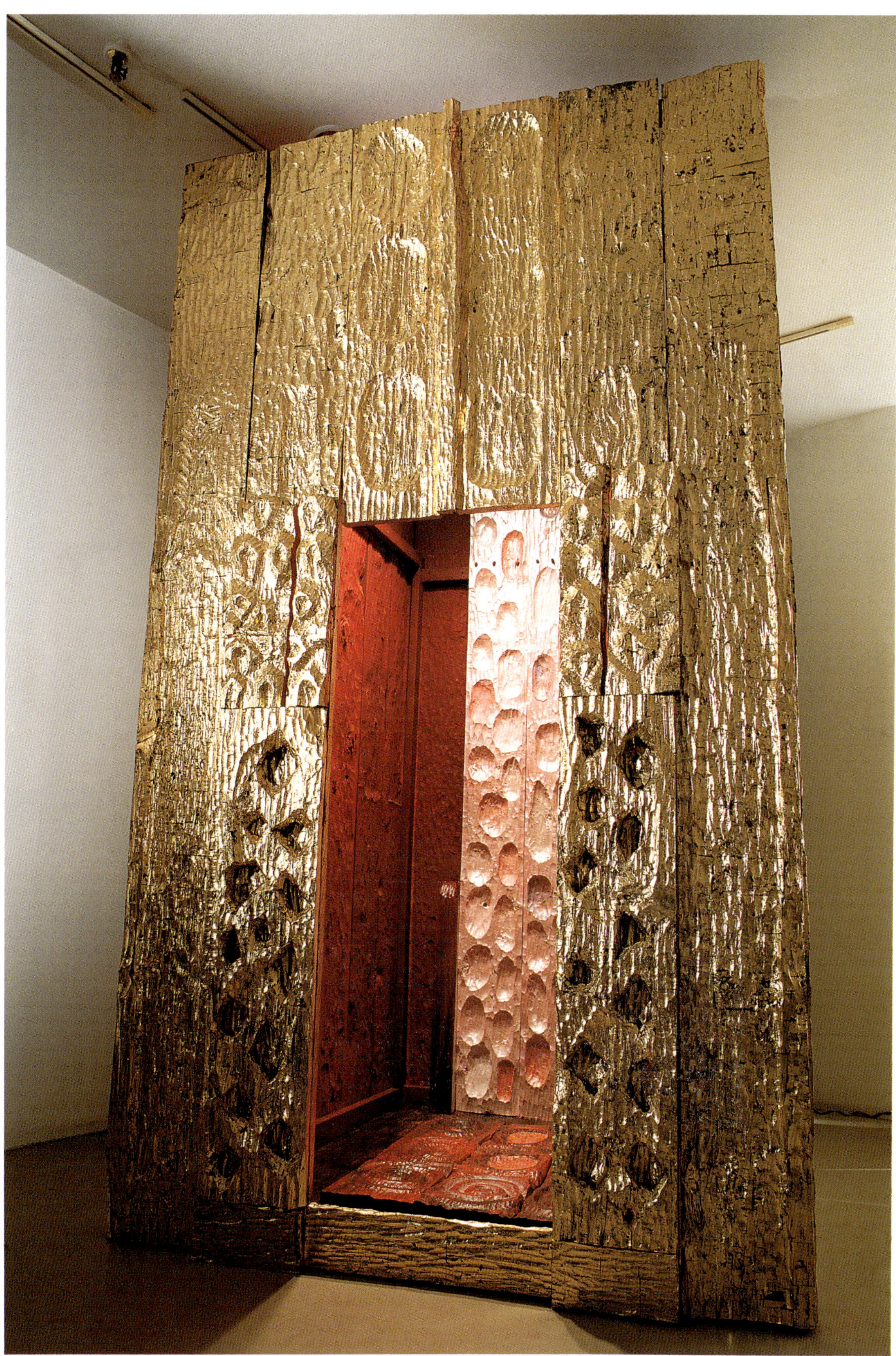

Photo: © by Christopher Burke

"Spirit House Of The Mother," 11′ x 6′ x 7′ carved and painted wood with gold leaf, 1994

"... I HAVE STUDIED MANY SYSTEMS
... INCORPORATING THESE TEACHINGS
INTO MY LIFE AND INTO MY ART HAS BEEN
AN EVOLVING PROCESS."

— BETH AMES SWARTZ

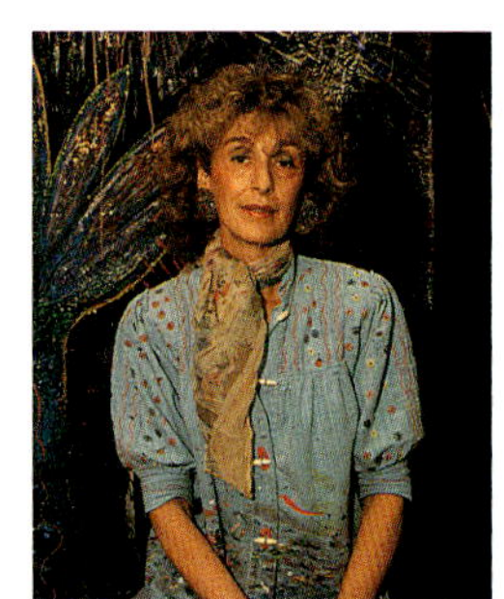

BETH AMES SWARTZ

I am fascinated with the interaction between art and healing. Can the energy of a painting actually affect the viewer? We can learn from the inherited philosophical wisdom of our kind. For 35 years, I have studied many systems, both ones well-known and those more esoteric. Incorporating these teachings into my life and into my art has been an evolving process.

The different phases of my work intertwine myth-like visual elements from many areas of wisdom ... including those of the American Indian, Buddhism, Christianity, the Kabbalah (an occult teaching with Hebraic sources), the chakra system of yoga and even more arcane learning such as that of the Seven Rays.

My early *Fire Work* series used fire as part of a "life-death-rebirth" process/ritual, with art arising through the transforming power of destruction. One continuing concern is the need for people, individually and collectively, to achieve harmony within ourselves and with our ecology.

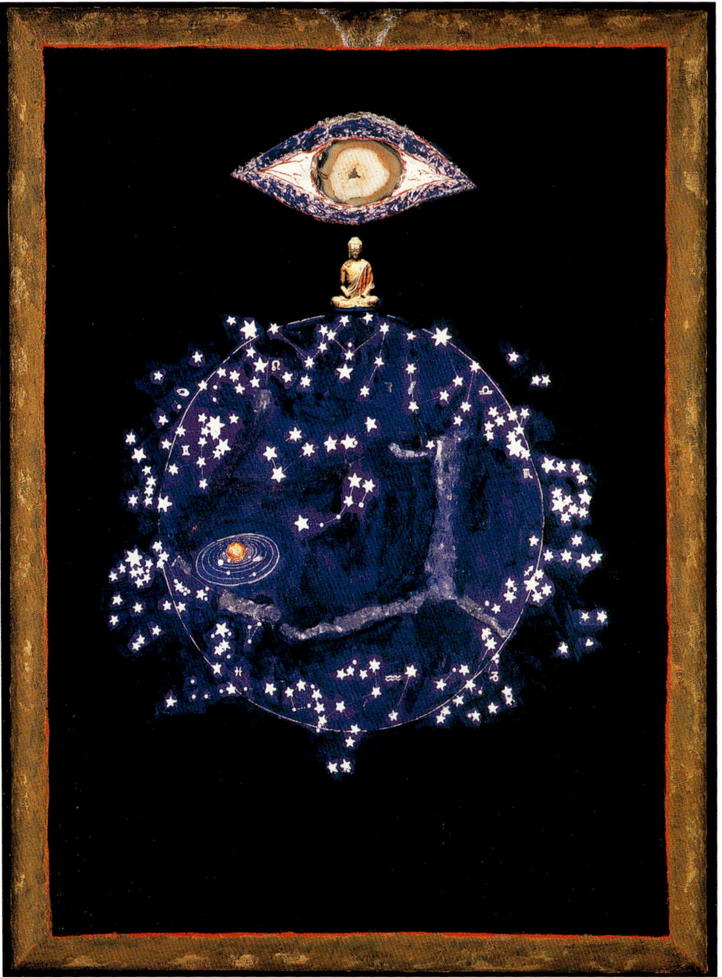

A Story for the Eleventh Hour, "Shantih, shantih, shantih,"
39 1/2" x 30" sliced geode, gold and silver leaf, mixed media on canvas, 1993

A Moving Point of Balance depicted the chakra system in seven 7′ by 7′ paintings using music and light baths in an installation designed to encourage the viewer to become a participant in their own healing process. This traveling museum exhibition was the source of a six year research study of audience reaction.

A Story for the Eleventh Hour visualizes a path to be taken by our species. The way travels from a time when the universe and life came into existence. It continues into our present world plighted by possible extinction (... at the eleventh hour). Finally, this visual prayer projects our collective story into a desired future where enlightened beings people the cosmos. The series employs a narrative sequence of related images, (such as that of an all-seeing eye and the Buddha) as icons symbolizing our race's potential for compassionate and enlightened behavior.

Currently, I practice Shen Qi while creating paintings in which I hope to infuse a quiet tranquillity and appreciation of the seeming reality of the moment.

Beth Ames Swartz ■ 5346 E. Sapphire Lane, Paradise Valley, AZ 85253-2531
Tel: (602) 948-6112 Fax: (602) 948-6092 email: RFArtsInc@aol.com

BETH AMES SWARTZ

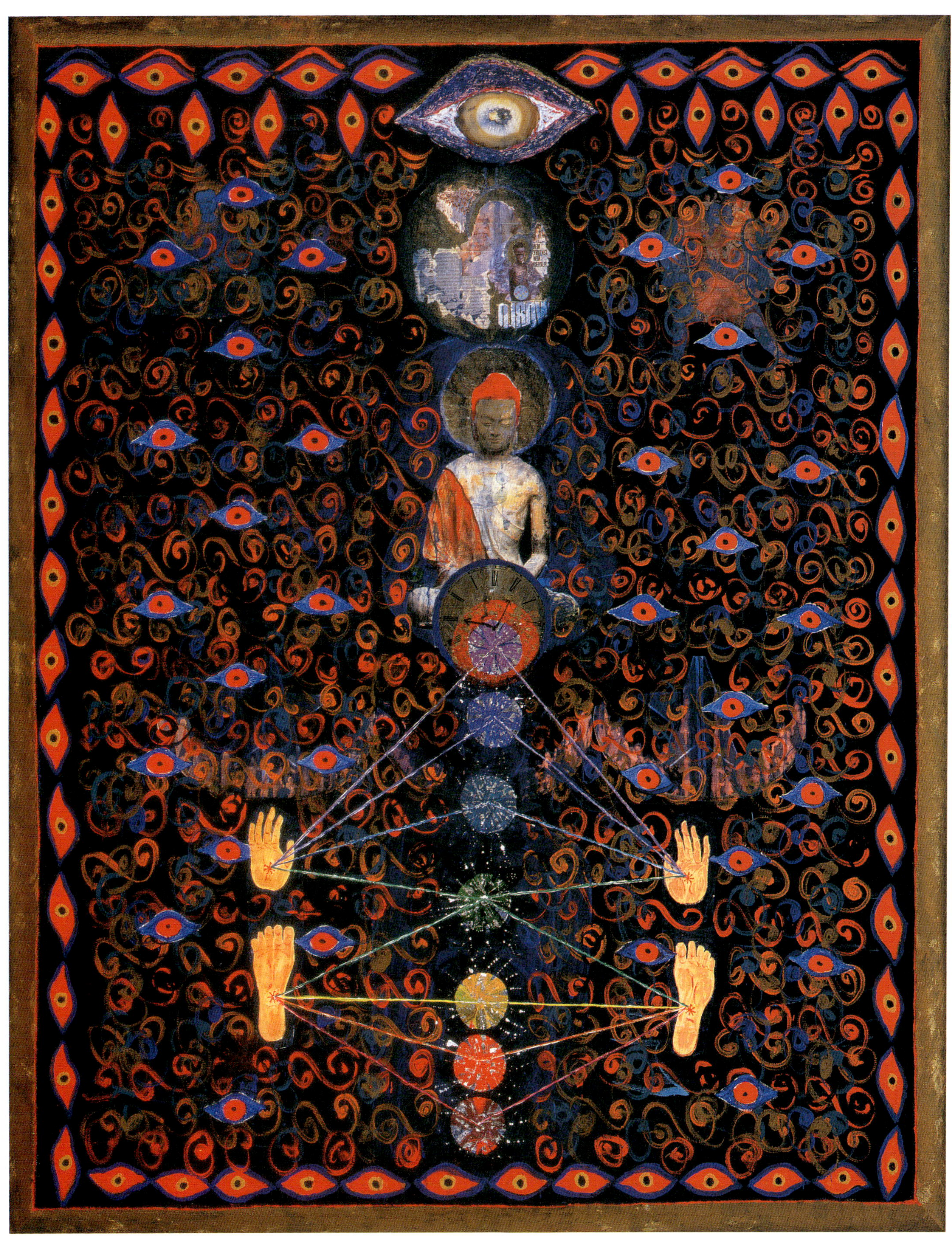

"The Return: Charging the Species at the Eleventh Hour," 60" x 48" sliced geode, gold and silver leaf, mixed media on canvas, 1993

ROBERT VENOSA

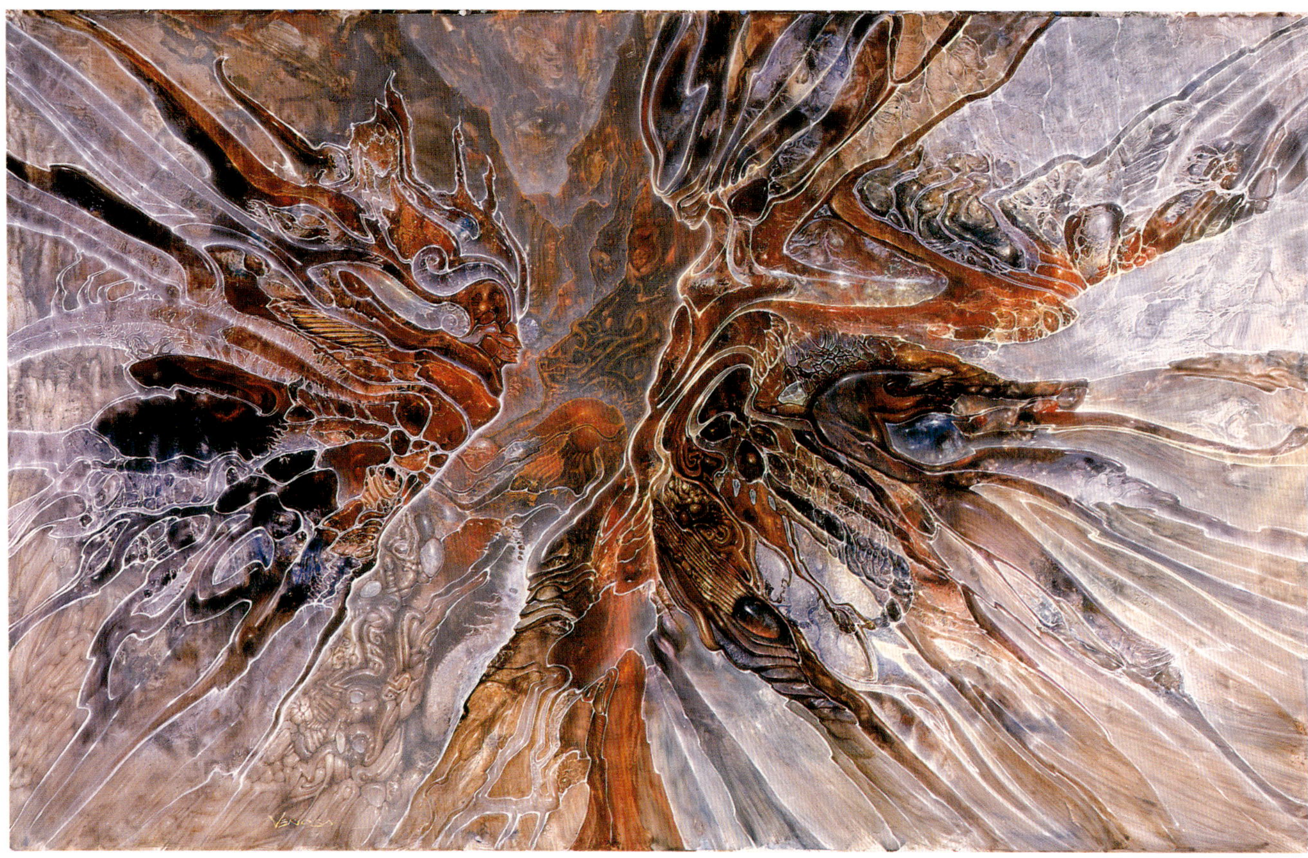

"Dos Angeles," 96" x 60," oil on canvas, 1995

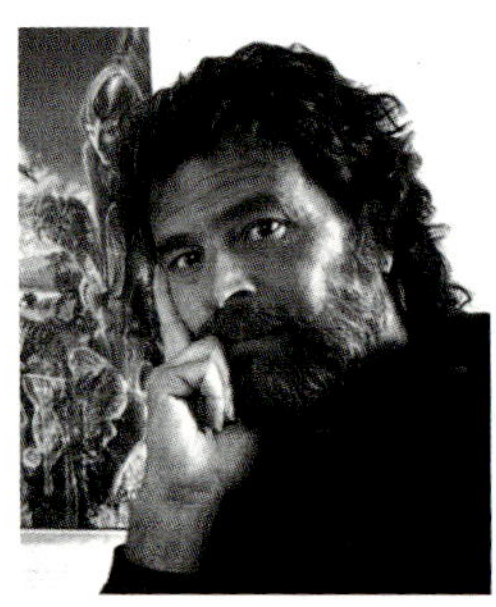

"THE PAINTBRUSH IS THE KEY THAT ALLOWS ENTRY INTO THE DIVINE MYSTERIES."
— *ROBERT VENOSA*

A work of art is no more than a flow of creative energy searching for form and manifestation through manipulation by the artist; its value/meaning is determined by the observer whose energy level and spirit capacity corresponds to that contained in the observed work. Many look at art, but few actually see it.

If we admit to an experience/thought-accumulating subconscious, then to be consistent we must also allow for a superconscious and the higher latitude of thought and creative potential it contains. Both are channels of time: the subconscious to the past, the superconscious to the future, and both contain the wish for expression. The artist, if he/she desires to be an architect of spirit-mind form, must ascend from the realm of subconscious symbolic representation and open up to superconscious guidance and experimentation.

During a recent exhibit of my work, more than one observer mentioned that the paintings opened up channels of vague otherworldly recognition, along with the feel of energy of a spiritual nature. If the true purpose of art is to foreshadow a higher state of reality, then the work of spirit-guided artists may not be as abstract or irrational as many of us are inclined to believe.

Robert Venosa
1430 High Street
Boulder, CO 80304
Tel/Fax: (303) 440-8905
email: venosa@csd.net

Opposite page: "Astral Circus," 36" x 46" oil on canvas, 1978

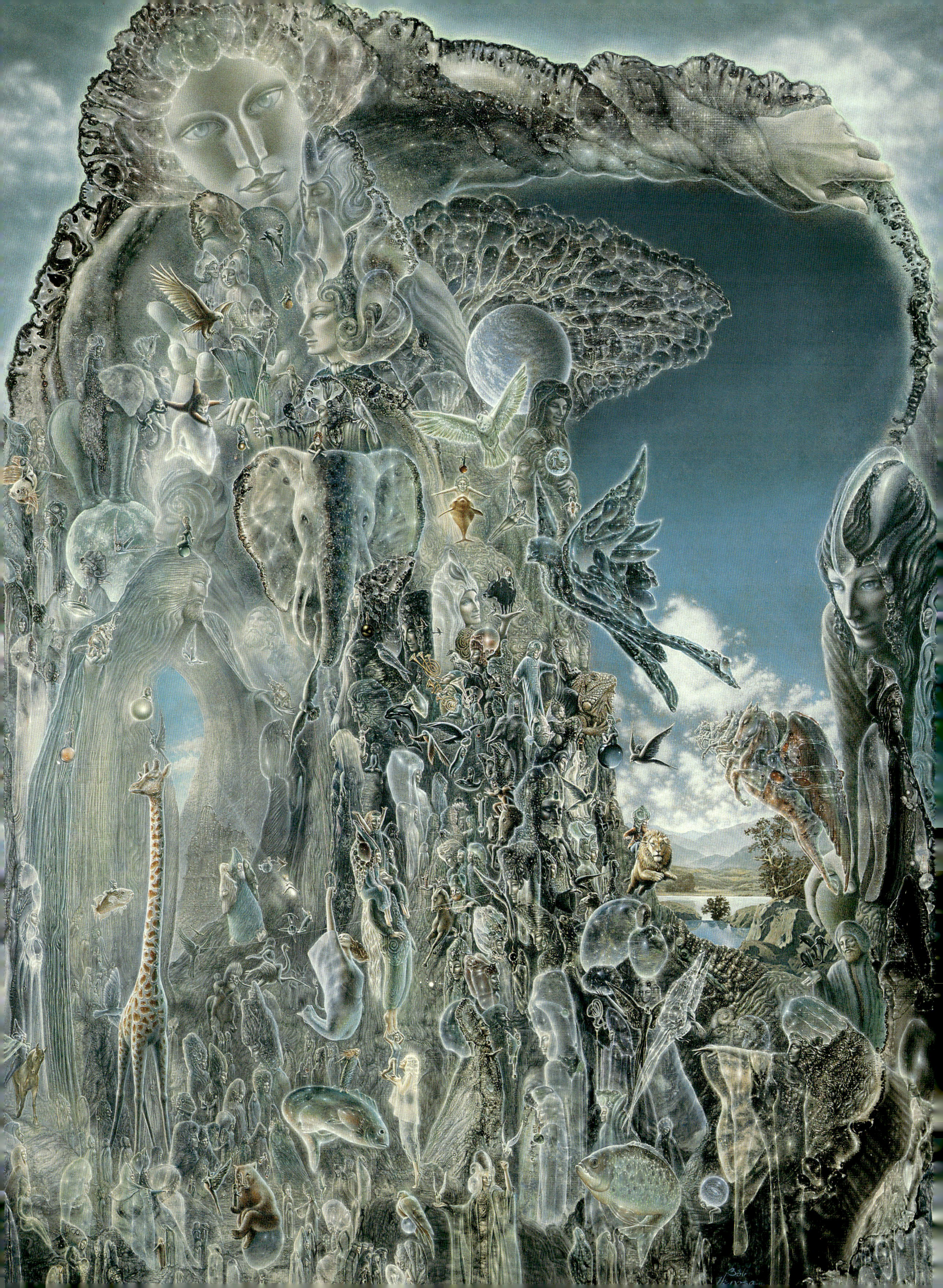

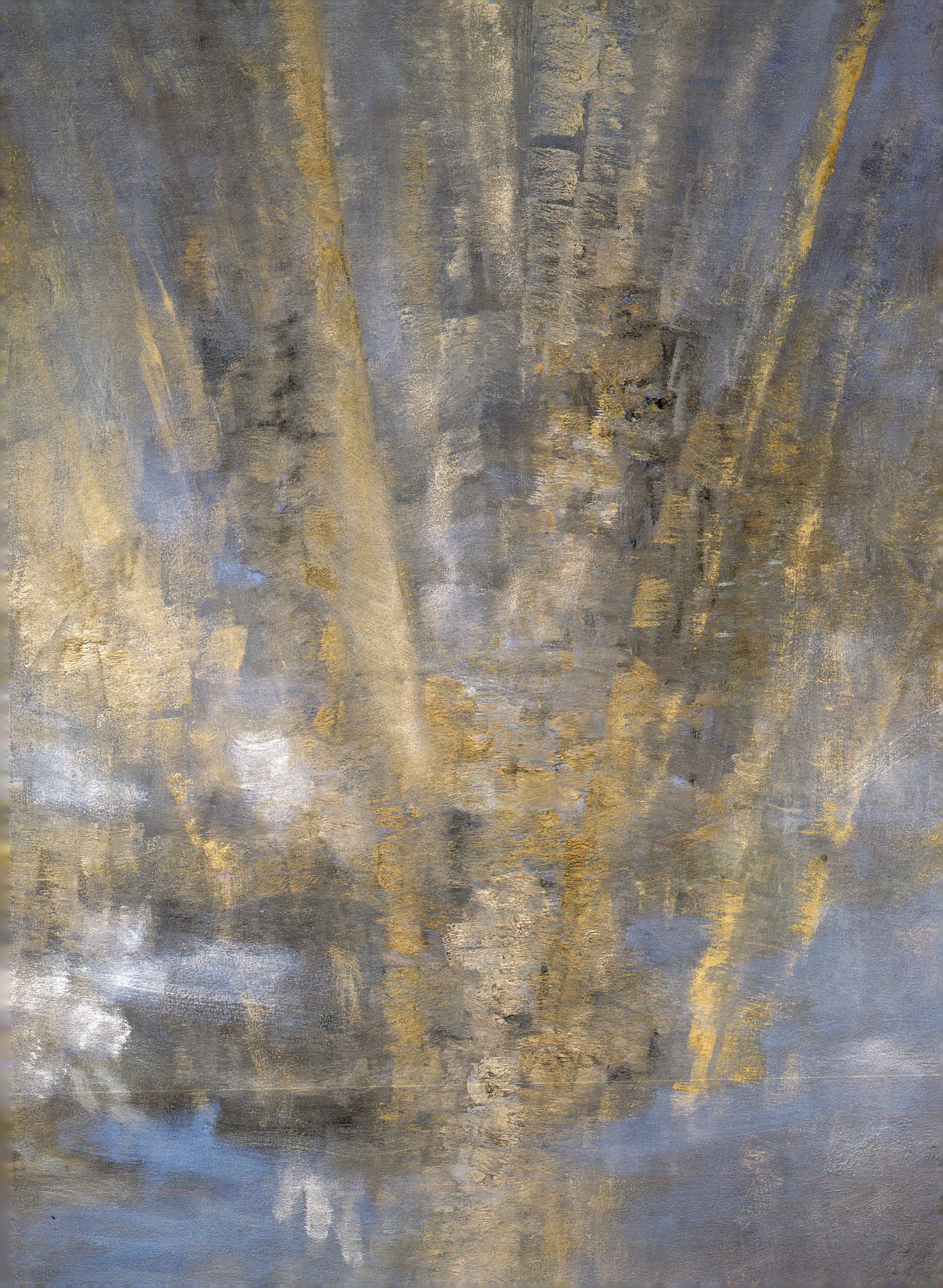

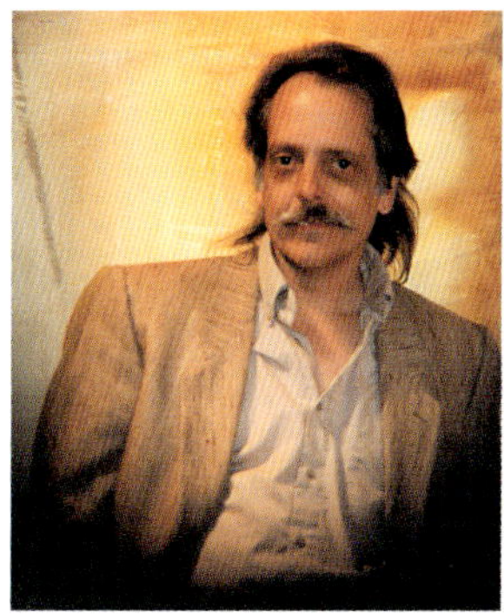

Vessels within vessels,
the container contained ad infinitum
Contained by the Universe we,
in turn, contain universes. Rather,
perhaps, multiverses.
Like some vast Chinese puzzle,
where bafflement leads inexorably to discovery.
— *Tony Walholm*

TONY WALHOLM

I view my work as opening up a space within the environment in which it dwells. As such the painting becomes a vessel, a container of energy to be dispensed or a craft to carry one across the great waters of our evolving beingness.

I have long considered abstract painting to be a vehicle for more than the recording of a gesture or providing a metaphor. Rather, I have gone about making paintings that create a space, providing a sense of nourishment, contemplation, and energy that extends to the environment around them.

At a showing of my work in Honolulu in 1982, Joe Campbell, the renowned scholar of things mythological, commented about my being "in the service of the White Goddess."

The White Goddess is that which represents the realm of the dream, of inspiration, of the compassionate and creative nature of God that stands before the God of reason. It is through the aegis of beauty, love, and harmony that life becomes more than bearable, but rather something to savor. It is my wish that, through my work, people receive such energy, and are strengthened by it. The veil of paint is but the flesh of that which bridges the material and spiritual realms.

Take of this and eat with your eyes.

Tony Walholm
Represented by:
NaPua Gallery
Grand Wailea Resort
3860 Wailea Alani Road, Suite 210
Wailea, Maui, HI 96753
Tel: (808) 874-0510
Toll Free Tel: (800) 800-6554
Fax: (808) 874-2522
email: twart@maui.net

Opposite page: "Out of the Depths," 60" x 48" oil on canvas, 1995

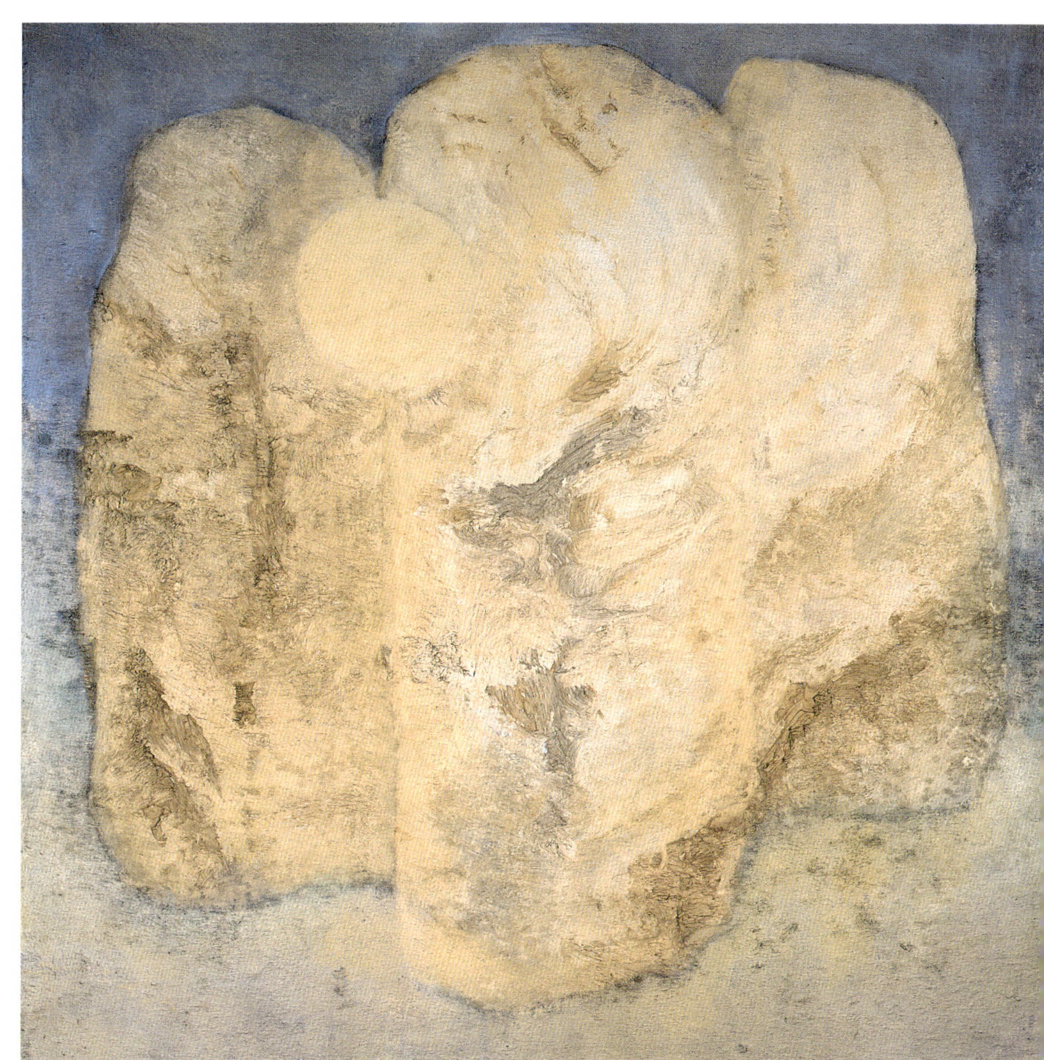

"Vessel of the Three Realms," 48" x 48" oil on canvas, 1995

TONY WALHOLM

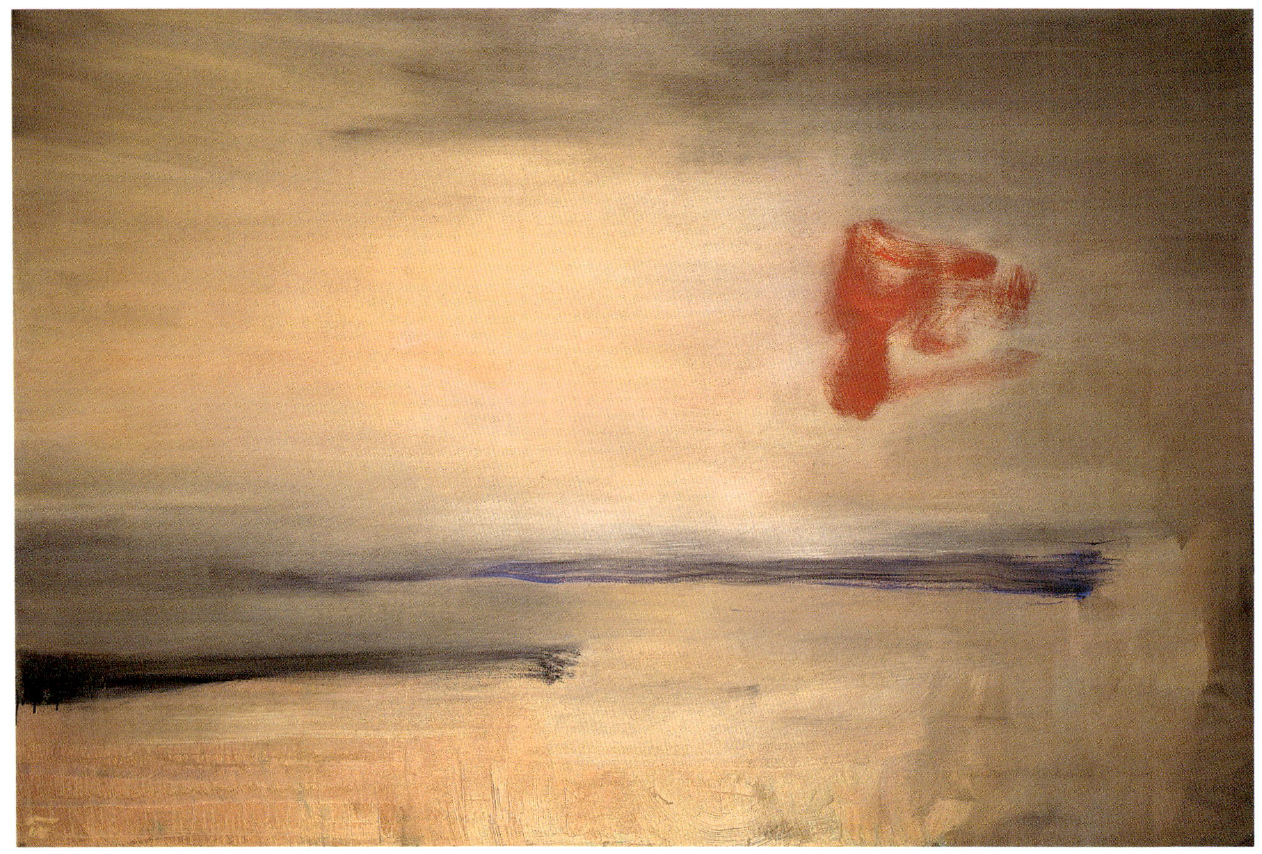

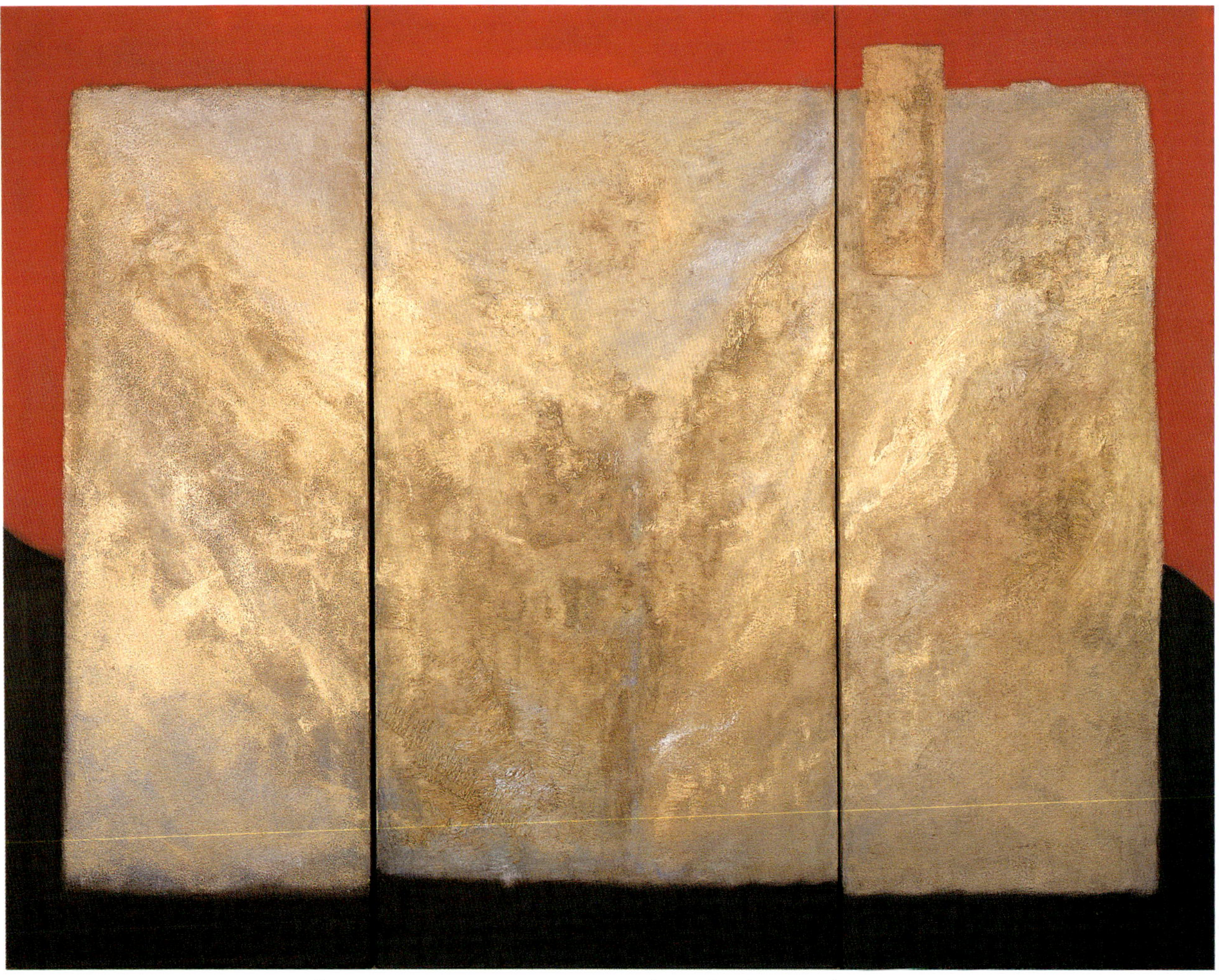

Top: "Satori Dances," 48" x 72," oil on canvas, 1994 Bottom: "Enter Radiance," 60" x 84" oil on canvas, 1996

TONY WALHOLM

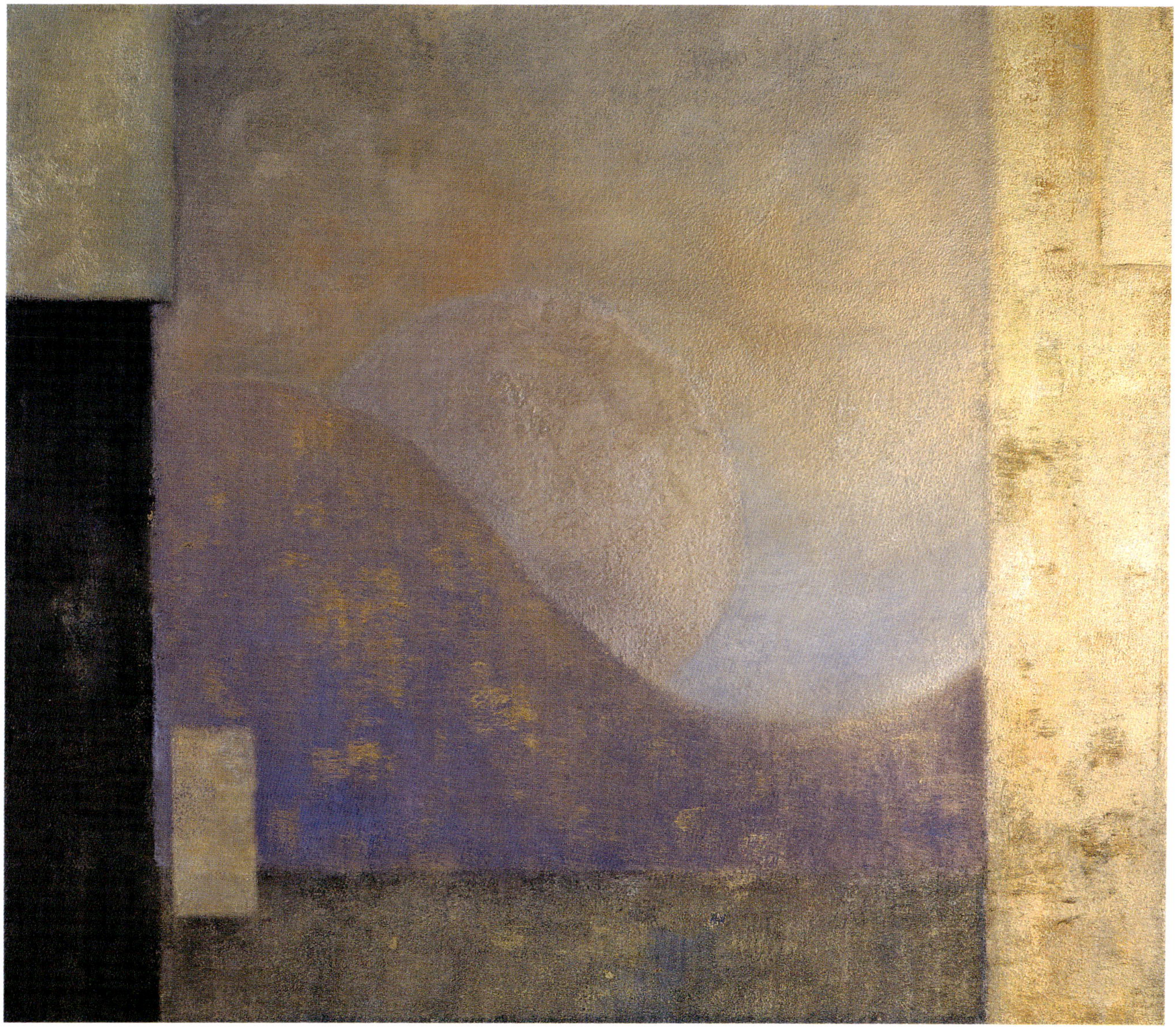

"Enlightenment," 48" x 56" oil on canvas, 1996

"The inspiration for the painting "Enlightenment" comes from a twelfth century sutra from the Hiroshima prefecture that tells the story of an emperor who becomes so despondent at the waste and suffering he himself has helped to create he thinks death would be the only answer. With such a mind he walks out into the wilderness that seems to echo his pain. With the rising of the moon, however, a transformation takes place and he experiences enlightenment. He returns to his realm as a Bodhisatta."

— TONY WALHOLM

TONY WALHOLM

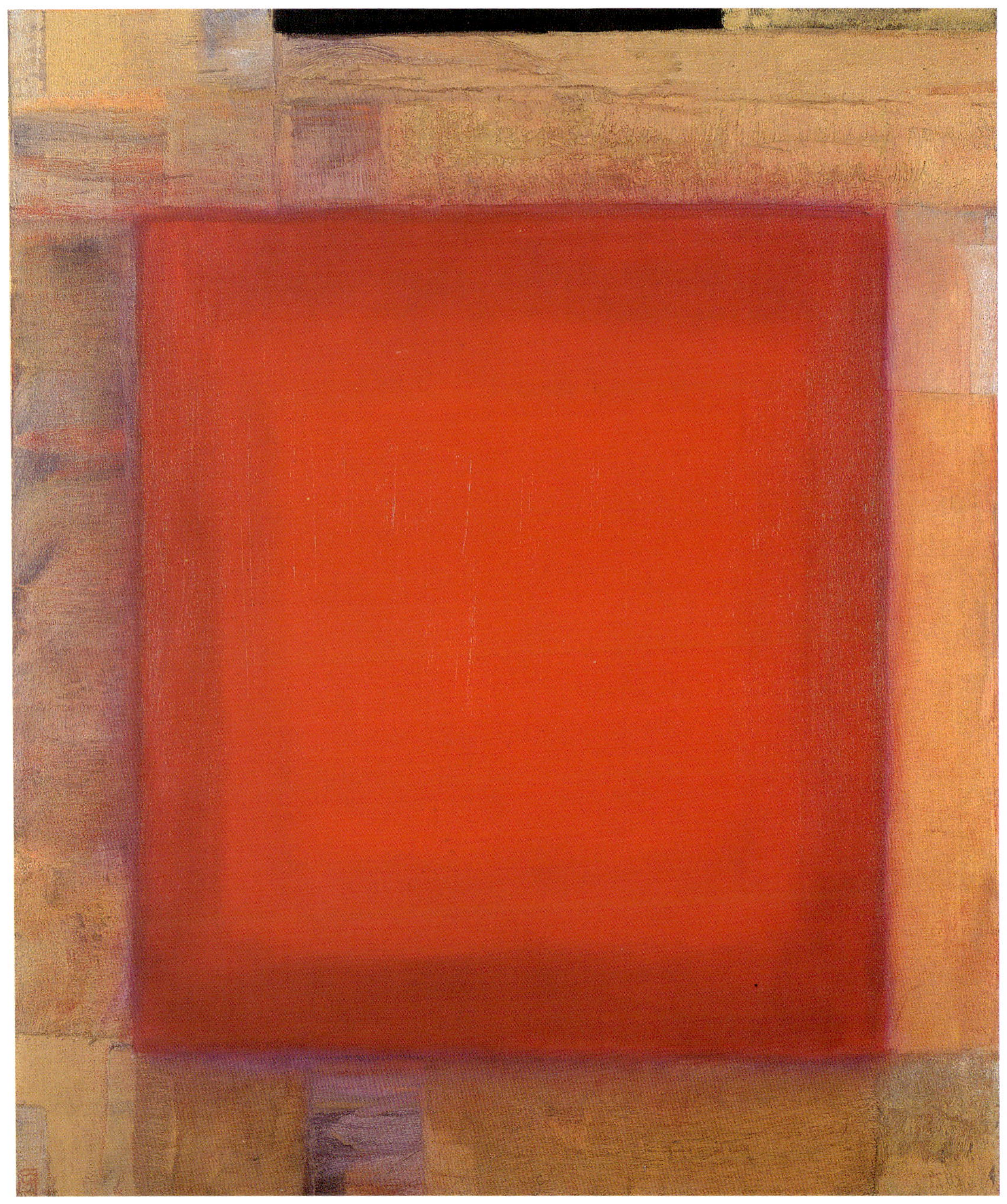

Above: "The Fire Within," 54" x 48" oil on canvas, 1996   Opposite page: "Resurrection, 72" x 48" oil on canvas, 1995

ENJOY THE WONDERMENT
the mystery,
the Not-Knowing
for there in the silence between the thoughts
the Silence of Space prevails
where we contemplate the Wholeness
of the Universe Eternal,
for in Space there is no matter
nor time.
The Silence of the Mountain
and the Song of the Stream
echo the Eloquence of the Mind of God.
Be still and Know that You are That.
— *Tony Walholm*

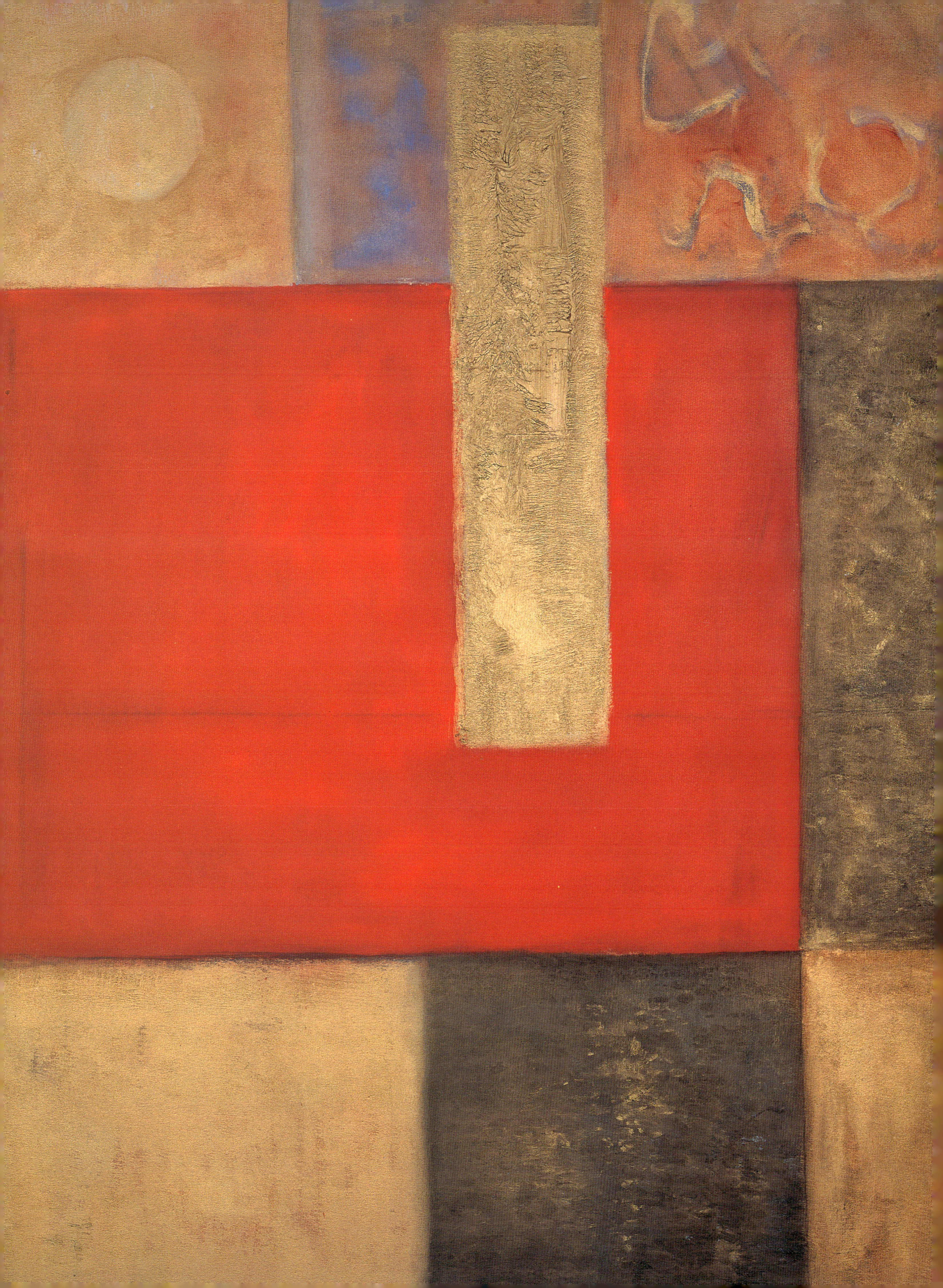

PHILIP RUBINOV-JACOBSON

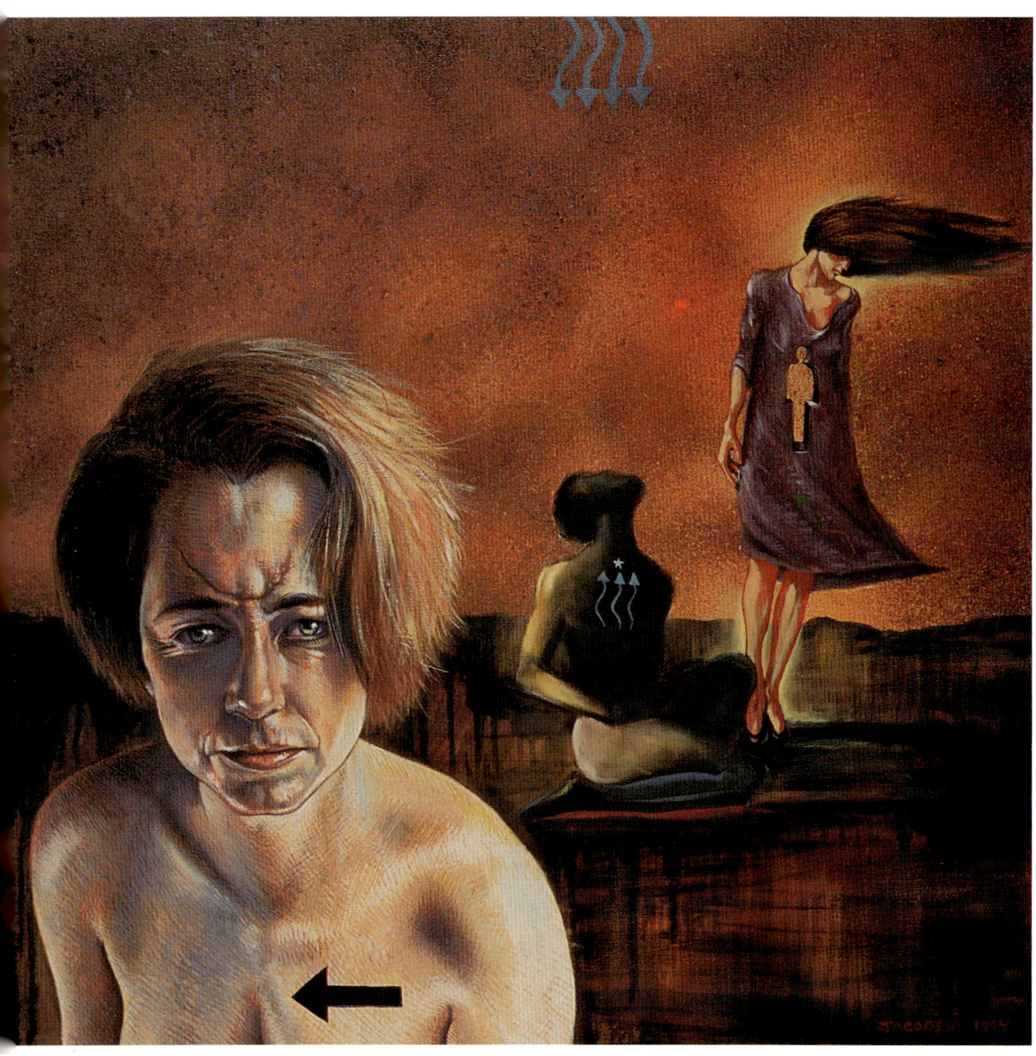

"Mary Jane," 36″ x 36″ egg tempera and oil, 1994

In my art, I invoke the healing potential of the creative act: delving into the artist's role as mystic and shaman while ecstatically exploring the realms of consciousness, unknown interior spaces and familiar faces. Painting in numerous styles, I express both personal and universal elements of the joy, pain, desire, mystery and bliss of re-connection to the absolute.

Art is a sacred path awakening the enlightened mind, healing and stirring the divine heart. A contemplative approach and understanding of the creative process has enhanced my work and what it means to be an artist. Breaking through the cultural trance — suspending the prescribed goals and expectations — allows alternative realities and solutions to be reached. I am not interested in making normal art nor administering to the existing mind-set. I wish to feed art into a new social hologram like seeds that take root. We have no future except what we can envision, and what we envision will draw us toward itself.

My eyes closed, learn what their
vision is for
they were fasting for lifetimes
now their fruit is harvested from the
beginningless beginning and the
endless end.

"ART IS A SACRED PATH AWAKENING THE ENLIGHTENED MIND, HEALING AND STIRRING THE DIVINE HEART."
— *PHILIP RUBINOV-JACOBSON*

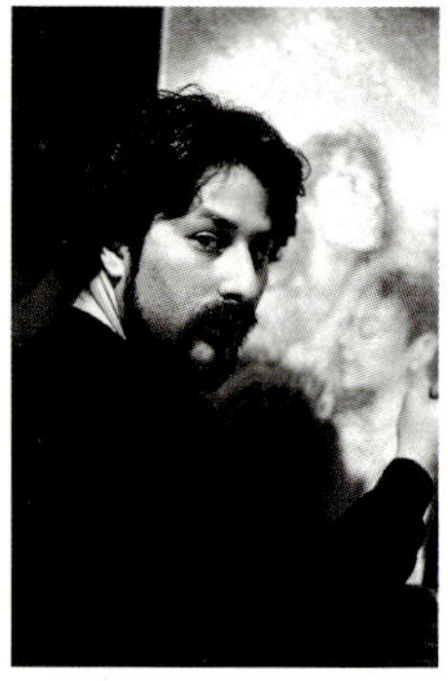

Photo: © by Carol Acquilano

Philip M. Rubinov-Jacobson
Artist & Writer
P.O. Box 20381
Boulder, CO 80308-3381
Tel: (303) 938-8586

Opposite page: "Aaron's Heart," 5″ x 6″ mixed media, 1986. Collection of J. Peter Chipmann

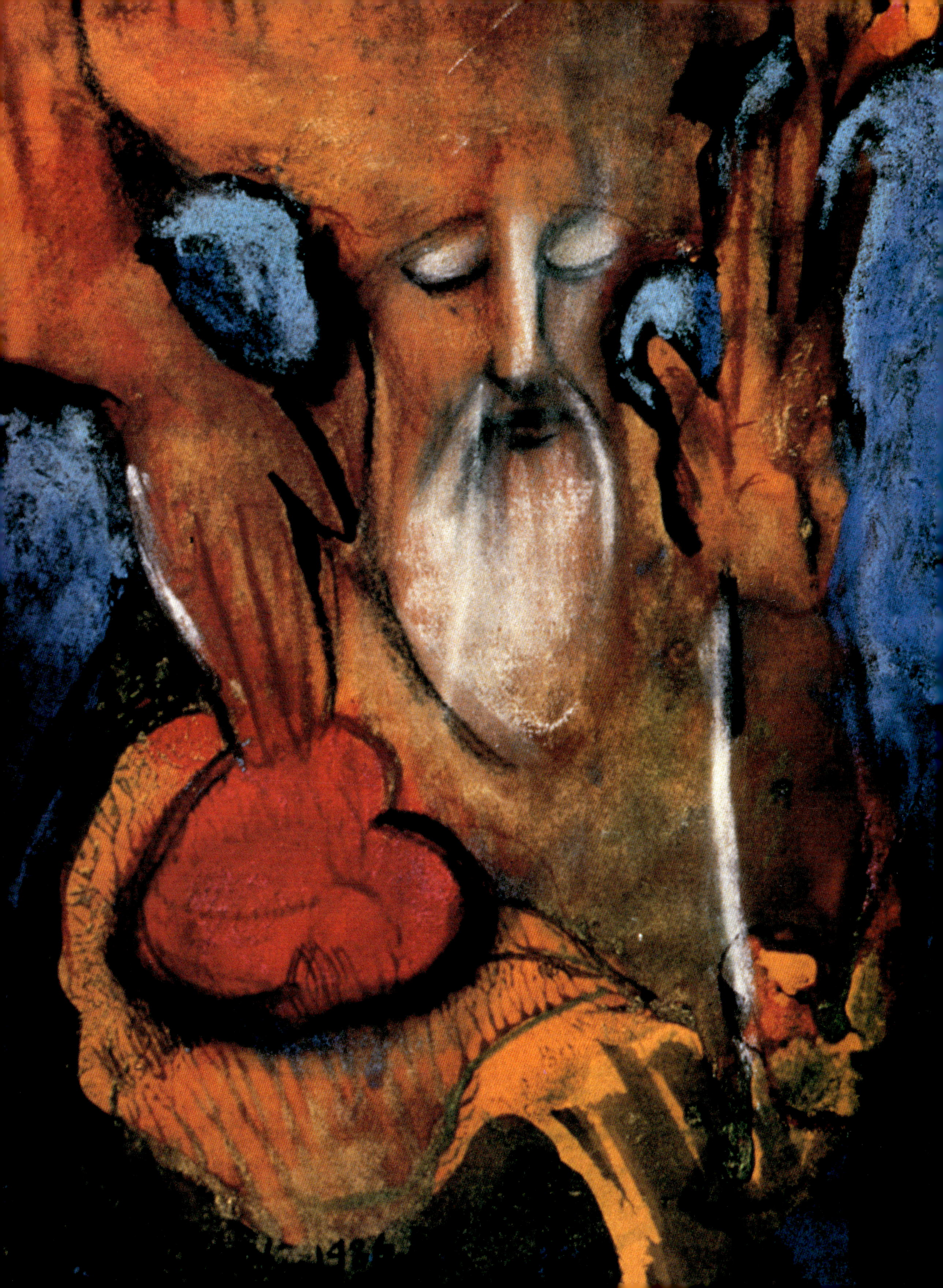

MARILYN SUNDERMAN

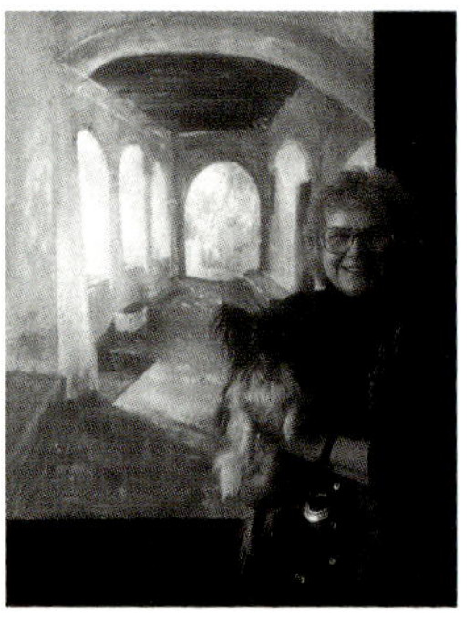

"I TRY TO CAPTURE THE 'LIGHT' — THE LIGHT THAT SHINES IN EACH OF US."

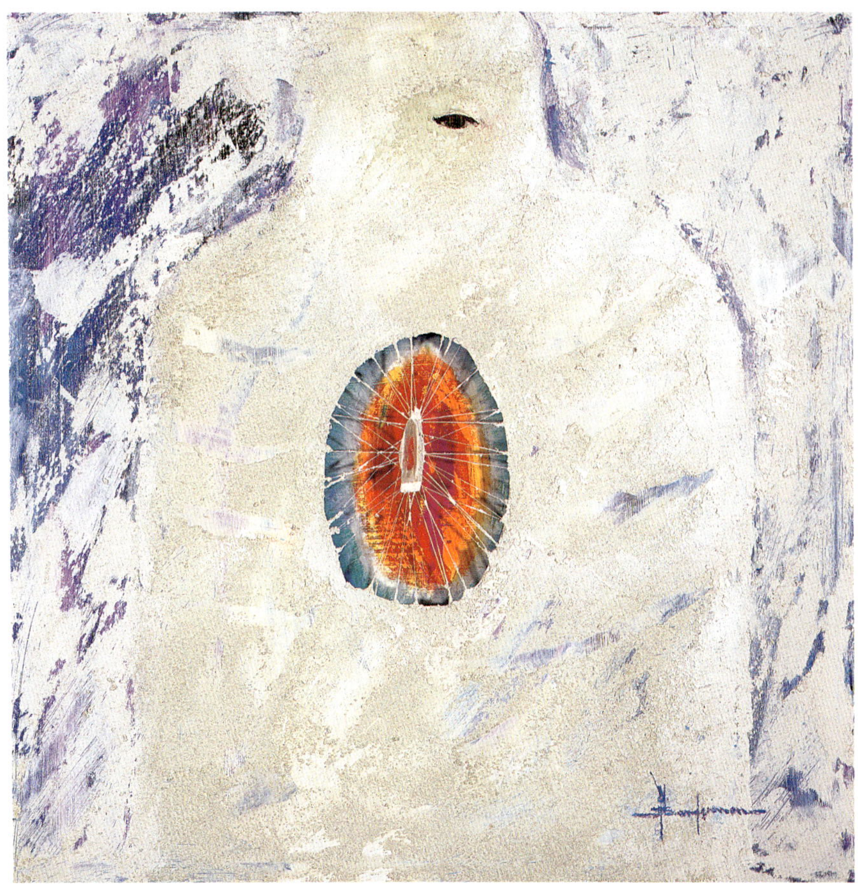

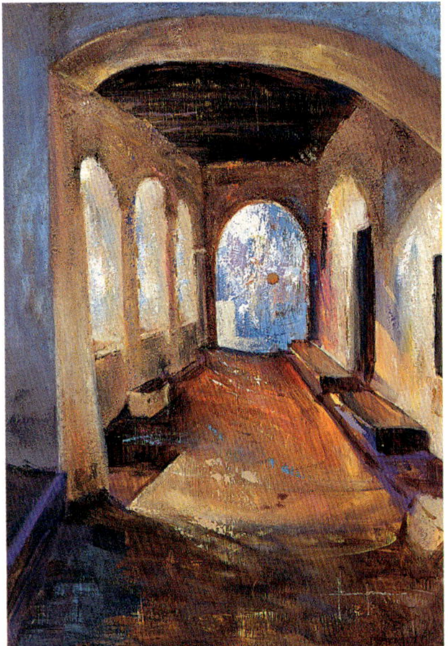

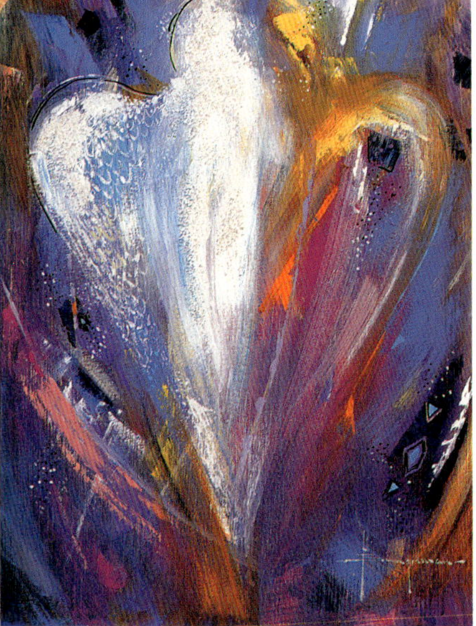

Top: "The Snow Walker," from the series "Keepers of the Universe," 36" x 36" acrylic on canvas, 1995 Bottom left: "Another World," 48" x 36" acrylic on canvas, 1996 Bottom right: "The Little Angel," 24" x 20" acrylic on canvas, 1996

Entering my studio, you are surrounded by angels. There are sculptures and paintings of them, as well as REAL ones. I always feel their presence as I'm painting or writing.

Sometime ago, while I was still doing portraits, I realized I was going deeply into the souls of people. Now, I do that with *life* and with my *work*. I try to capture the "Light" — the Light that shines in each of us.

The world is transforming and it is compelling us, pleading with us, to transform with it. We have the opportunity now to build a world of *Peace*, not war, *Love*, not fear.

With the paths and arches I paint, I try to draw the viewer into my canvases, and suggest there is a *Path* for them.

With my *Light Beings* and *Creation of Light*, I try to awaken the viewer to deeper parts of themselves.

Through my writings as well as my paintings, I want to show other dimensions, other worlds, and invite people to enter them.

Always I imply there is hope for transformation. *And always there are angels.*

Marilyn C. Sunderman
Sunderman Studios
P.O. Box 2633
Sedona, AZ 86339
Tel: (520) 282-5499

Opposite page: "Metamorphosis and the Soul," 60" x 48" acrylic on canvas, 1994

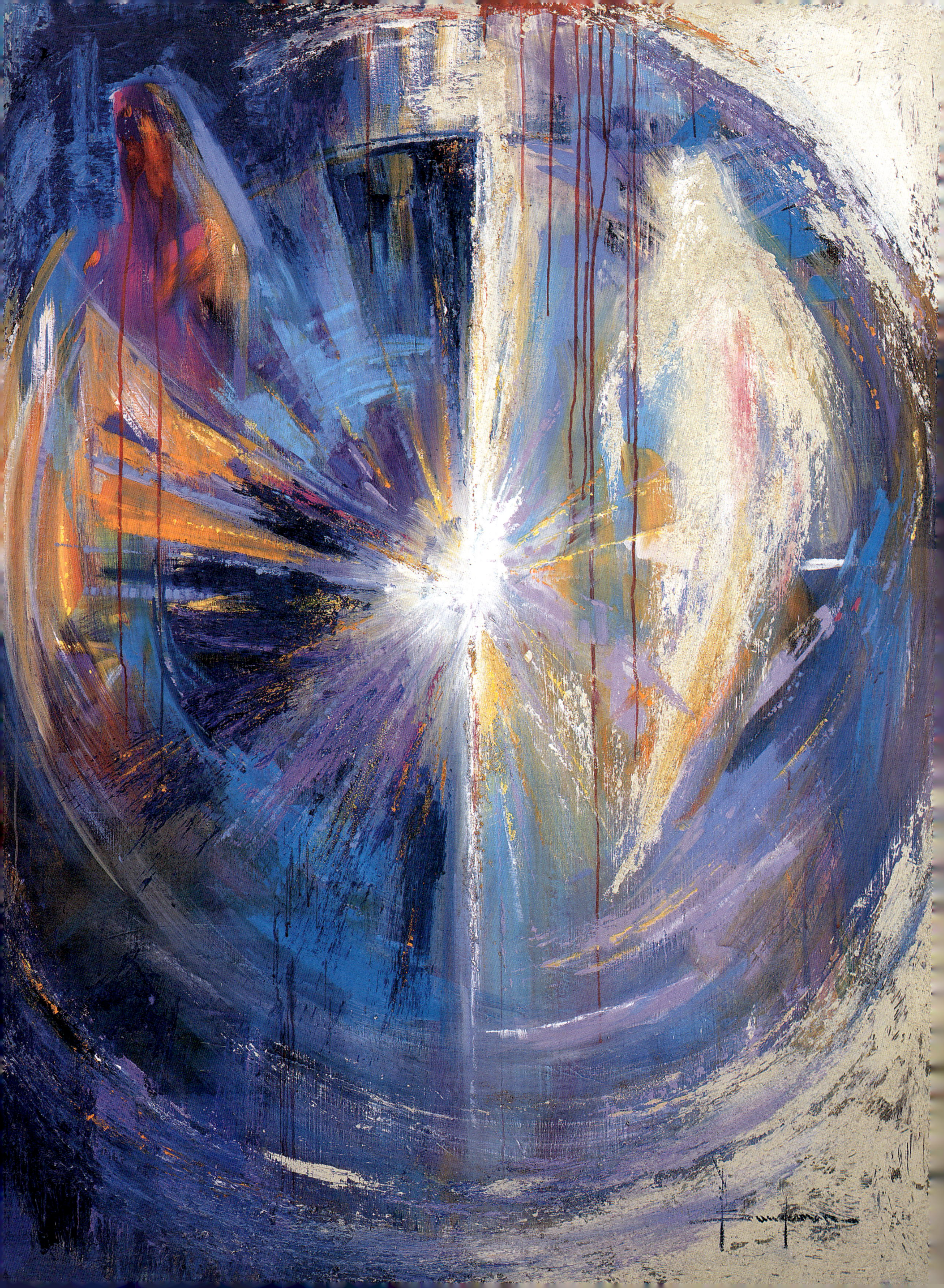

DEBORAH KOFF-CHAPIN

THE CENTER FOR TOUCH DRAWING

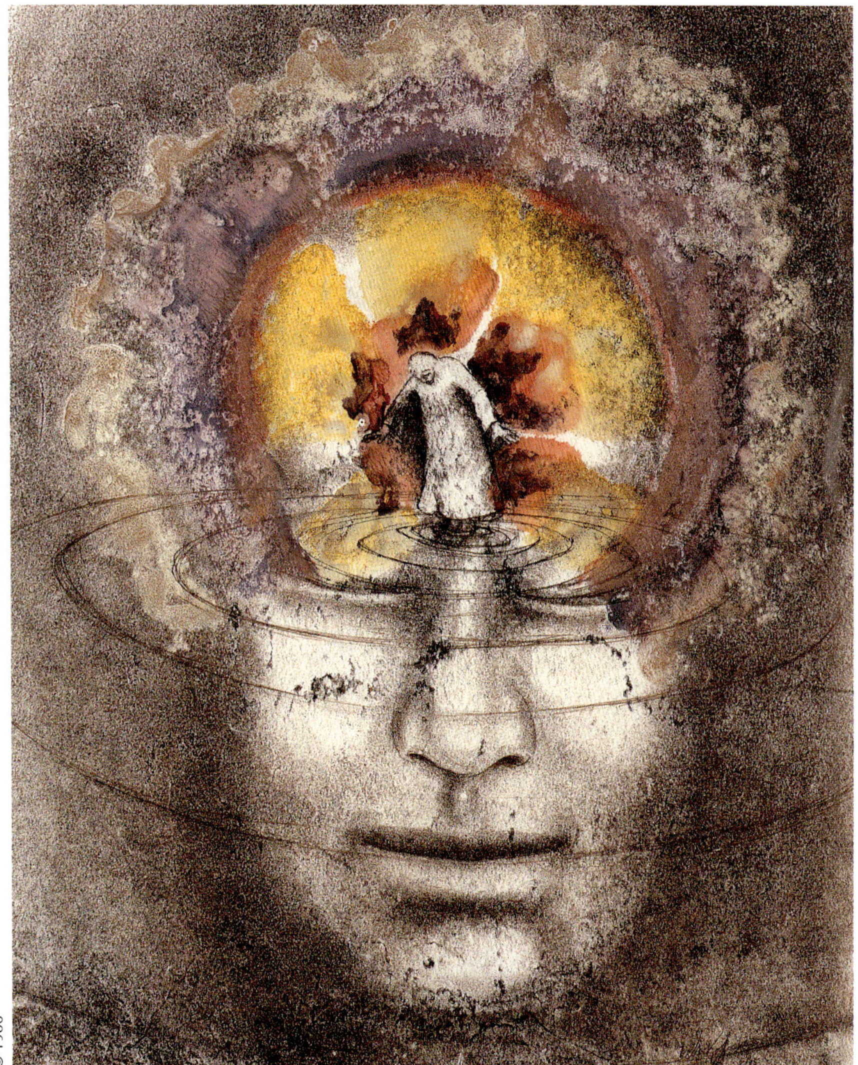

© 1986

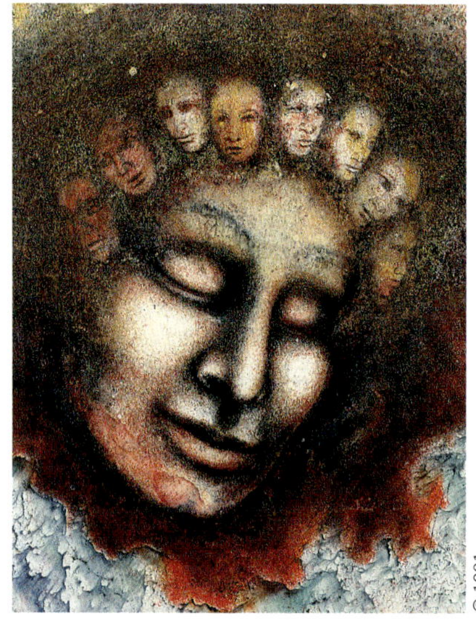

© 1991

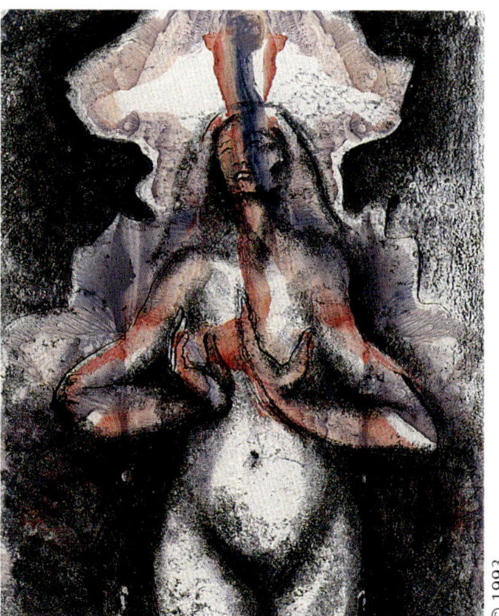

© 1993

Touch Drawings, selected images from a series of 60 published as "SoulCards." Printers ink on paper.

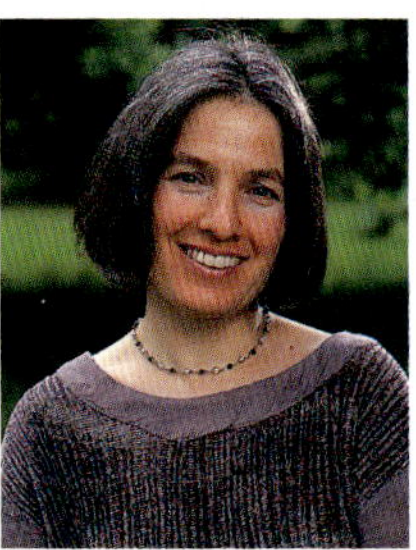

"SURRENDERING TO SUCH PRIMAL EXPRESSION TAUGHT ME THE ART OF LISTENING WITHIN."

— Deborah Koff-Chapin

From my earliest awareness, I have felt a calling to express the depths of the soul through human images. During my years in art school, I became fluent in the language of abstraction. This was pure and essential, but foreign to the eyes of all but those educated in the esoteric knowledge of the art world. I was stunned into this realization one day when an old friend came to my studio and stared blankly at the abstract paintings on the wall. In the past I had shared the depths of my soul with friends through images. Where had I gone in those art school years to draw such a blank? The seed of an answer came one day as I scribbled some words onto a page ... "What's wrong with drawing a face?" With a shudder of guilt, I tentatively doodled some raw, primitive heads. It felt as if as if I was drawing something "dirty." I tucked the embarrassing doodle away.

Within several weeks the seed that had been germinating in my being burst forth in the form of Touch Drawing. On the last day of my last year in school, I was helping a friend clean an inked glass plate in the print shop. Before wiping the ink off the plate with a paper towel, I playfully moved my hands over the towel, and lifting it, saw lines which had been transferred to the underside of the

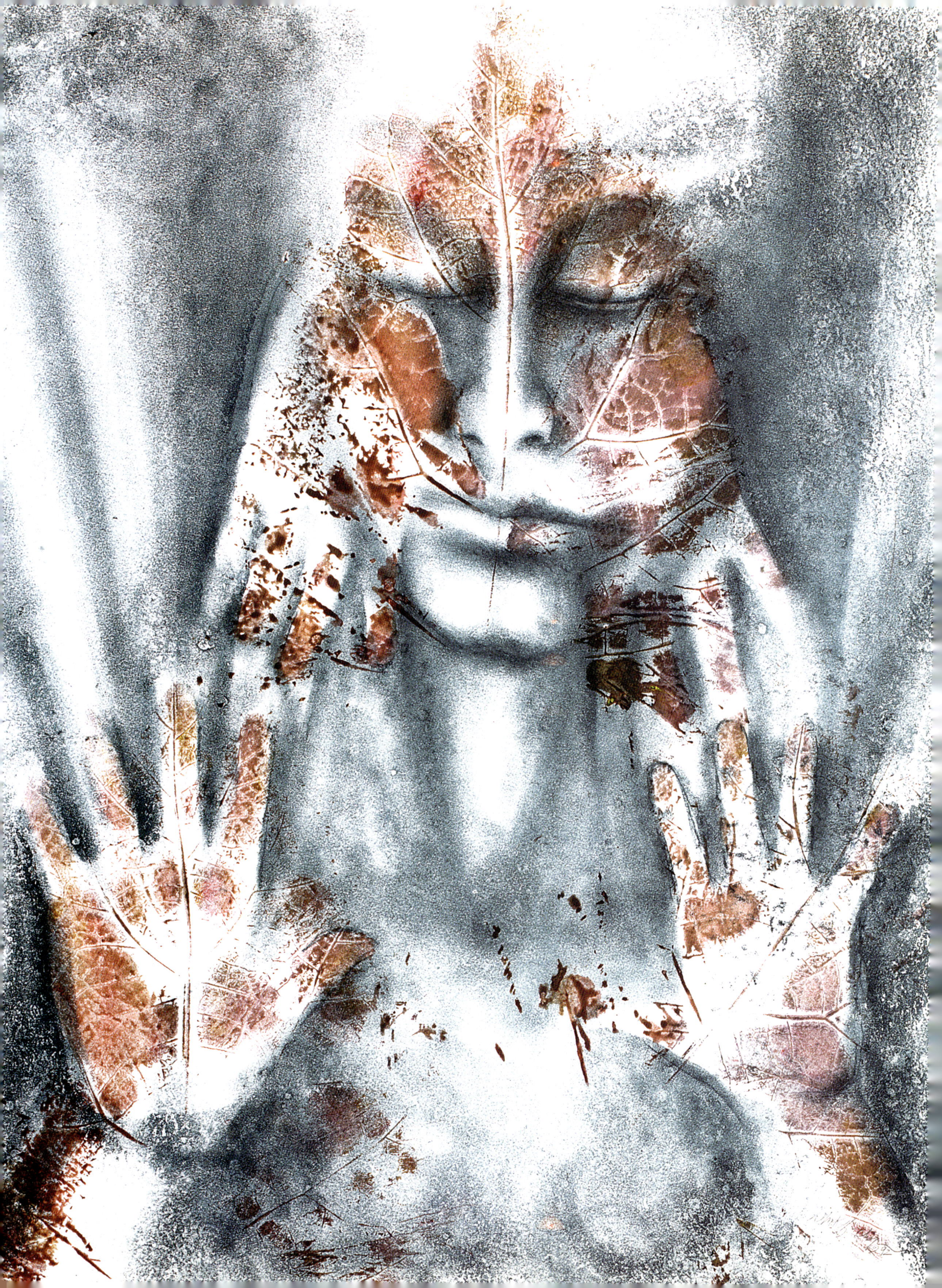

DEBORAH KOFF-CHAPIN
THE CENTER FOR TOUCH DRAWING

towel by my touch. Lines coming directly from my fingertips! I laughed hysterically with this discovery and crawled around on the floor, gathering up more discarded paper towels. In a state of ecstatic revelation, flowing lines poured from my hands. They were a natural extension of my being onto the page, a record of each moment as it passed. Within minutes I was drawing faces with both hands. My ever-changing soul was being reflected before me, childlike and primitive, honest and direct.

Although this experience had the appearance of simply being play, under the surface was something profound and powerful. It felt as if I was receiving a gift from outside of time, from an invisible knowing presence. I had a sense that Touch Drawing was being given for more than my own personal use. Along with this gift came a responsibility. Somehow, I would have to share this process with the world. While sensing that I was acting on behalf of a great evolutionary force, I began to pour my soul into Touch Drawing. During difficult times I would turn to the drawing board to release emotions. As I accepted my feelings and allowed them to pour onto the page through my hands, I was drawn more deeply into myself. It was as if I was sculpting my own being — transforming, literally before my own eyes. At the end of a session I had a record of this transformation — images of my soul in motion. And I would feel clear and whole.

The images that emerged in the early days were personal and therapeutic. Surrendering to such primal expression taught me the art of listening within. Over time, I began to tap into a transpersonal consciousness. Gradually, I have become aware of a subtle overlighting presence as I draw. Now when I bring my attention to the drawing board, my hands trace the beginnings of a sensed image. In deep focus and trust, I abandon myself to the process and watch as an image emerges onto the page. When I rise to leave the drawing board, I realize that I am disengaging from a deep communion. Silently, I offer my thanks.

Through the years I have sought to answer the call to share Touch Drawing that came in the initial moments of its discovery. My original intuition that this process was not for myself alone is confirmed again and again. It is confirmed each time I witness people who had been expressing fear and limitation, relax and dive into themselves through the mirror of the drawing board. It is confirmed each time I see hands moving on the page in an unselfconscious dance, and by the healing power that is unleashed through this pure act of creation. And it is confirmed by the deep satisfaction felt as people recognize the honesty, power and beauty reflected in their drawings, each other and themselves.

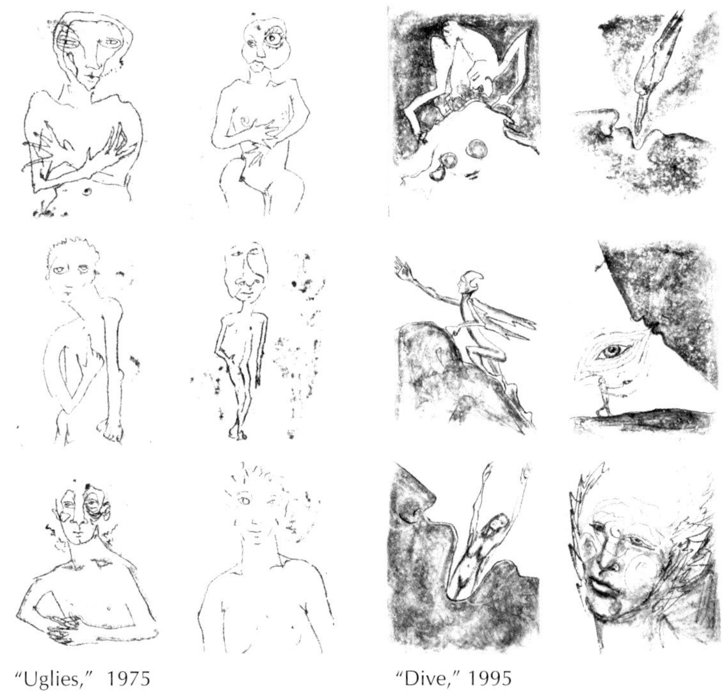

"Uglies," 1975 "Dive," 1995

"In the early years of Touch Drawing, my images were primal expressions of emotion and body awareness. With time, the images began to emerge from a deep interior attunement."

My hope is that Touch Drawing will sprout up in the gardens of so many lives that it will continue to reseed itself long after I am gone. My vision is that Touch Drawing becomes rooted in many facets of human culture through the natural seeding of person-to-person contact. My prayer is that Touch Drawing can serve in the healing and blossoming of the human soul. I invite you to help make this a reality. The future use and development of Touch Drawing is in the hands of those who hear its call.

Deborah Koff-Chapin
The Center for Touch Drawing
P.O. Box 914
Langley, WA 98260
Tel: (360) 221-5745
Fax: (360) 221-5931

Opposite page: Touch Drawing selected from "SoulCards," 1988

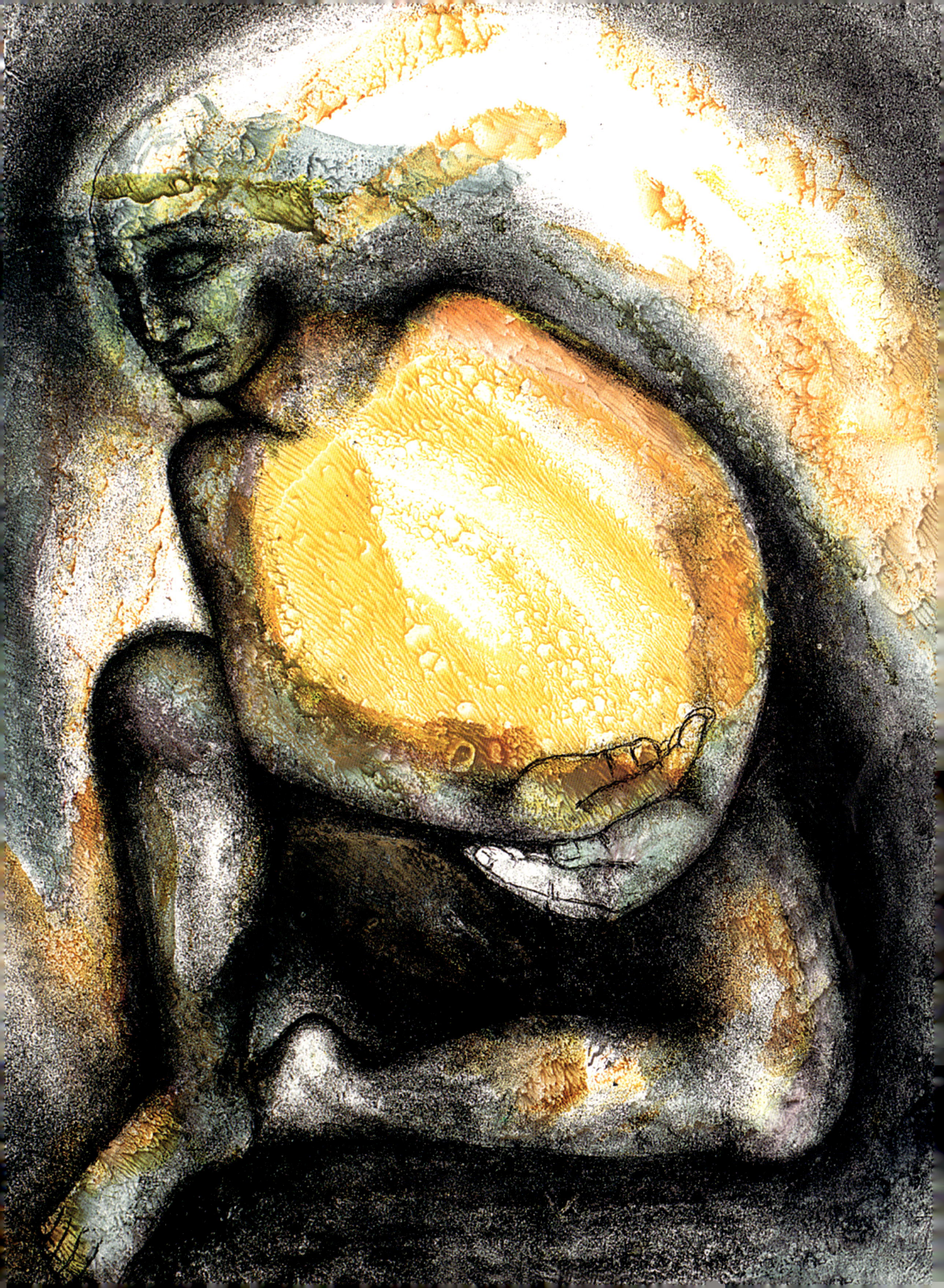

"FOR ME, THE ACT OF CREATING IS ABOUT ENERGY AND OPENING TO MOVE DEEPER INTO THE MYSTERY OF LIFE."

— SANDRA REAMER

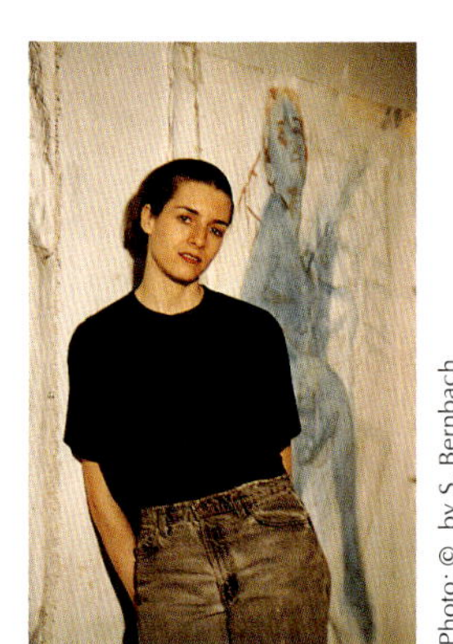

Photo: © by S. Bernbach

SANDRA REAMER

My images are born out of my living. My experience of what life is and the energy that is life nourishes me as maker and moves me to create. Art-making for me is intimate and personal requiring full participation of my body. What I mean by body includes emotional, mental, physical and soul layers of being. When I'm painting or drawing, my art-making acts as an interface for these layers of being, fostering a harmonic, visceral intelligence and intuition within the vastness of reality and my being. The vastness of reality is so large, and yet, in its largeness are the contents that make up life. That which is known and not yet known offers me the opportunity to participate in the gift and mystery of life through the art-making process.

My body is my instrument played by the energy that moves me and the life that I am. An integral part of my art directly involves my physical body. I rub, press, scratch and mark the surface primarily with my face, hands and feet or use unconventional tools. The marks that I apply to a surface speak as a resonant cord and visually resound my state of being in the moment of making. I form my compositions in the immediacy of a feeling as it is fired by the energy that flows through my life. In this way, my compositions serve as a lens, imaging states of being through the various filters of my awareness.

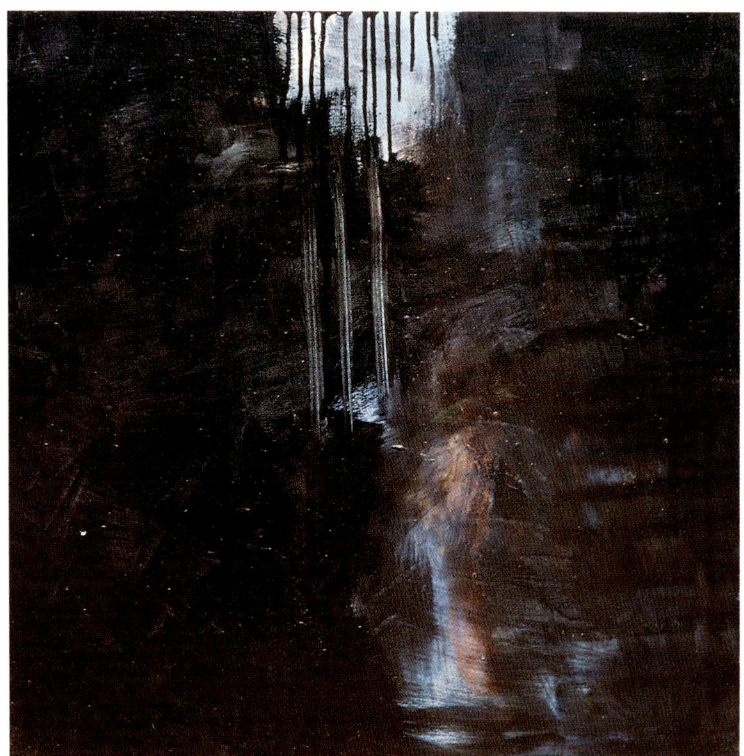

"Cavern Of The Warrior's Heart," 30" x 30" oil, 1996

The surface holds parts of my body as image recording my physicality in a very personal and direct way. It is not necessary that this be apparent for the viewer. My physicality with the surface is an attempt to bring my subconscious reality through my physical form. In a way, I'm penetrating emotion as the end result of something I experience to get to the underlying energy. Through the immediacy of the gesture, the mark and the process of painting, there is a representation happening in some way of energy, where form is a consequence, an end result. For me the act of creating is about energy and opening to move deeper into the mystery of life. Within the grand scheme of life, my evolution is cultivated through an embodiment of art.

Sandra Reamer Studio
P. O. Box 1459
New York, NY 10013
Tel: (718) 399-8281 (303) 938-8586

Opposite page: "Chthonic Spirits," 36" x 36" egg tempera on oil, 1996

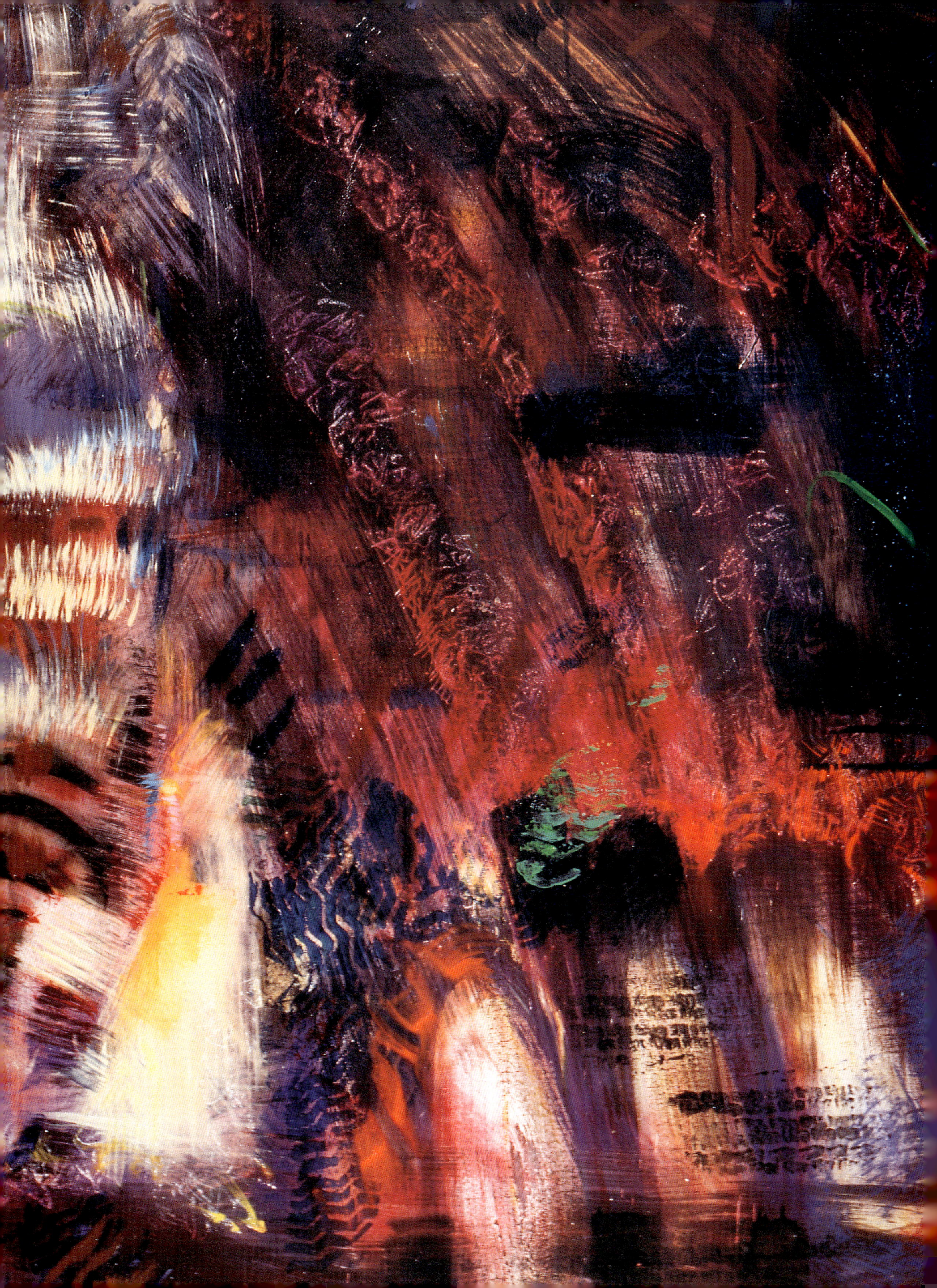

EL DIECKVOß

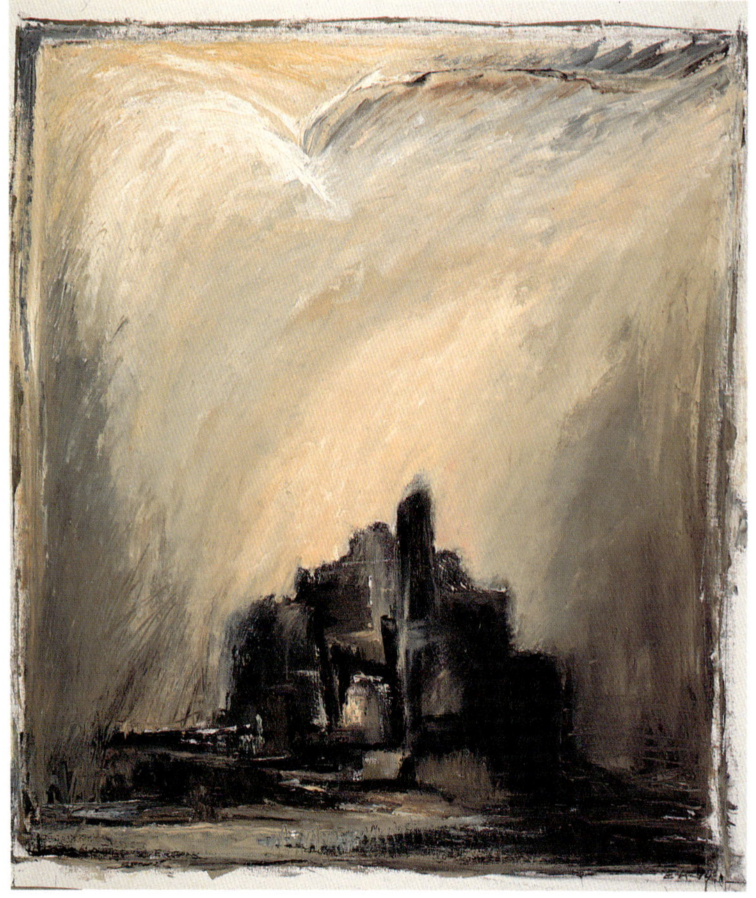

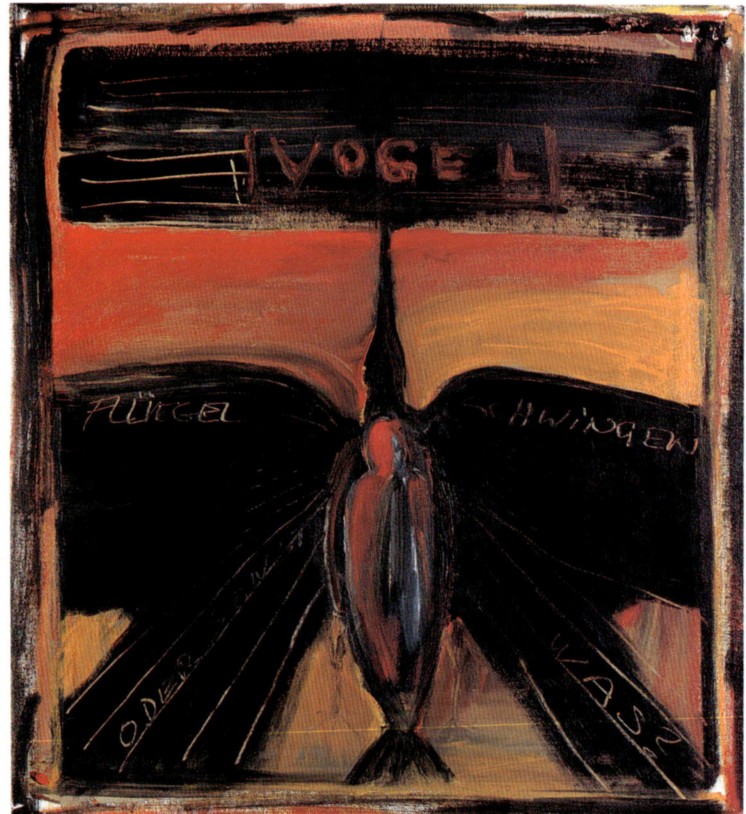

Top: "Circling the Ancient Tower," 32" x 37" oil on canvas, 1994
Bottom: "Encompassed," 31"x 41" oil on canvas, 1994

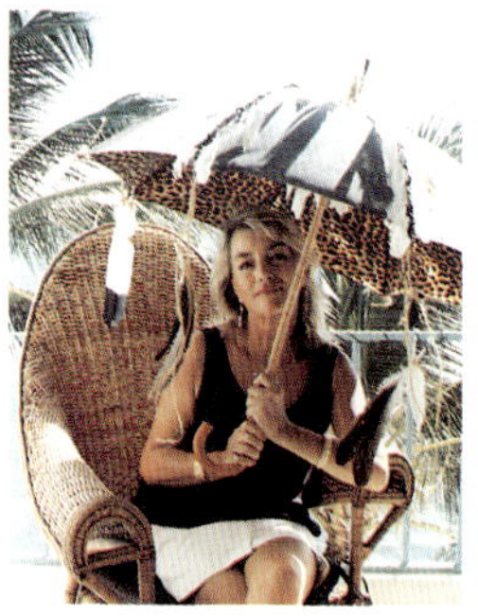

YOU,
wings and birds,
appearing in dreams,
paintings and visions,
tell me, what is the message?
SILENCE
— El

The transplanting of myself from Europe to Hawai'i has opened me to experience new paths. As part of that path I journeyed frequently to New Mexico. During my quests I encountered creatures — mainly birds — that played the role of messengers, providing messages my inquisitive Western mind did not understand. It was not until I began to express and explore those teachings and visions in my work, that the images unfolded, taking on their own life. It was then that I experienced the awesome freedom of flight of birds.

For several years the messengers have traveled with me in all walks of life. They mystify me and motivate me. It was not until I surrendered to a higher wisdom that I realized the gift I had received: that I had been given a link between Germanic, Hawai'ian, and Native American mythology ... and with that a sense of universal belonging.

El Dieckvoß
Atelier EK
2999 Kalakaua Avenue #601
Honolulu, HI 96815
Tel/Fax: (808) 923-1711

Opposite page: "Shedding Old Skins," 31" x 53" oil on canvas, 1994

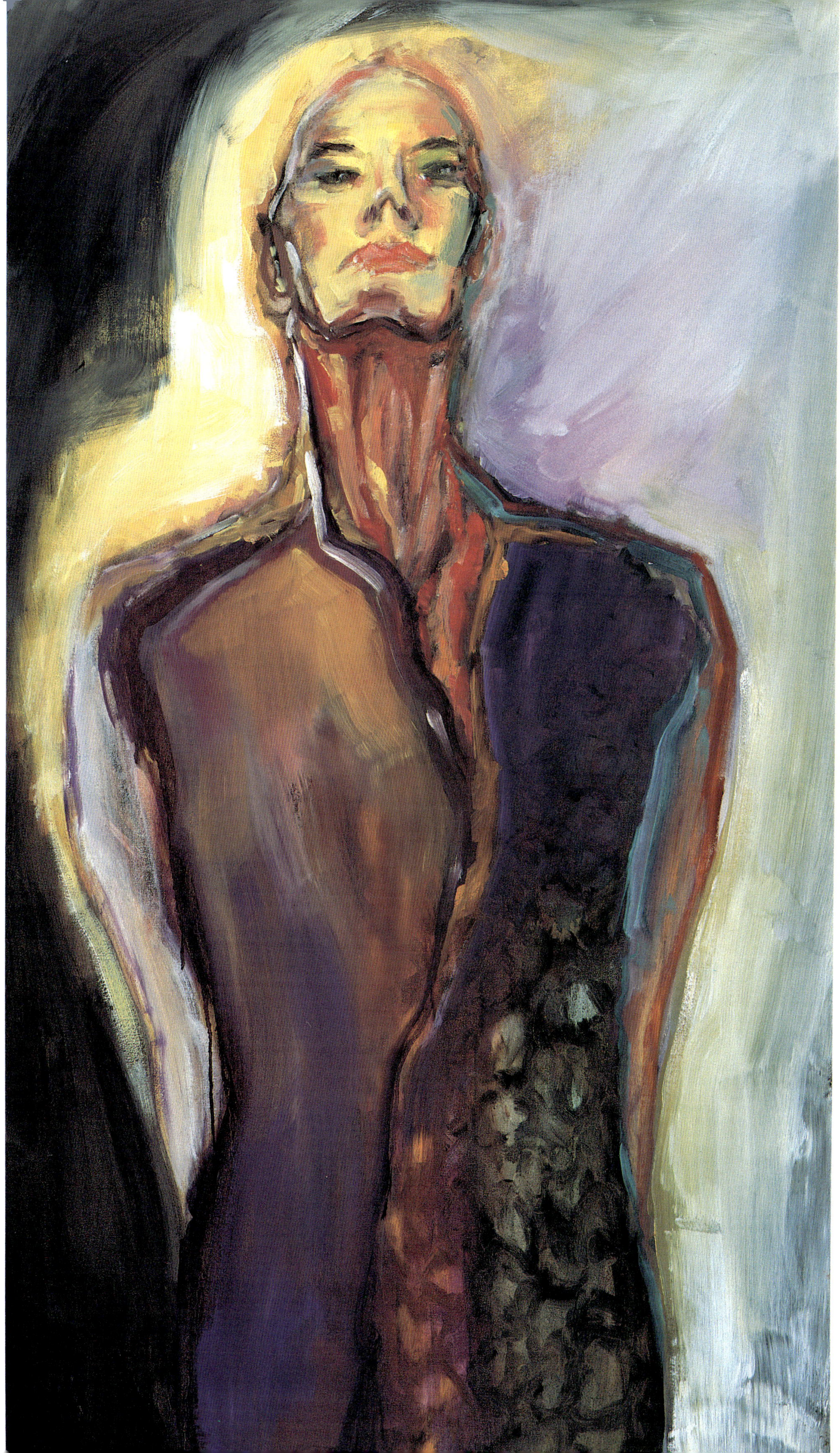

CHRISTIE FERTAL

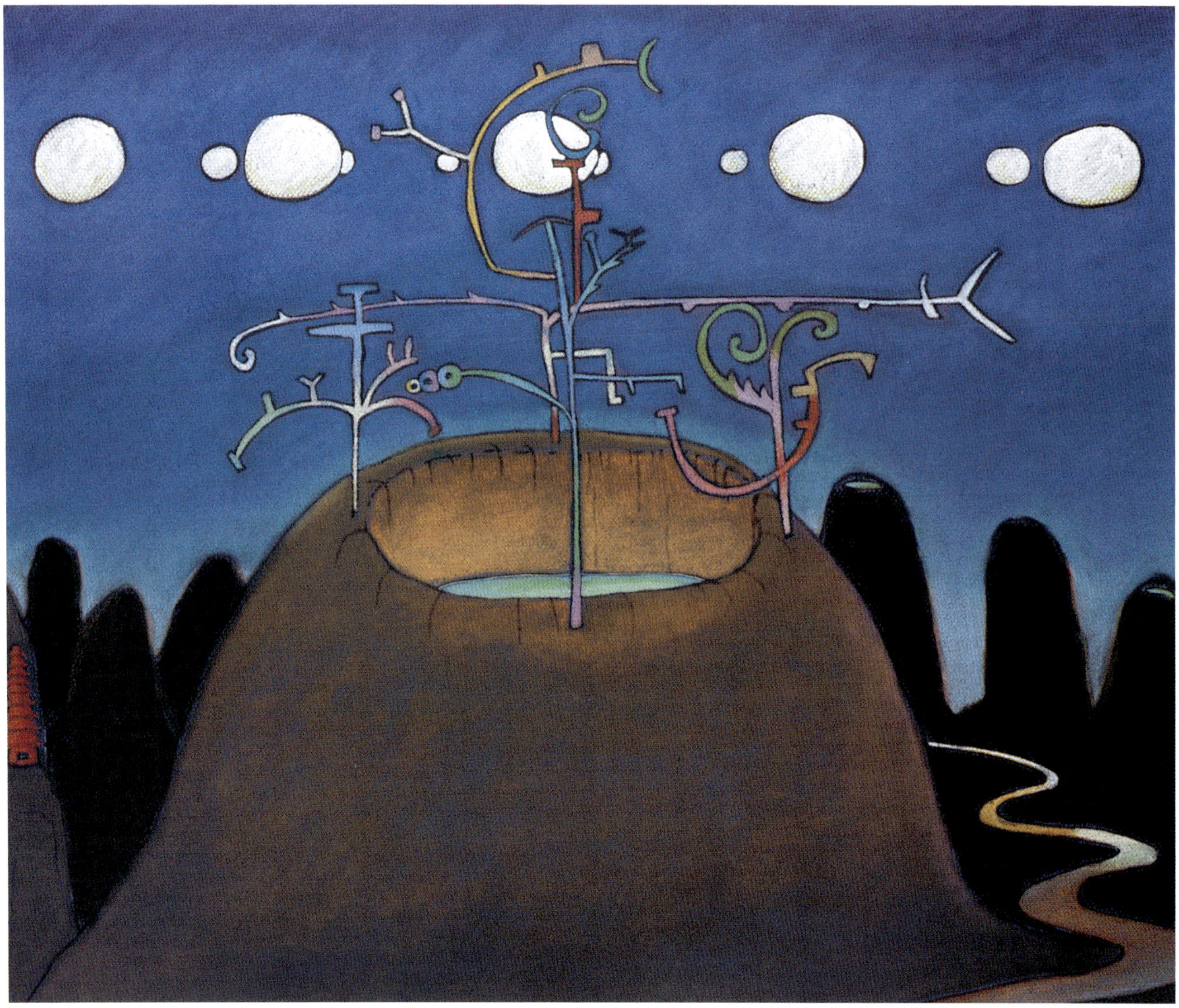

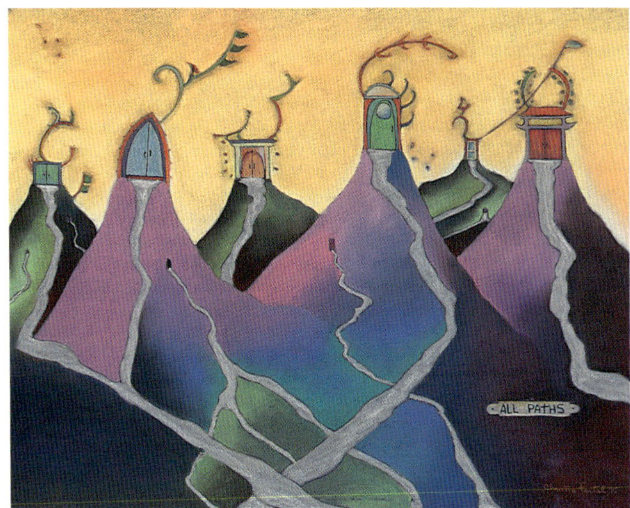

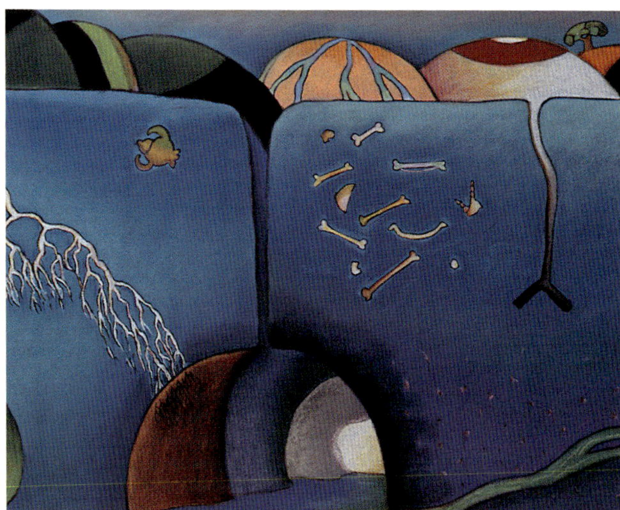

Top: "Dismemberment Pagoda," 19" x 25" pastel, 1996 Bottom left: "All Paths," 19" x 25" pastel, 1996
Bottom right: "To the Underworld," 19" x 25" pastel, 1996

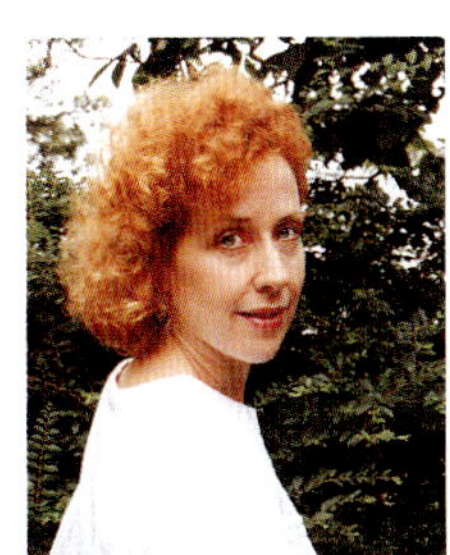

"... THE SPIRIT OF MY ART IS ABOUT PLAYING IN THE MYSTERY, BEING FULLY PRESENT IN THE MOMENT ..."

— *CHRISTIE FERTAL*

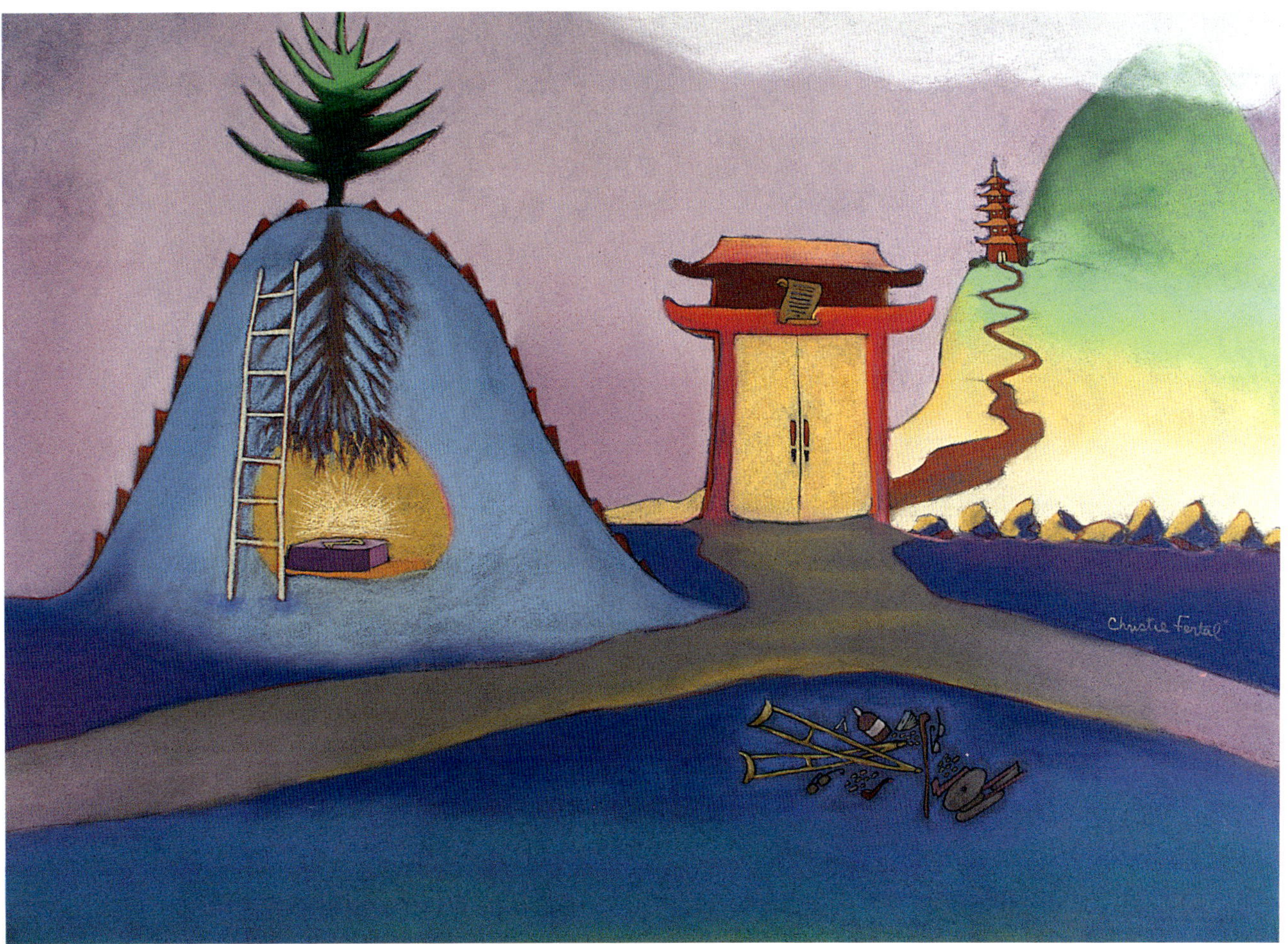

"Doors of Transformation," 19" x 25" pastel, 1996

I use shamanic journeying as a method of accessing personal and universal information through my heart. I call my work contemporary shamanic art because it is earth-centered and magic-centered. Many of my images come directly from my experiences in journeying. Other images come from my studies of Hinduism and Vedic literature, Taoism, Buddhism, Cabalistic Judaism, sacred geometry, the Bible, dowsing, and Feng Shui.

I have generally perceived my consciousness as a landscape — always a sky and an earth. Underground is my subconscious, where my impressions reside as boulders, roots, hibernating animals, hidden treasures and objects. Water represents many things to me — my prana, chi, life blood, the sap, rain, rivers and streams (blood flow of the earth); the love I feel in my being — deep, still ocean or active flowing river. My veins — the earth's veins — ALL ONE.

The Bible says you cannot enter the kingdom of God except you become as a little child. My personal transformation and the spirit of my art is about playing in the mystery, being fully present in the moment, and receiving abundant love and support from my mother universe. My past reality of effort, alone-ness, fear and conflict has vanished. My new reality of ease, all one-ness, love, clarity, and abundant care for my creation is here now. I decree it. My art tells the stories of my experiences. Blessings.

Christie Grady Fertal
Many Mansions Studio
304 E. Brow Road
Lookout Mtn., TN 37350-1212
Tel: (423) 825-2067

"IF A PAINTING IS SUCCESSFUL
IT LEAVES OPEN A DOOR
INTO THE SPIRITUAL WORLD ..."

— *K. MARTIN-KURI*

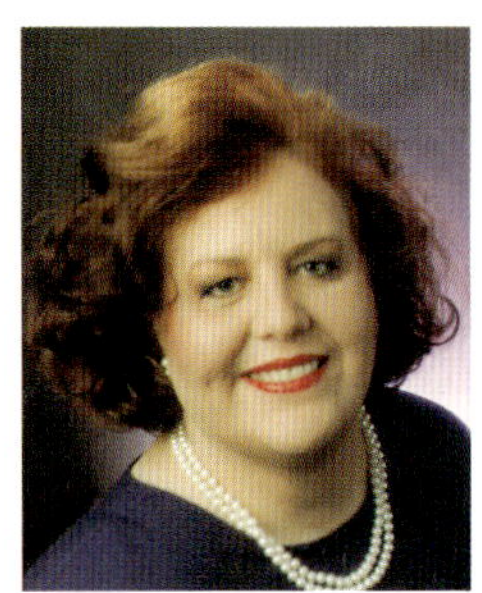

K. MARTIN-KURI

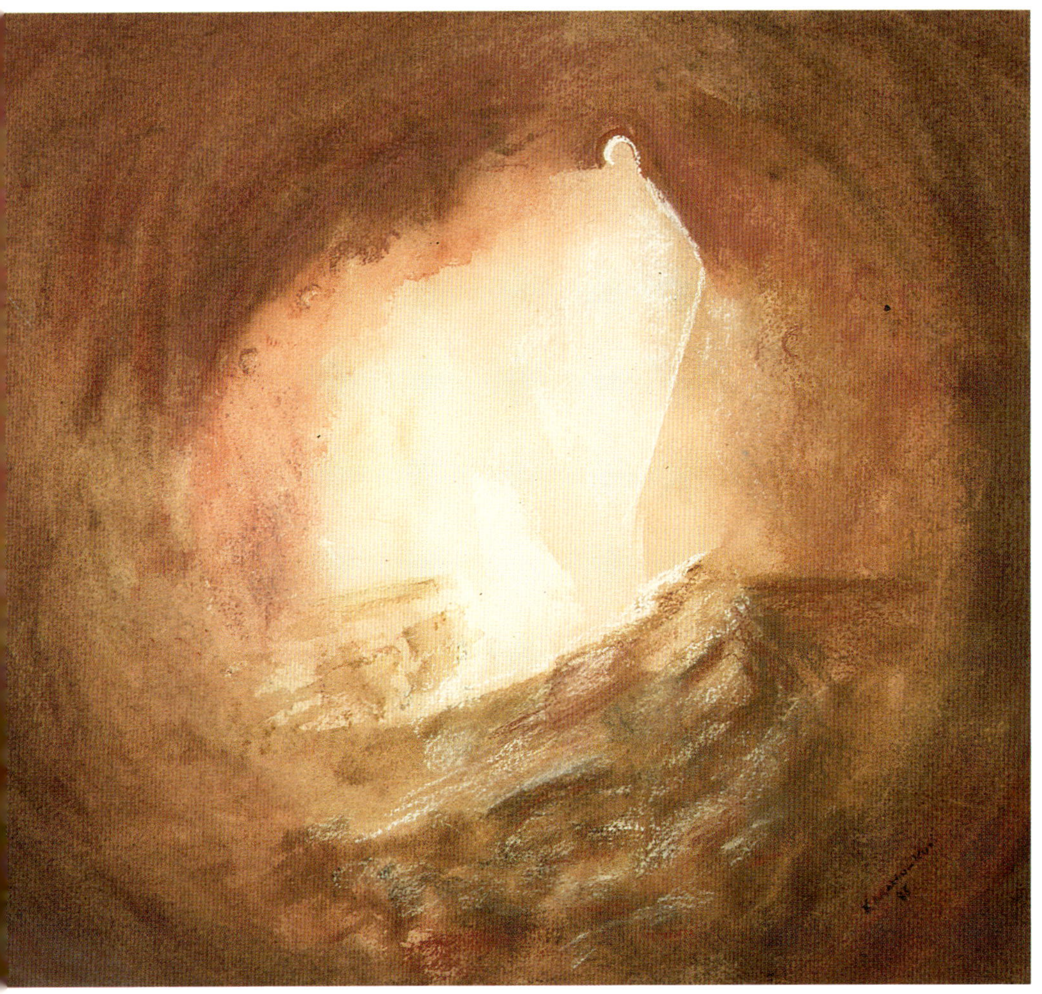

Above: "On the Mountain," 16" x 22" watercolor and chalk pastel, 1983
Opposite page: "Peacemaker," 10" x 16" watercolor and chalk pastel, 1983

It has been a life-long goal of mine to create an artform that would reveal loving images from heaven. My paintings are created out of a process of deep inner contemplation and prayer. The watercolors are done by using a wet-on-wet technique followed by thin veils of color. The final stage involves the use of chalk pastels to heighten the effect of radiance. The oil paintings have a special process that took many years to develop to overcome the natural heaviness of the medium and allow for the remarkable vibrant light to be released. My paintings have been compared to the artist and poet William Blake and have been described as carrying further the impulses of the English painter Turner, and the impressionist Monet.

There has been a growing recognition that the paintings serve as pathways or windows into a realm of consciousness that exists on a Universal level but which one rarely sees in a visible art form. The heavenly energy of the paintings help people become balanced on spiritual and emotional levels.

I consider my talent to be a spiritual gift that was received as a result of years of prayer and inner preparation. I approach my work with great seriousness that requires becoming extremely balanced within before entering the creative process. The painting process is a devotional practice which honors God. Each piece is created through a direct experience rather than portraying a memory. If a painting is successful it leaves open a door into the spiritual world that will enable the viewer to share the same experience.

K. Martin-Kuri
28 Angels Inc.
P.O. Box 116
Free Union, VA 22940
Tel: (804) 978-3990
Fax: (804) 978-4508
Toll Free: (800) 28Angel

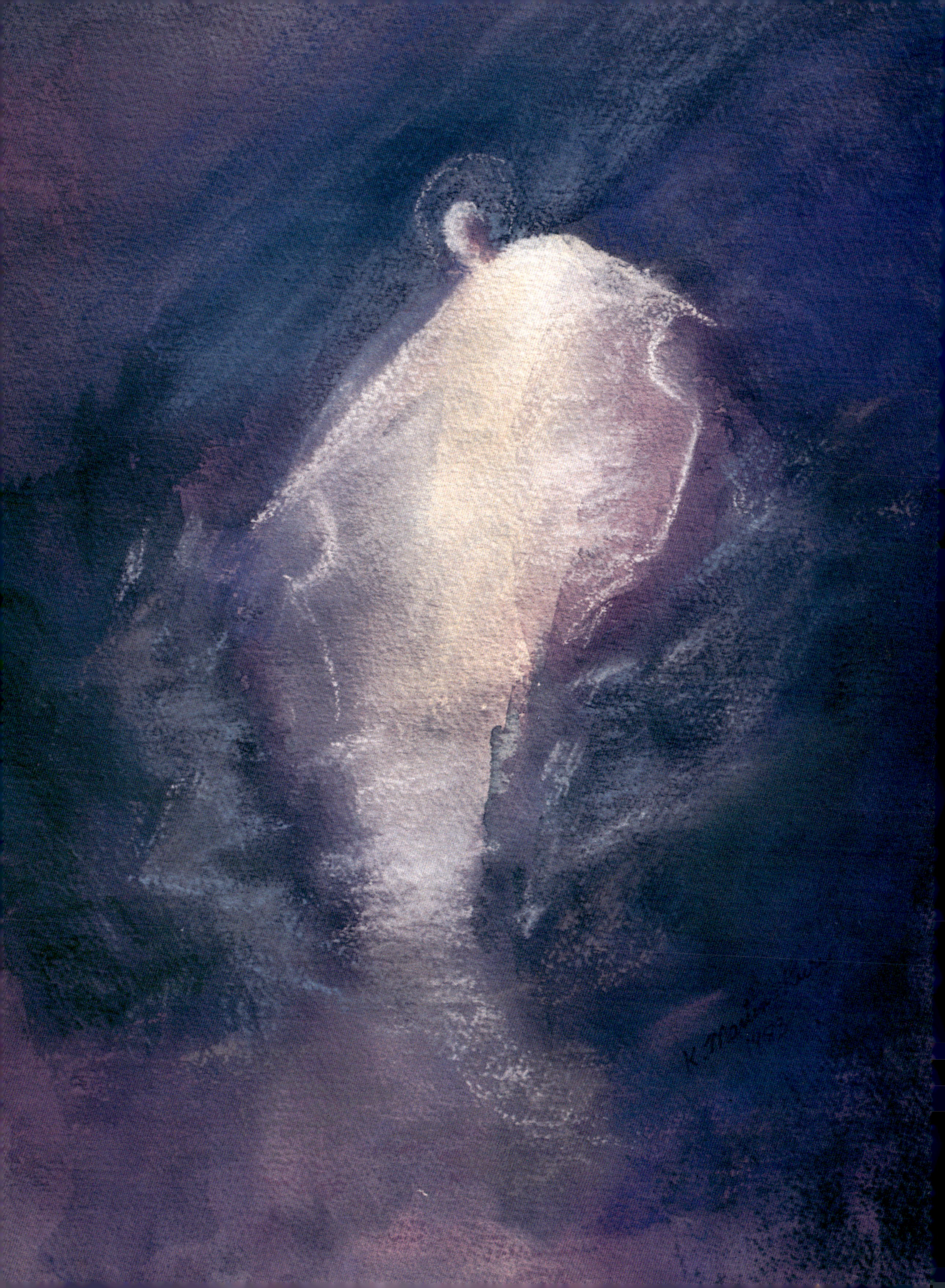

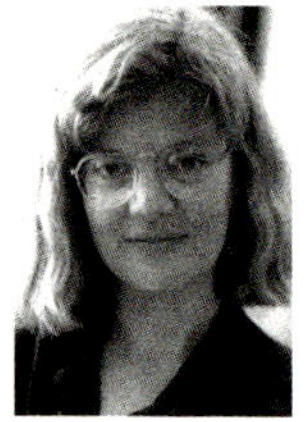
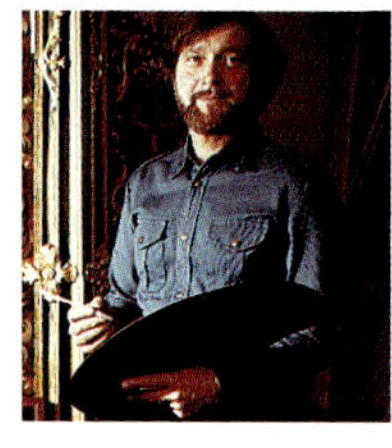
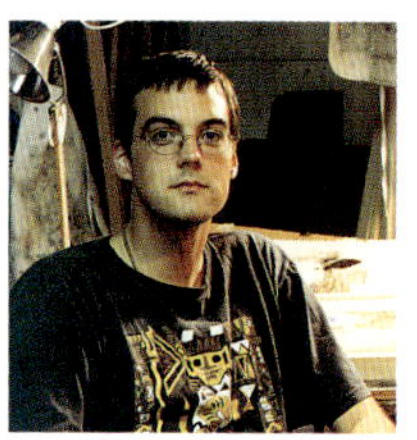
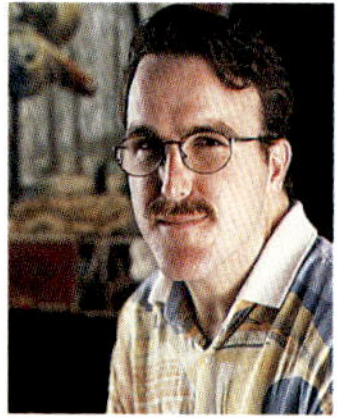

GALLERY ART CONSULTING

REPRESENTING CAROL AUST, KONSTANTIN K. IVANOV, MARK FREDRICKS AND TIM TIMMERMAN

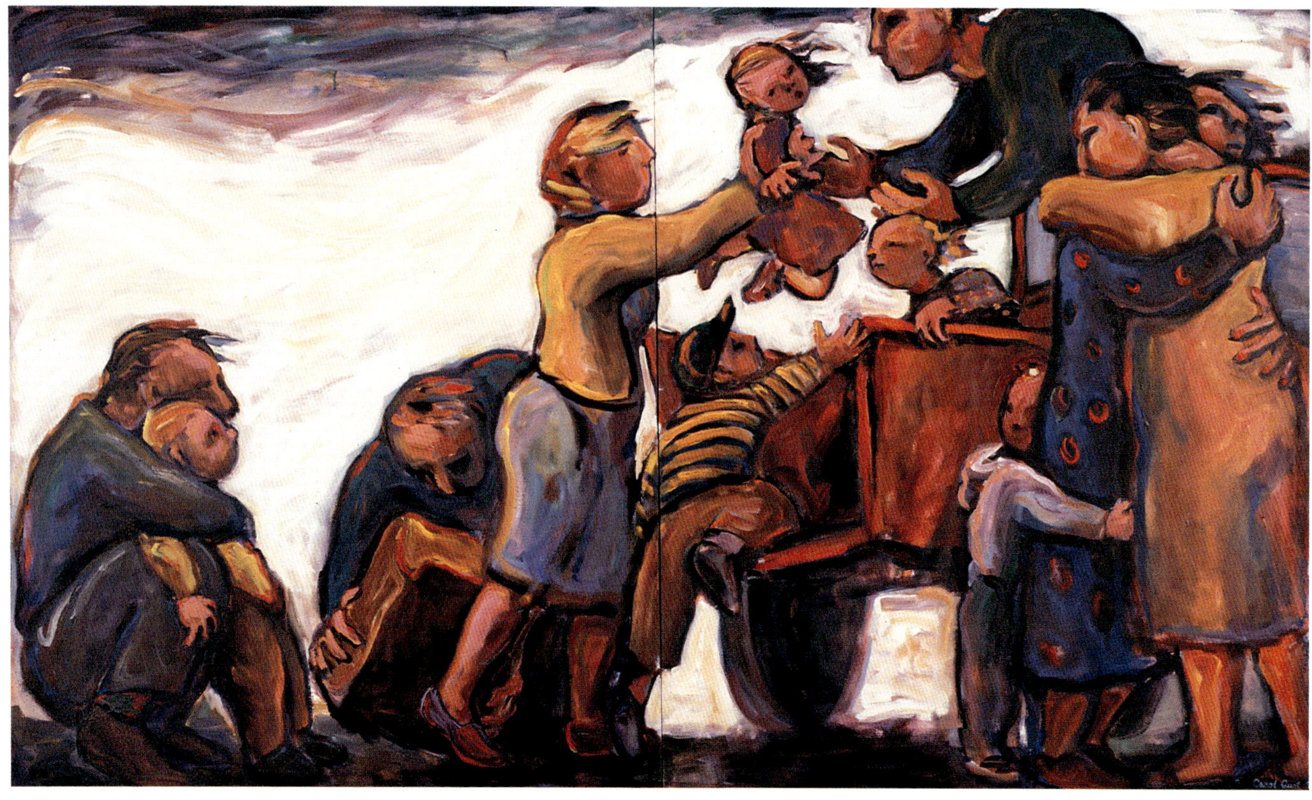

"Unknown Destination" by Carol Aust, 53" x 90" acrylic on canvas, 1993

"... THEY EACH HOPE TO REVEAL TO THE OBSERVER AN AWARENESS AND ILLUMINATION OF A LOVING GOD."
— *CASSANDRA DEARBORNE*

Carol Aust, Konstantin K. Ivanov, Mark Fredricks, and Tim Timmerman cultivate personal anecdotes into their art which imply visual moral fables. Similarly, biblical narratives are often the inspiring messages in which they each hope to reveal to the observer an awareness and illumination of a loving God.

Aust's "Unknown Destination" draws the viewer in to see the occurrence of a family leaving on a long voyage. There is no indication of where this family is going or why; yet many possibilities are visually implied through the juxtaposition of body language and tensions that interact between the characters in the painting. On a closer look, a sense of regret or happiness is expressed in the faces of the movers and friends present for the bon voyage.

Aust, "For me, the paintings aren't just narrative. They are about resolving issues and using the family as a metaphor. After grappling with the kids all day, I can go out to my studio and see with fresh eyes. I may be drained, but I feel energized after working on my art."

Konstantin K. Ivanov, from St. Petersburg, Russia, has suffered by seeing what is dear and sacred to him destroyed and left to decay. The Ivanov family has a two hundred year history of Russian Orthodox priests, so to be an Ivanov for Konstantin is to be a servant to the church he loves. Before the end of communism, it was only through his painting that he was able to preserve his desire and faithfully serve his fellow man. His painting, "Legend," is symbolic of all that was and is Russia in his eyes. By placing the tattered icon outside in the elements, Ivanov is visually illustrating the tale of hope and preservation that he kept in his heart for his country and belief. Yet, like all great work, "Legend" transcends the standard symbolism of the traditional icon and expresses the spirit of survival that persists in spite of oppression.

Ivanov, "Living in the darkness of communism and experiencing its still misguided breakup is often difficult. But one thing prevails, the spirit lives."

Fredricks' "Pierce Me Of These Desires" cuts to the interior man more directly. Gone from this work are the trappings of common phenomena. The man that Fredricks portrays is a man taken with the passions and hopes of lovers, writers and poets that inspire great art. His small renditions of life read like the pages from the heart, unfolding out to the observer like a book from our interior being. And though this particular piece is a more direct reference to our inner world, Fredricks' images always use the physical symbols of present reality to remind us of what is only felt, dreamed or sensed.

Fredricks, "My work exists in a context of meditation. It seeks to send someone inside, slightly beyond words and thought. It seeks to 'pour out,' as John of the Cross writes, 'secrets and mysteries rather than rational explanations.' At its very heart, it is a simple cry out to God."

Tim Timmerman takes the high road of humor and combines it with

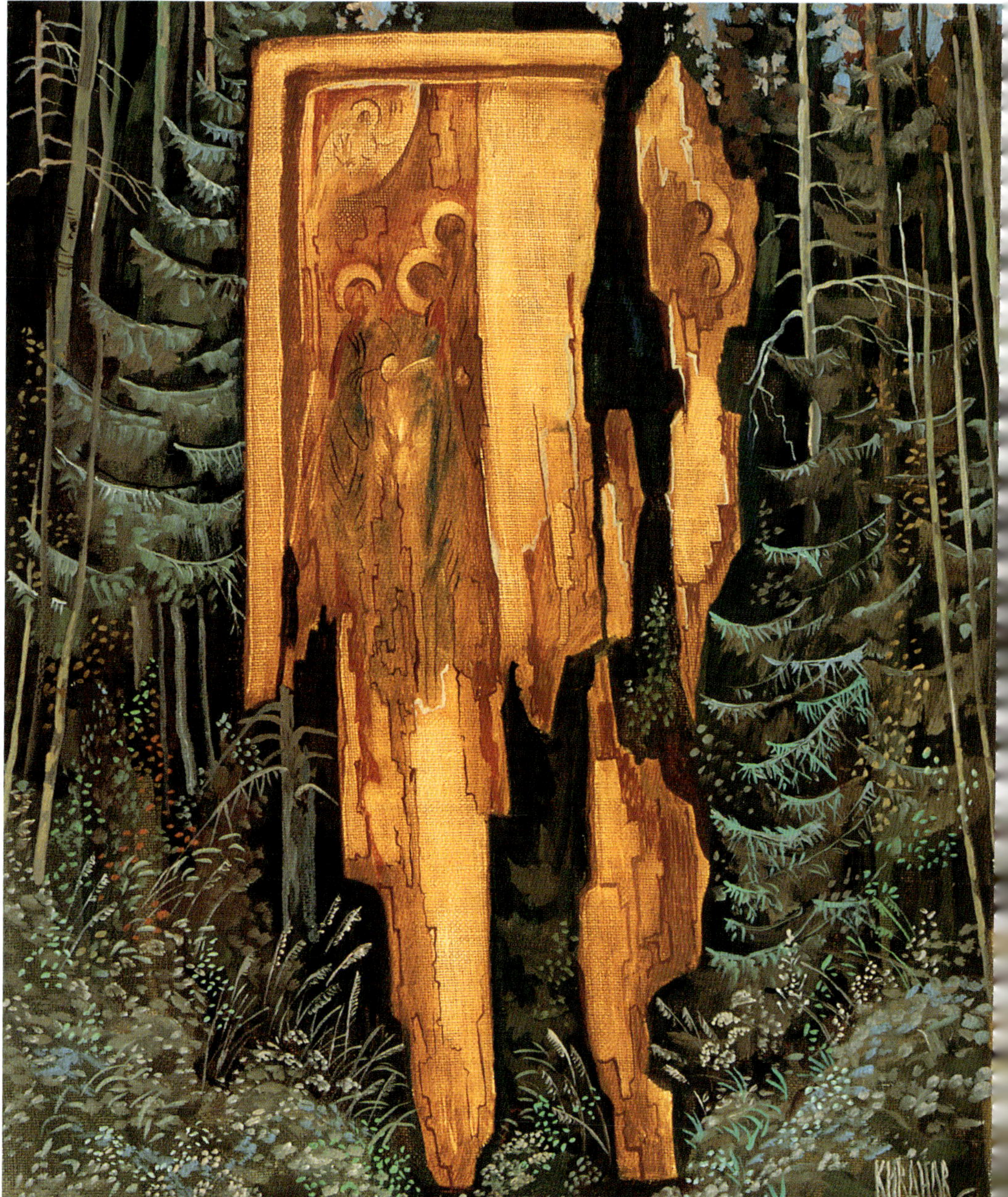

"Legend" by Konstantin K. Ivanov, 24" x 20" oil on canvas, 1991

GALLERY ART CONSULTING

REPRESENTING CAROL AUST, KONSTANTIN K. IVANOV, MARK FREDRICKS AND TIM TIMMERMAN

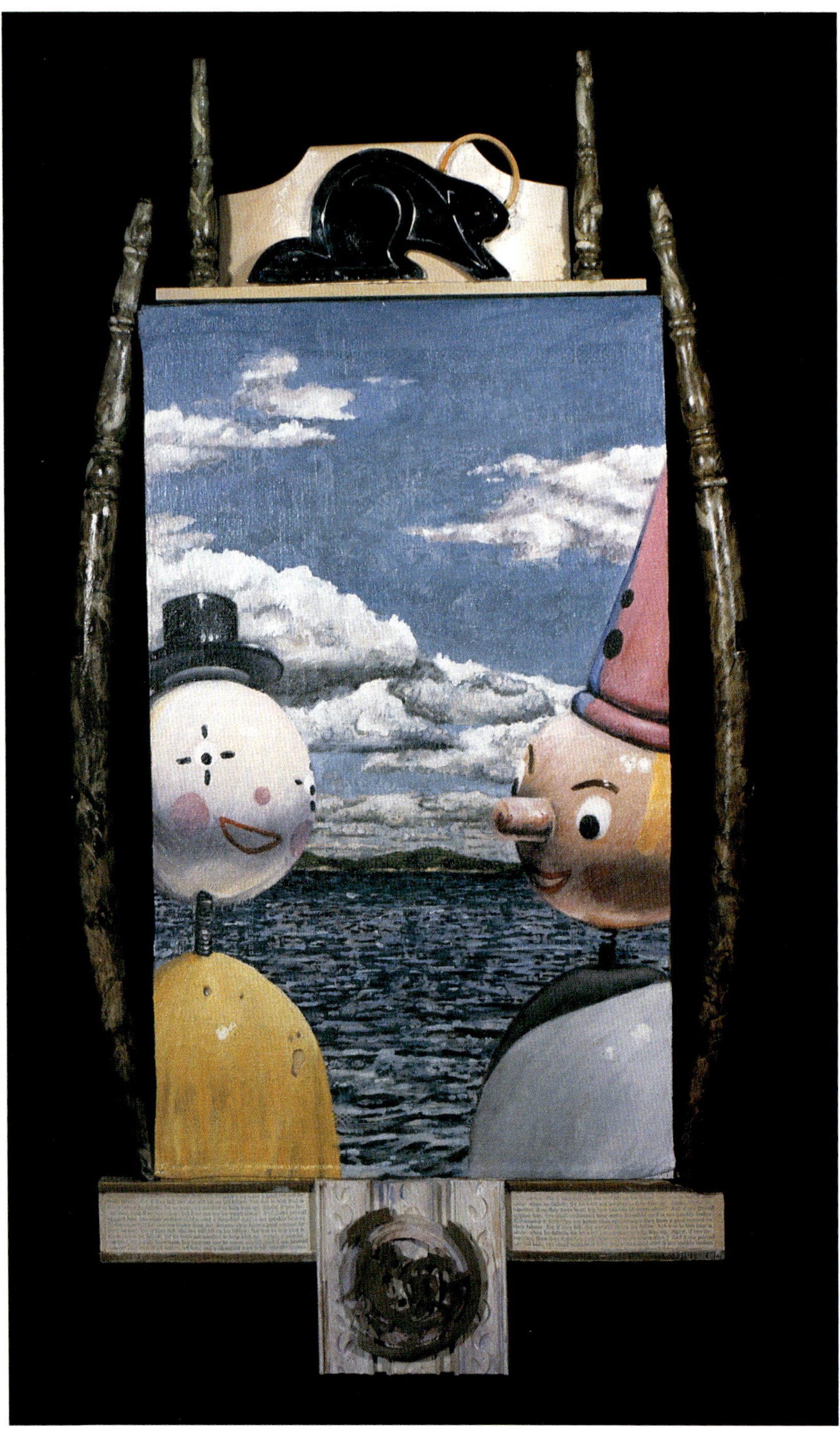

"Count On Me" by Tim Timmerman, 35" x 18" oil on linen/assemblage, 1996

dry wit and irony, often to the delight and terror of the observer in one viewing. Here, in "Count on Me," a more direct, funny version of life is seen. Two wooden stick dolls smile and grin at one another. The doll on the left, wears an old fashioned black bowler on his head, cocked to one side. His right eye is easily interpreted as a wink, while his left eye is in sly profile. His friend, a clown or dunce, is smiling and agreeing with whatever is being said, as Saint Beaver at the top of the frame watches over it all as the holy guardian of conversation. Only a divine saint disguised as a common fool can make such inspired dialogue. And for Timmerman, the divine fool is an enlightened soul who acts out many of the roles in his deadly, funny plays on life.

Timmerman, "I would have to say, the promise in my work is in the honesty, odd humor, introspection, and the assurance that no matter what may happen in this life, love wins."

— *Cassandra Dearborne*

Gallery Art Consulting
G. Eric Pleschner, Director
P.O. Box 254492
Sacramento, CA 95865
Toll Free Tel: (888) 542-3456

Gallery Art Consulting, directed by G. Eric Pleshner, began in 1990 to facilitate the business of Gallery W. The focus of Gallery W and Gallery Art Consulting is to exhibit critical contemporary art by regional, national and international artists of a Judeo-Christian world-view. The gallery serves as a place of meditation, education and artist support.

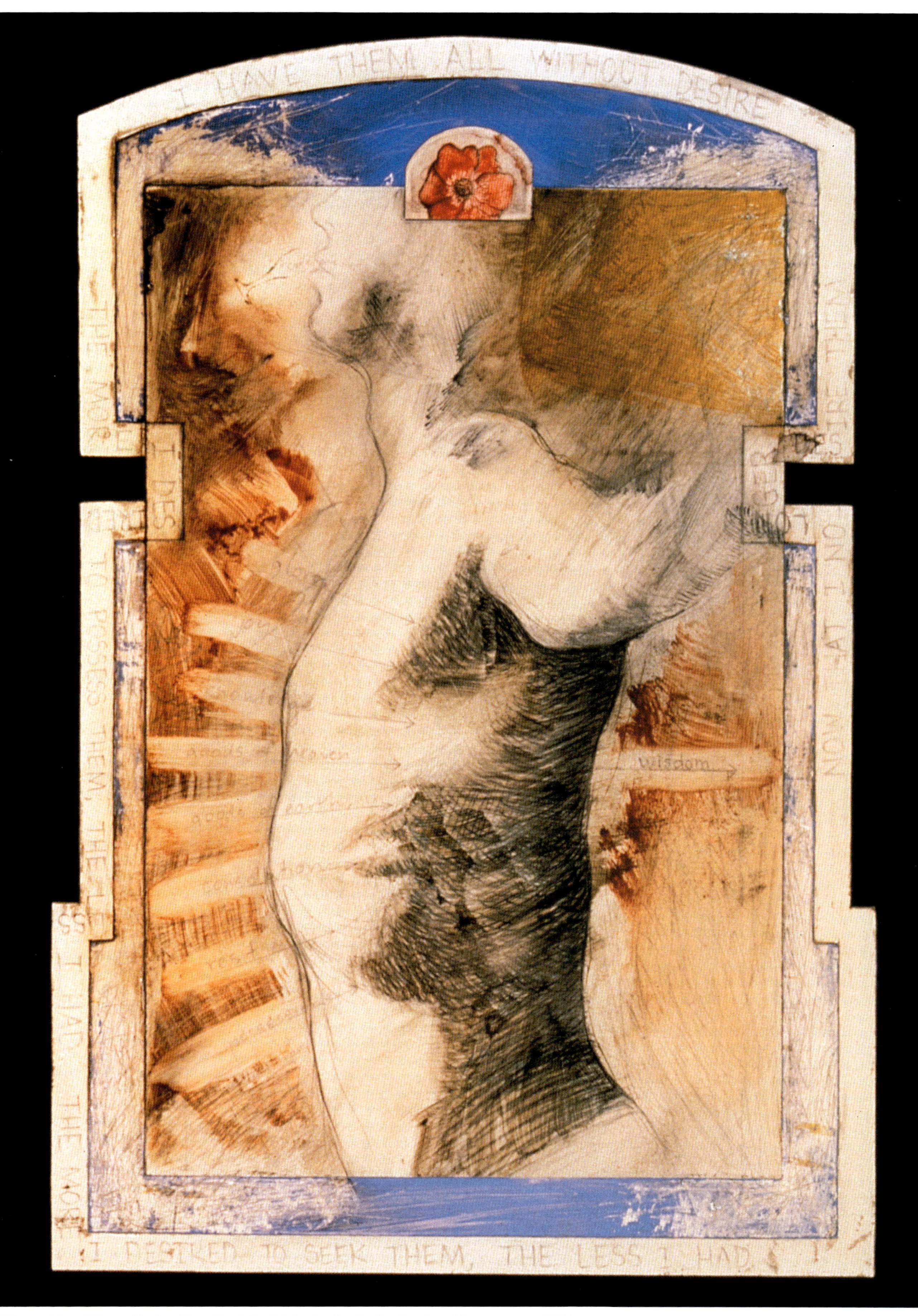

"Pierce Me of These Desires" by Mark Fredricks 73/4" x 51/4" mixed media on paper, 1996

"I CHOOSE TO WORK IN PASTEL
BECAUSE CHALK IS REALLY MUD;
IT'S PRIMAL STUFF AND
IT REMINDS ME OF INDIA
WHERE MY WORK WAS BORN."

— BENTZION

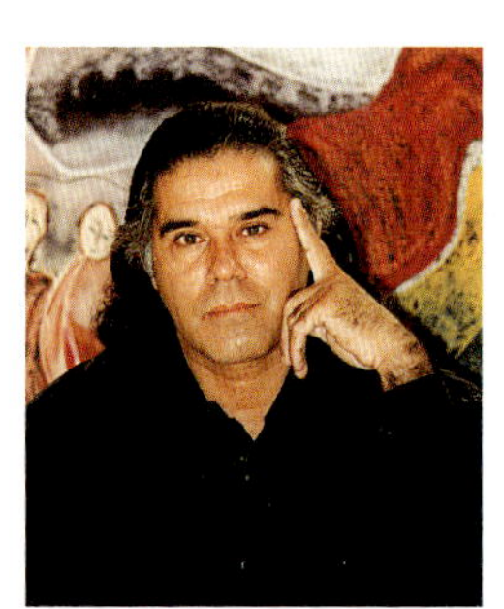

BENTZION

(BEN JACOBS/BENTZION BEN YOSEF YAKOV)

As an artist what is my task? I push myself to generate a visual energy that is inspired by soul, to transfer it to the board so the viewer can have a dialogue with the work. That dialogue I fervently hope will expand his spiritual and moral point of view. My paintings call for a deeper understanding of the spiritual level within ourselves. Art critics and art historians have said that I am an intuitive visionary expressionist.

Art for me is sensory. There is a Kabbalistic belief that wisdom is in the hands and in the feet. By using the cushions of my fingers, and my wrists and arms, I use my whole body to translate images from my imagination to visual concepts others can enjoy. I choose to work in pastel because chalk is really mud; it's primal stuff and it reminds me of India where my work was born.

The images and colors come from my childhood in India and youth in Israel as well as my travels to eighty countries around the world. My philosophy and knowledge of history come from my Hebrew Jewish tradition, my foundation in Kabbalah, as well as from my contacts with mysticism and the religious practices of India and Christianity. I represent in my person the unity of East and West. Although I am a self-taught artist, I owe a deep gratitude to my mentors in painting: Moshe Melamed and Yitzchak Frankel (Frenel), as well as to the influences of Chagall, Van Gogh and Kandinsky and the town of Safed, Israel in the Galilee where I lived.

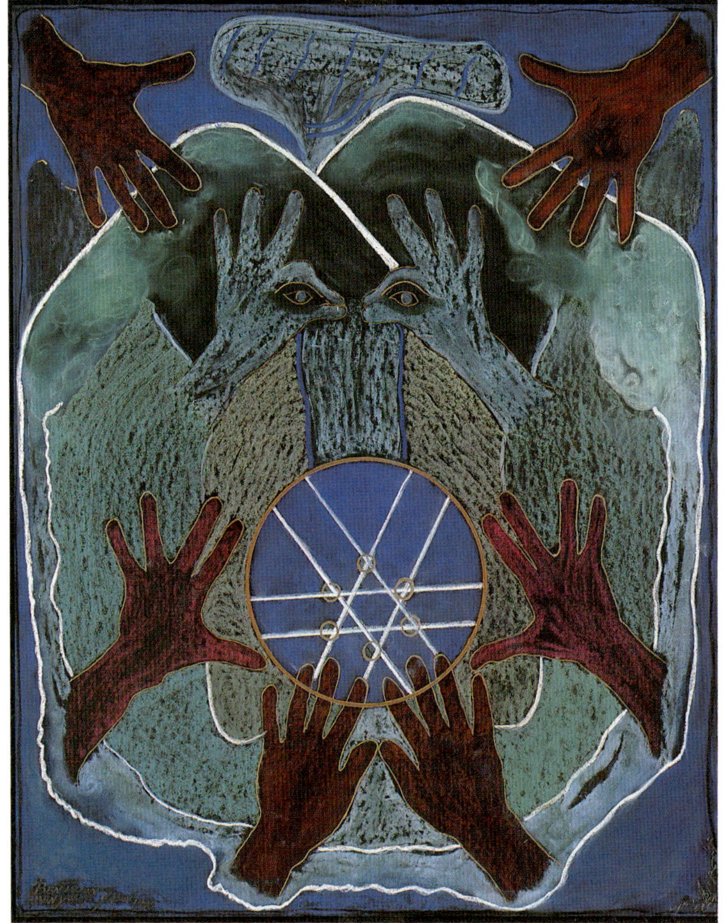

"Breath of Life," 32" x 40" pastel and metallic gold, 1996

If I have a mission, it is to encourage mankind, through my art, to begin to understand the unity that exists in all things. The unity between man and woman, the body and soul and God and his handiwork. Only tolerance and effective collaboration between nations will allow a convergence of the spiritual and material worlds. My dream is to one day have exhibitions at the Museums of Jerusalem and Tel Aviv, as well as in Bombay, New Delhi, and New York. I want to give something back to the countries that gave me so much.

Opposite page: "Adam & Eve" from the series "In Search of Adam," 32" x 40" mixed media, 1996 (limited edition print)

BenTzion ■ 11423 Pepperdine Lane, Houston, TX 77071
Toll Free: (800) 524-8084 Tel: (713) 723-2123 Fax: (713) 354-2088
Web: http://www.econonet.com/bentzion/index.htm email: neveh-shalom@juno.com

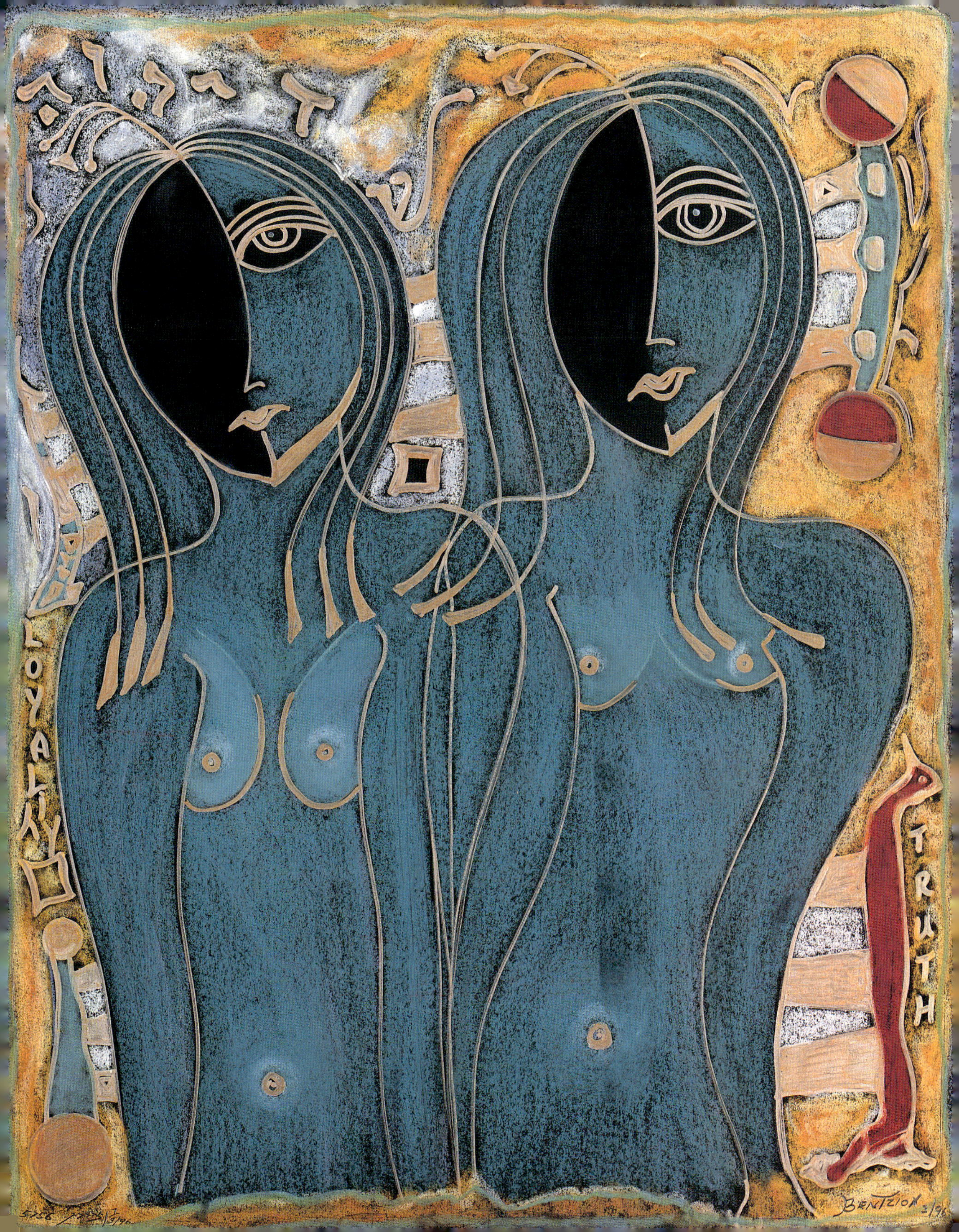
LOYALTY
TRUTH
BENTZION 3/96

KAREN CHASTAIN-HAUGHEY

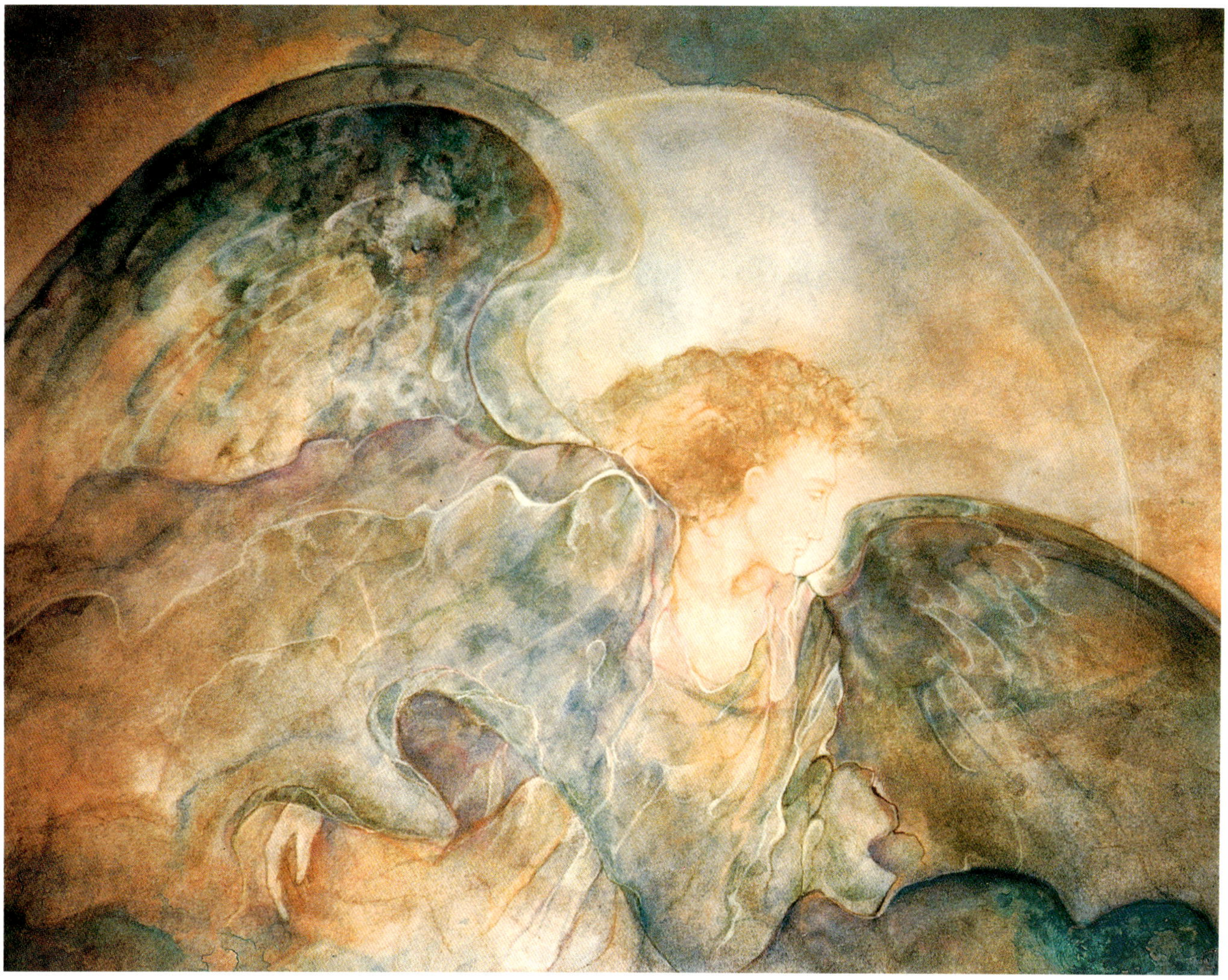

"Saint Michael," 20" x 30" pastel and watercolor, 1990

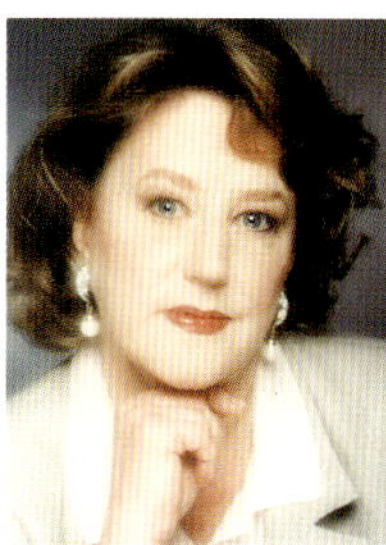

"... IF WE COULD ONLY PERCEIVE EACH OTHER LIKE WORKS OF ART... WE WOULD THEN SEE LIFE AS HEAVEN ON EARTH."

— *KAREN CHASTAIN-HAUGHEY*

Art is a personal vibration, one which reflects how the artist evaluates life, either consciously or subconsciously. I personally believe there is no "bad art" ... art is a visionary vehicle which reveals the individual impressions of the creator.

For the past twelve years I have painted from my heart, without expectation or worry about acceptance from the general public. Yet when my work was embraced by some, I was grateful and satisfied deep within my soul. There is always the hope that the work will convey a message to the viewer, objectively or passionately. However, ultimately, the goal of the artist is to always paint selflessly, without expectancy or motive.

Although controversial at the time of its first delivery in 1984, I realized my subject matter had a message — of spirit, light and subliminal love. I found it interesting that people from all walks of life were able to accept as their inner reality what I was trying to convey through the creation of superhuman images of angels and elementals.

If we could only perceive each other like works of art without judgement or prejudice, each being different and totally unique, we would then see life as heaven on earth.

Karen M. Chastain-Haughey
4141 Stevenson Road
Fremont, CA 94538
Tel: (510) 252-9646

KAREN CHASTAIN-HAUGHEY

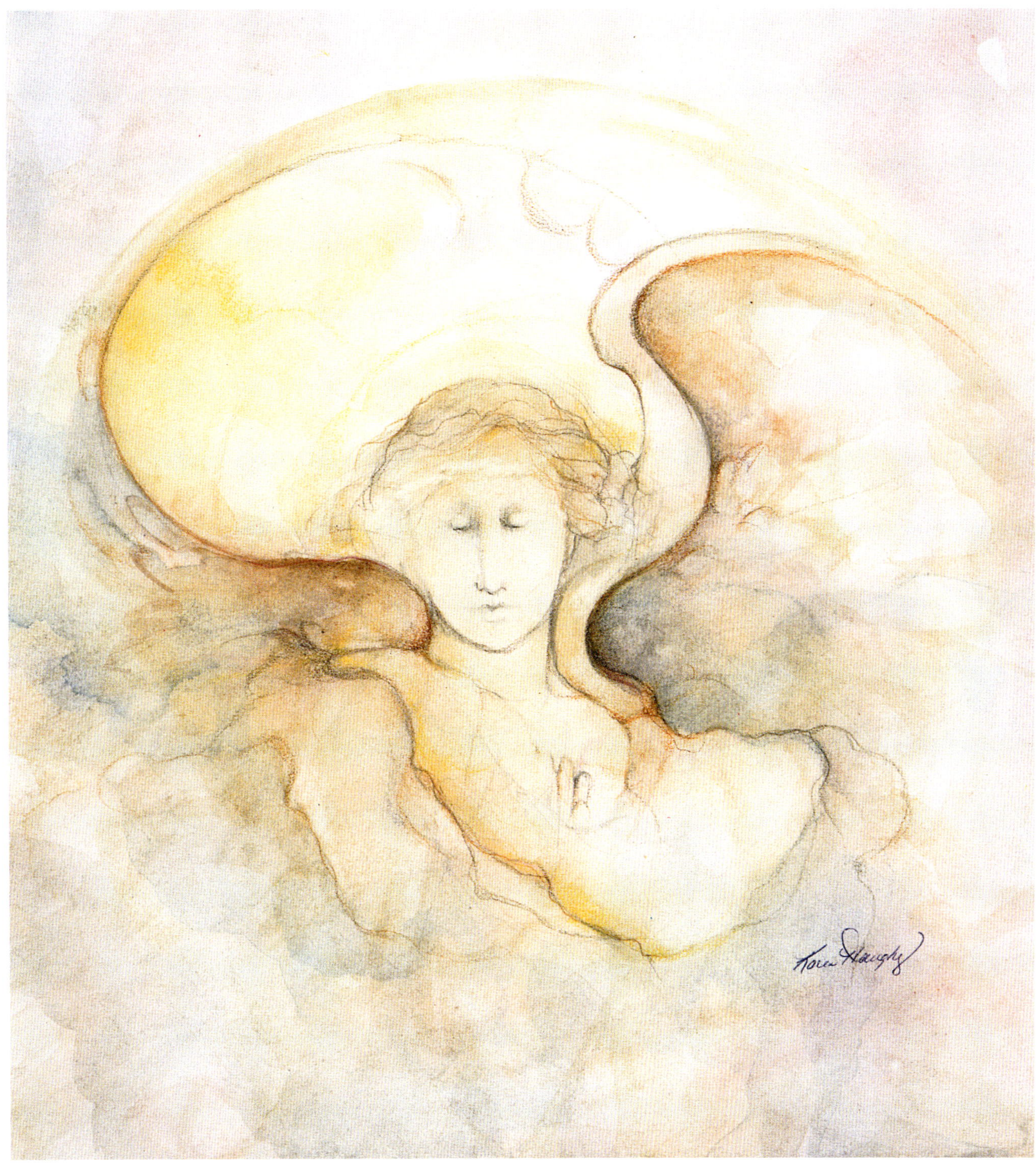

"Untitled," 11″ x 14″ pastel and watercolor, 1995

"... PAINTING IS MY MEDITATION. IT IS MY GIFT FROM SPIRIT, A TOOL TO HELP ME AS I JOURNEY DOWN ALL THE ROADWAYS IN THIS LIFE ..."

— *JEANNE PROM*

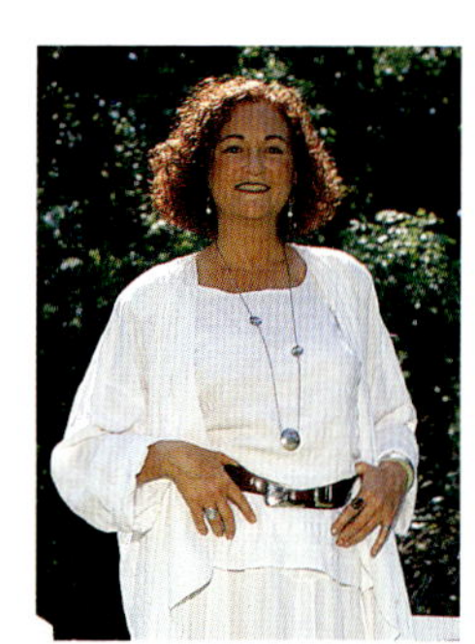

JEANNE PROM

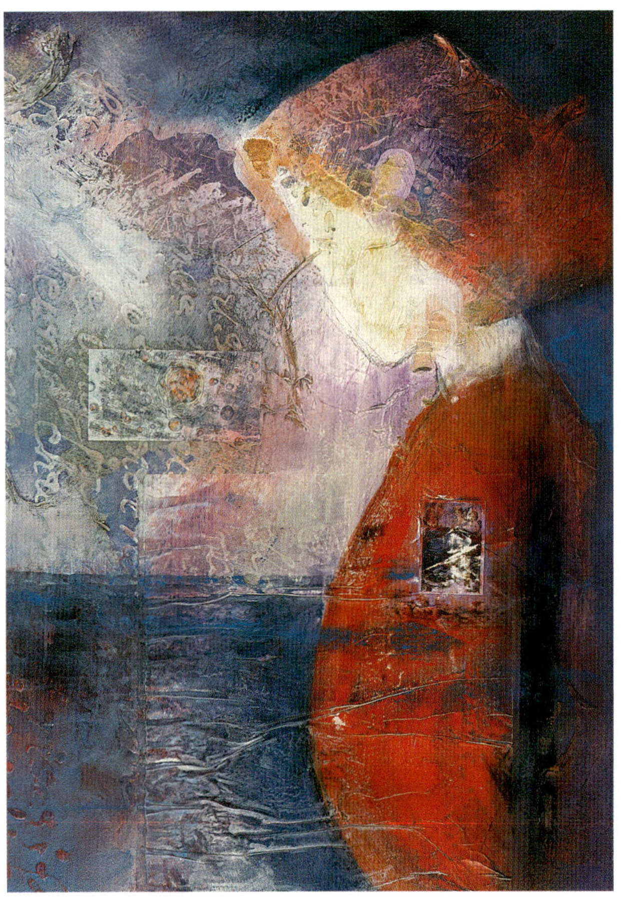

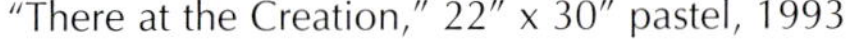

"There at the Creation," 22" x 30" pastel, 1993

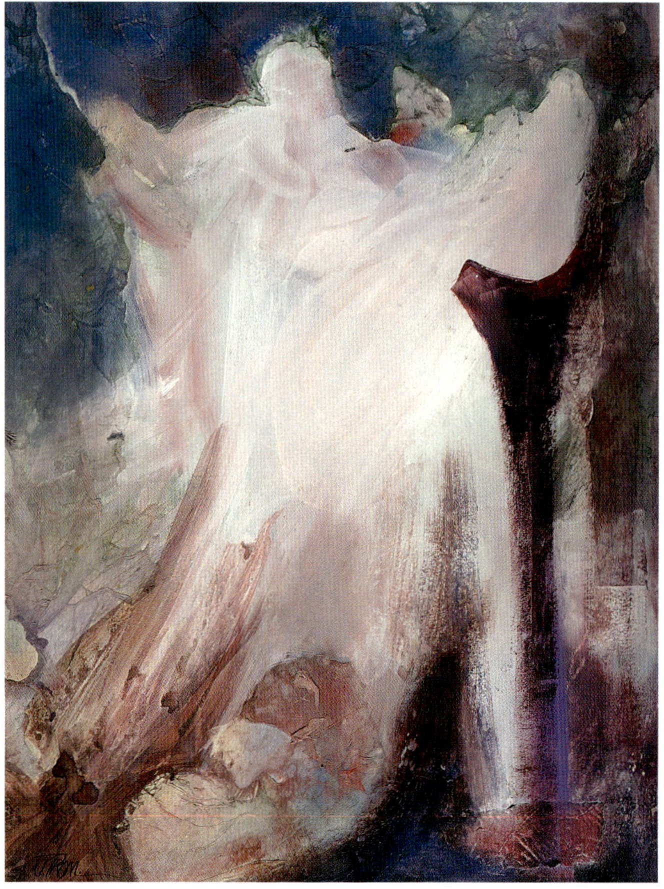

"Creative Spirit," 28" x 36" pastel, 1993

Painting and working with color, texture, and design has always been an integral part of my life. It has been and continues to be "the" activity that consistently enables me to enter into the place of balance and peace within. Here, the millions of thoughts that can bother, bring worry or fear, confusion, and feelings of frustration cannot reach me. Traditional methods of prayer and meditation have been elusive for me in the past ... for me, painting is my meditation. It is my gift from Spirit, a tool to help me as I journey down all the roadways in this life; the quiet streets of status quo, the highways of change, the winding ups and downs of foggy paths where patience is developed and loneliness eventually embraced, and the veiled and intricate trail I walk daily towards the joyful discovery of who I really am.

While painting I feel a deep contentment and a sense of accomplishment in that I am communicating to myself and others my most intense and intimate (and many times subconscious) thoughts, beliefs, and feelings.

I am enthused about life and its mysteries that parade by us each day clothed in bold costumes of human form, flesh and bones we call "each other." Even more so am I intrigued by the mysteries of the unseen world, that of Spirit, and what their relationship to us really is.

Eighteen years ago while working through the process of accepting that I had just had a one on one meeting with cancer, I was catapulted into the world of spirit in a much more profound way. I knew then that someday I would paint angels.

Jeanne M. Prom
38 Wood Duck Lane
Tariffville, CT 06081
Tel: (860) 658-2827

Opposite page: "Unaware," 21" x 28" acrylic, 1994

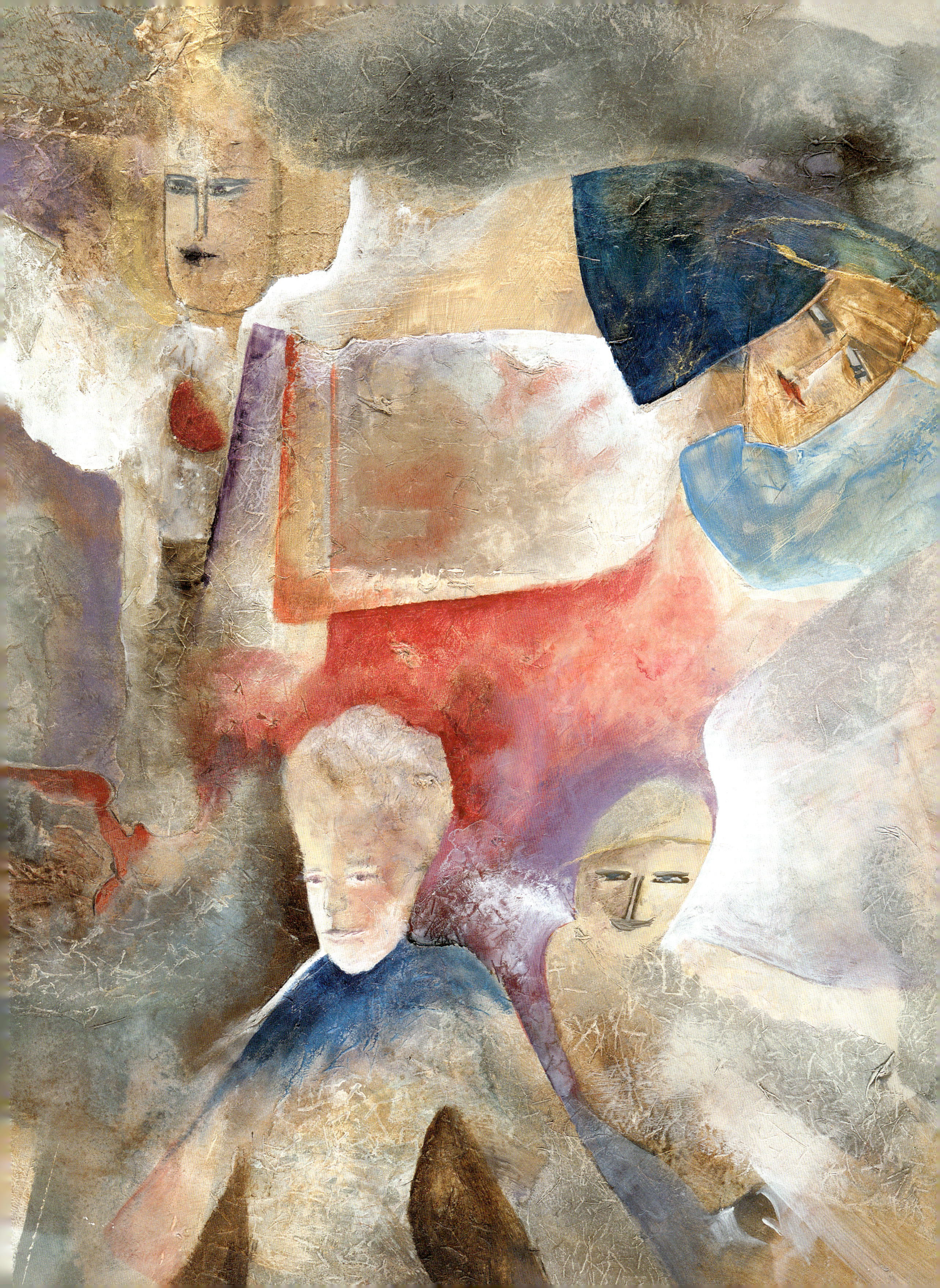

JONATHAN WILTSHIRE

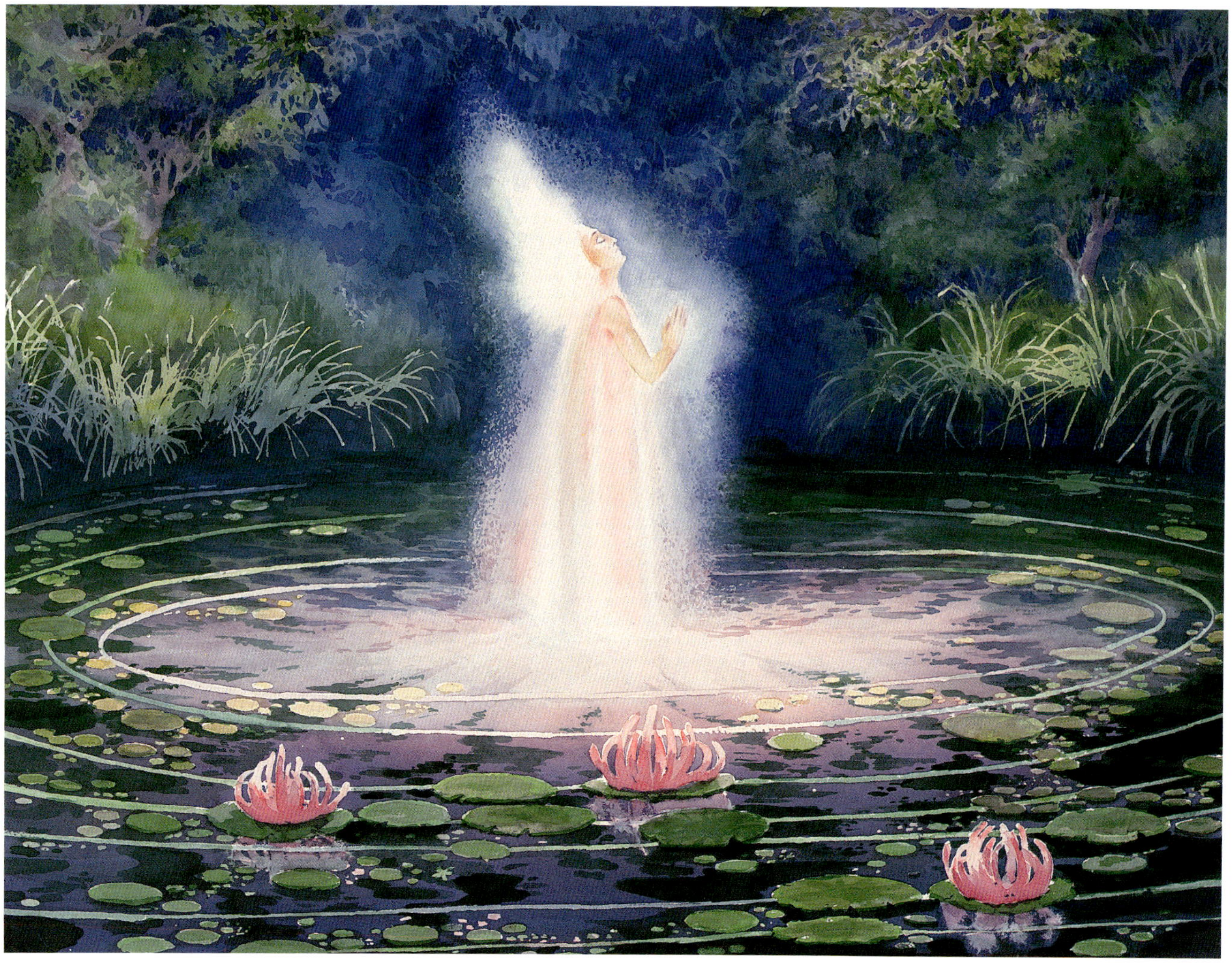

"A Deva of the Pond," 18" x 24" watercolor, 1994

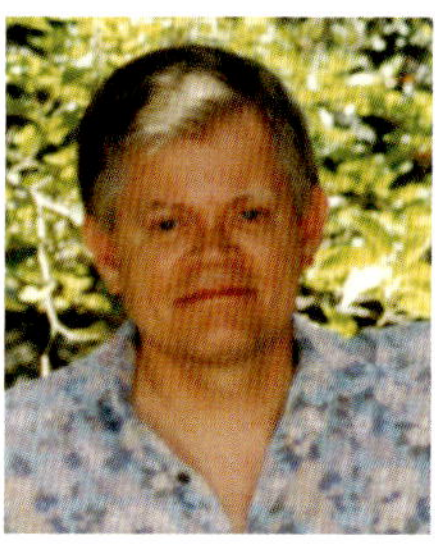

"AN ERA OF NEW SPIRITUAL ART WILL EXPRESS MYSTICISM — THE DIRECT, CONSCIOUS 'EXPERIENCE' OF THE DIVINE."
— *JONATHAN WILTSHIRE*

Life is an evolutionary journey toward an ever more perfect union with God. To pursue the highest course of art is to follow a path leading to the discovery of the visible and invisible expressions of God's Reality. And when Divine Spirit influences our work, images and ideals of Truth emerge, imparting to music, dance, literature, and the visual arts a power which elevates human consciousness by speaking a universal language our soul consciousness under-stands.

Art contains spiritual power when its expression flows through the artist's higher self, or soul consciousness. It's here an artist touches the heaven world and senses dimensions of unspeakable beauty, music, color, harmony, and the presence of beings whose purity and love are beyond human experience. Art expressions from this realm, though only a dim reflection of Divine Reality, begin to serve the greater purpose of lifting human consciousness.

Jonathan Wiltshire
826 So. Rancho Sante Fe, #H
San Marcos, CA 92069
Tel: (619) 727-0735

JONATHAN WILTSHIRE

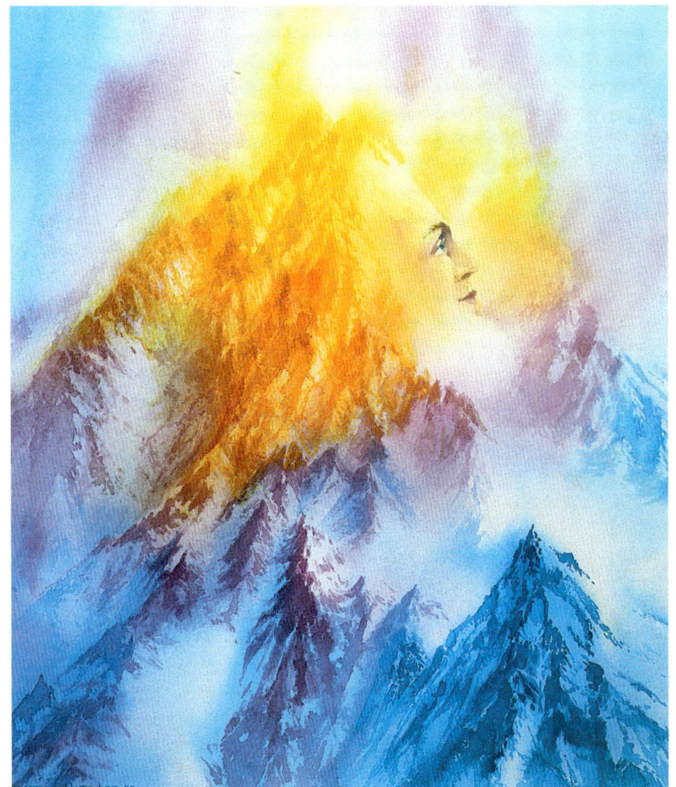

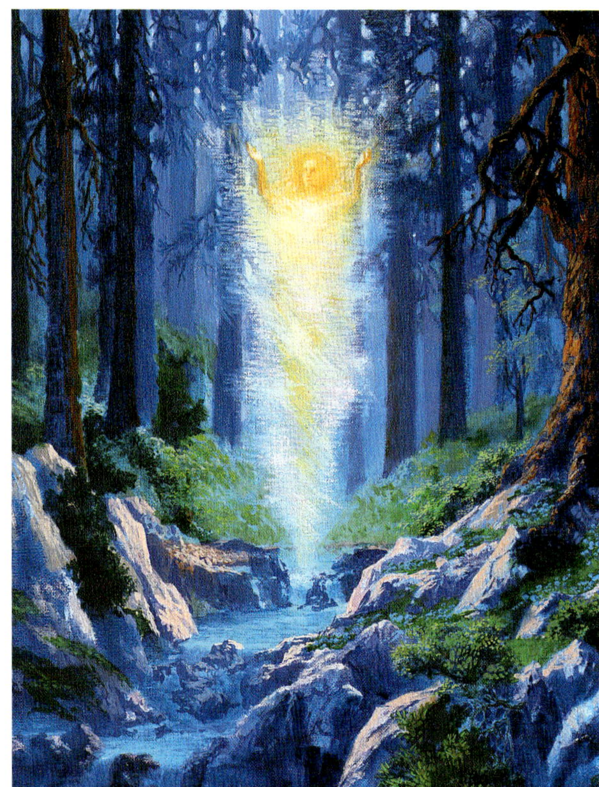

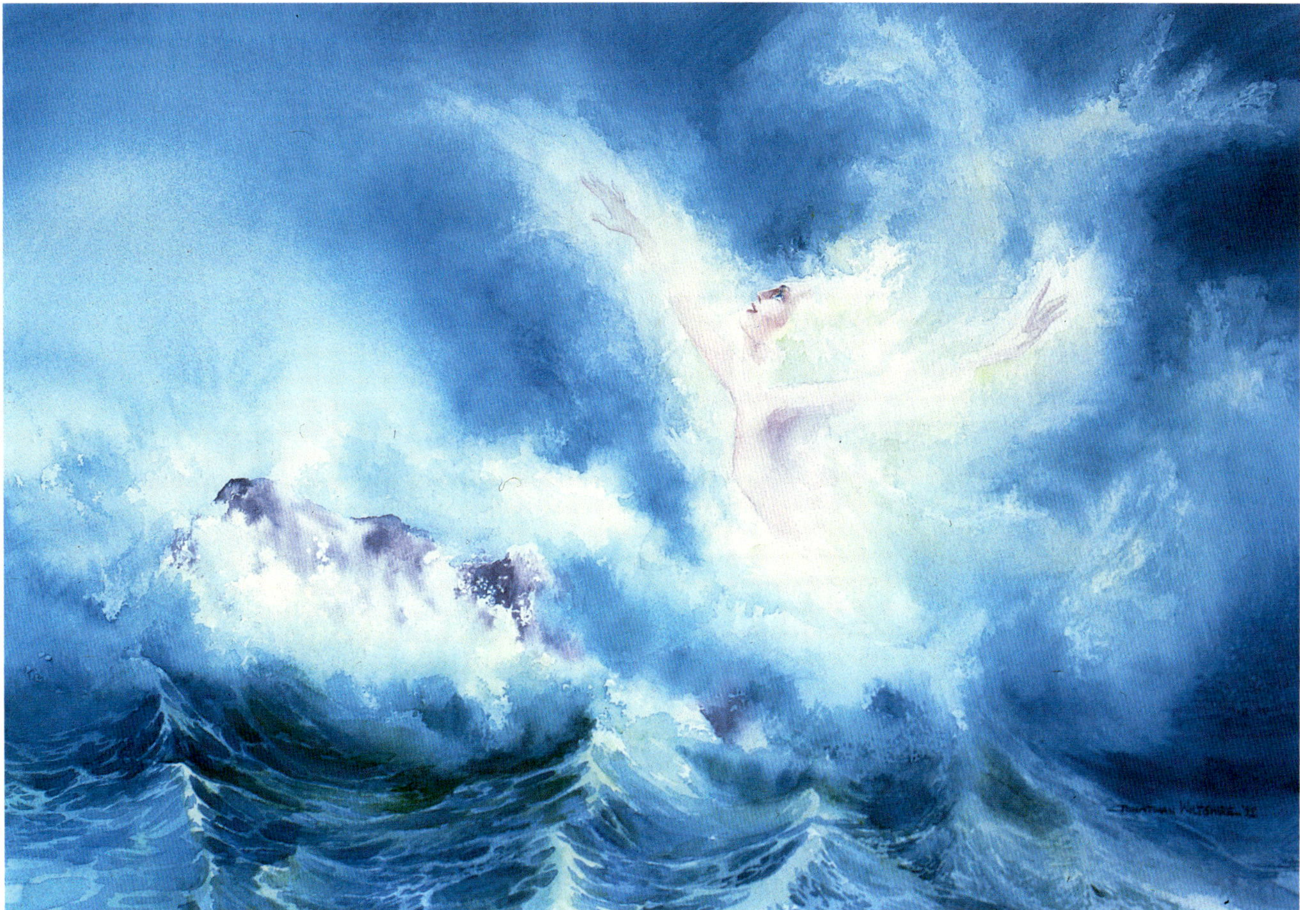

Top Left: "A Mountain Lord Communes with His Logos," 18" x 24" watercolor, 1992 Top Right: "A Forest Healer," 18" x 24" acrylic and oil, 1980
Bottom: "A Sea Nymph Riding on a Current of Joy," 18" x 24" watercolor, 1992

MELANIE MAUNG

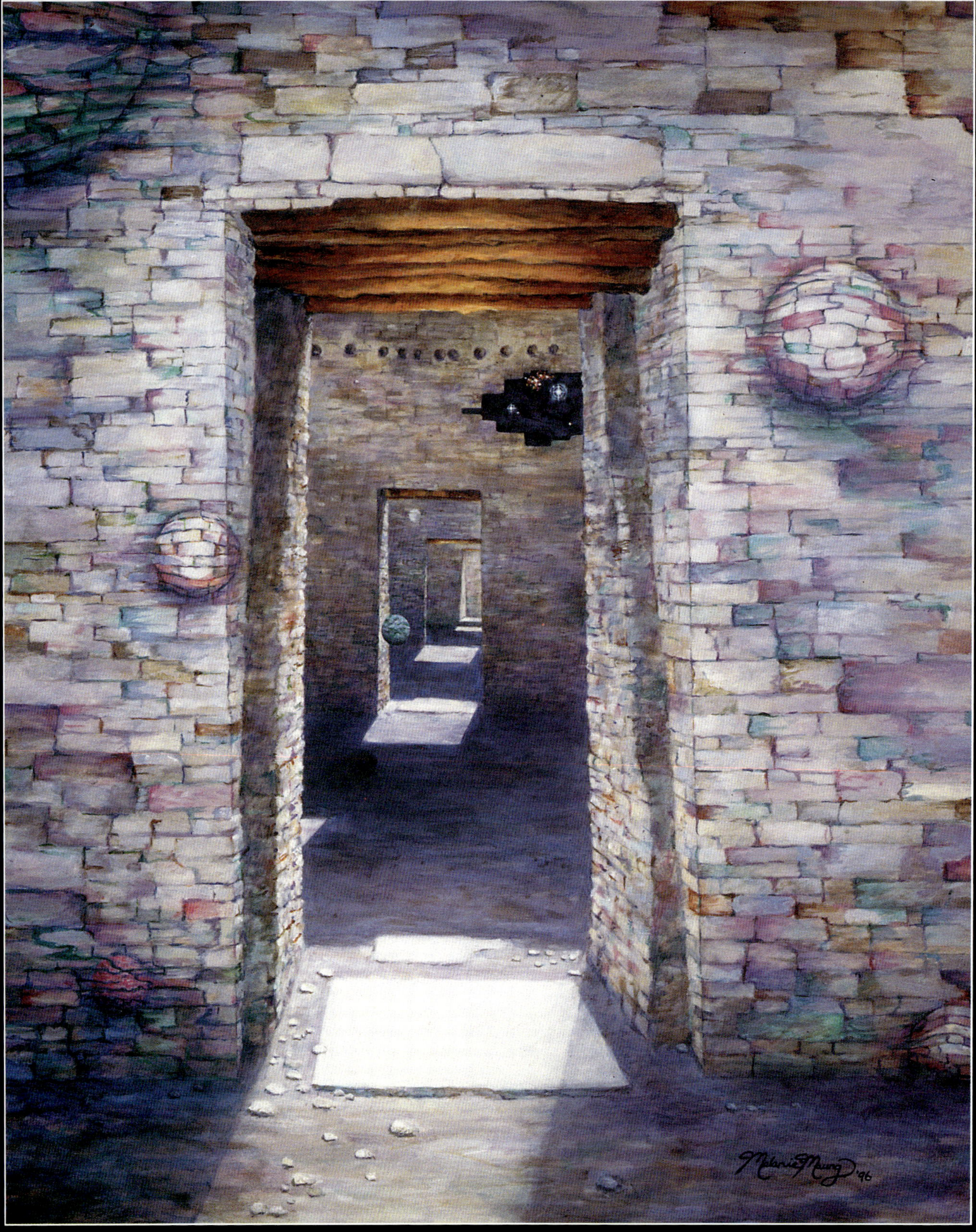

"The Visit," 24" x 29" acrylic, 1996

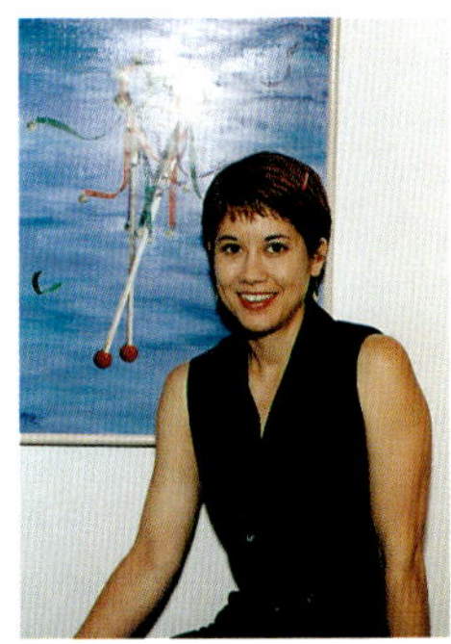

"THIS PATH TOWARD SPIRIT AND OPENING OF THE HEART HAS ALWAYS EXISTED WITHIN US."

— *MELANIE MAUNG*

All things are connected by strands that weave through time and space. Artists, musicians, writers and poets, healers and shamans are the bridge between the mystical realm and that of everyday life. We record both the struggle to survive with all of its sorrows and those moments of transformation, the way of love and compassion. We are guides into the world of imagination who travel as part of the dream journey that never ends. It is in this spirit that I paint, and I am a storyteller through my art.

I often work with images using doorways or portals, and galaxies to represent the mind and new experiences. It is the potential for expansion and great joy which gives someone the courage to move forward in the face of the unknown. This path toward spirit and opening of the heart has always existed within us. And if a person is ready and chooses to walk through, the doorway is open.

Melanie Maung
P.O. Box 604
Boston, MA 02102-0604
Tel: (617) 237-5111

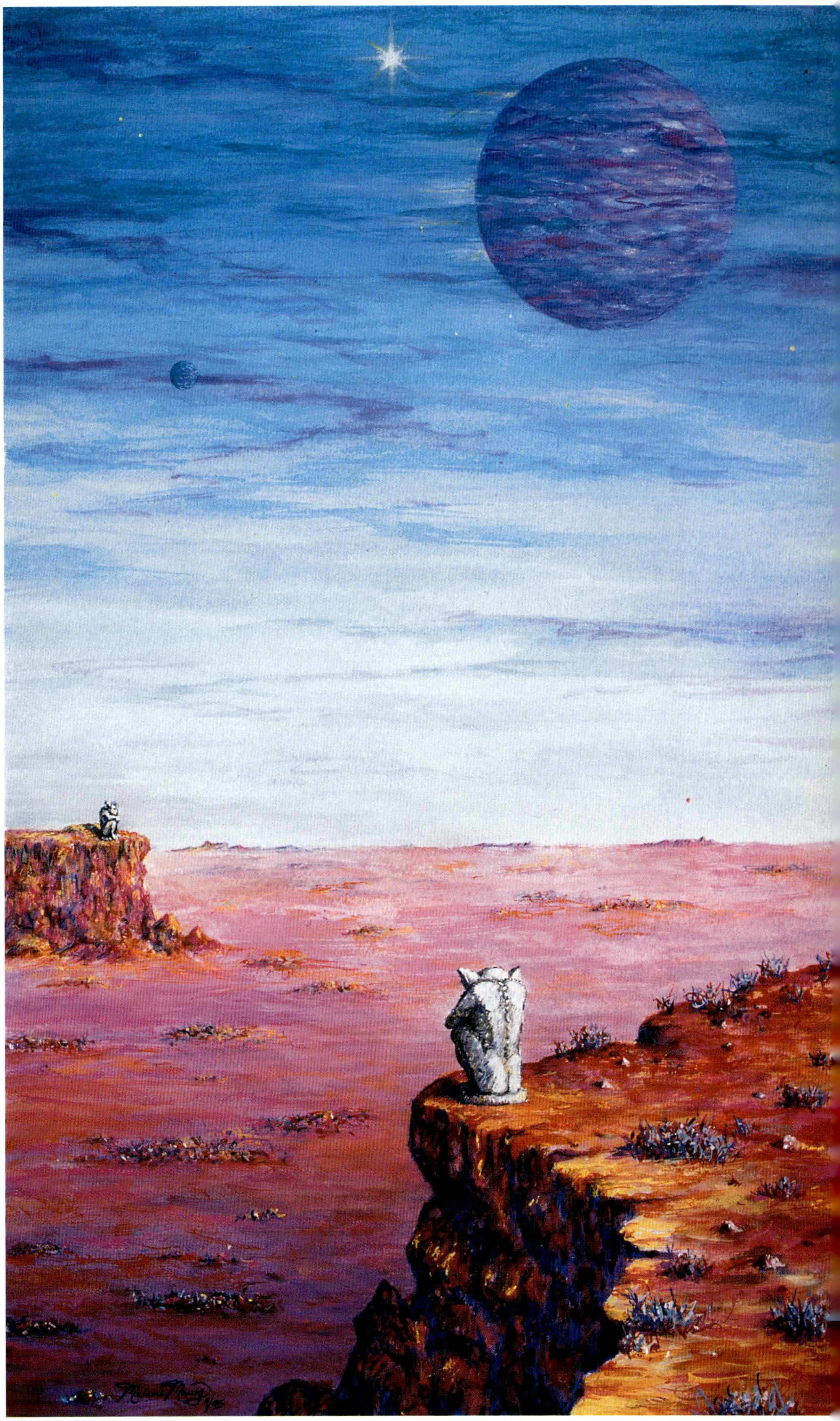

"Them," 12 1/2" x 20 1/2" watercolor and gouache on paper, 1995

ANN ROTHAN

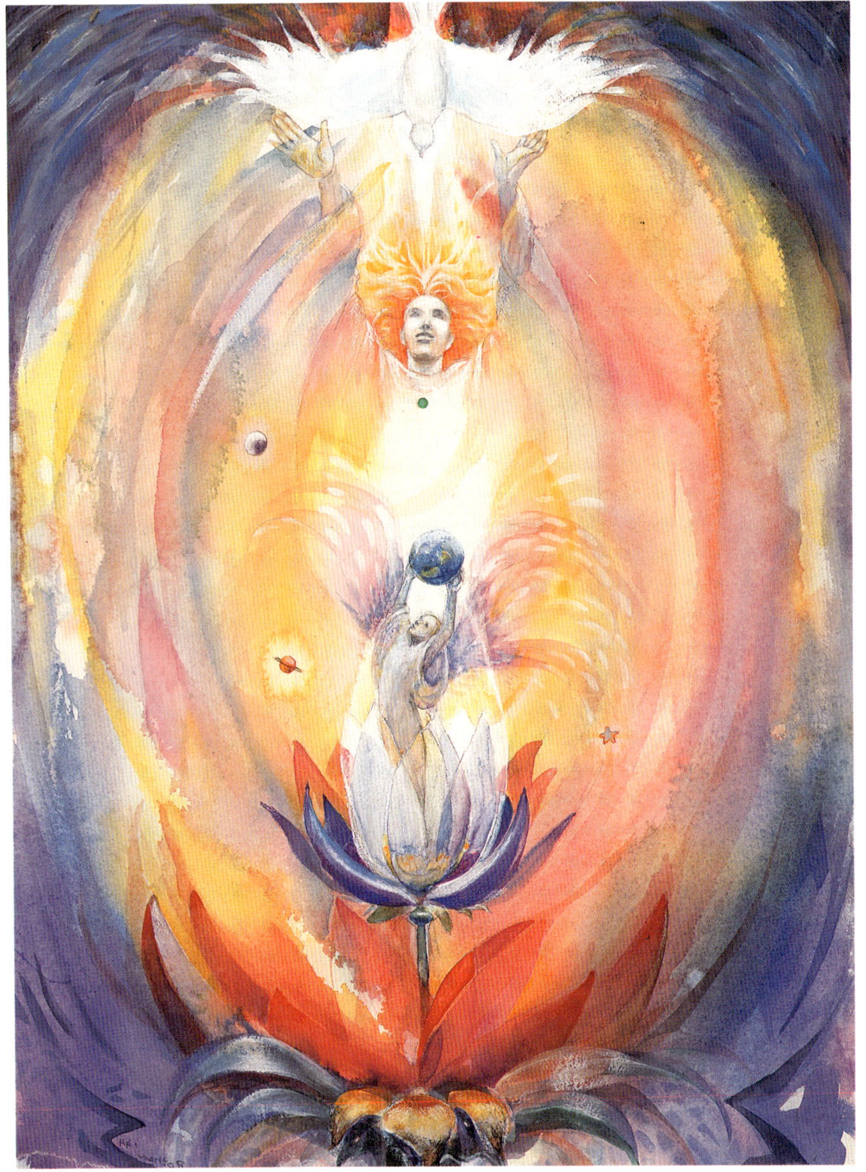

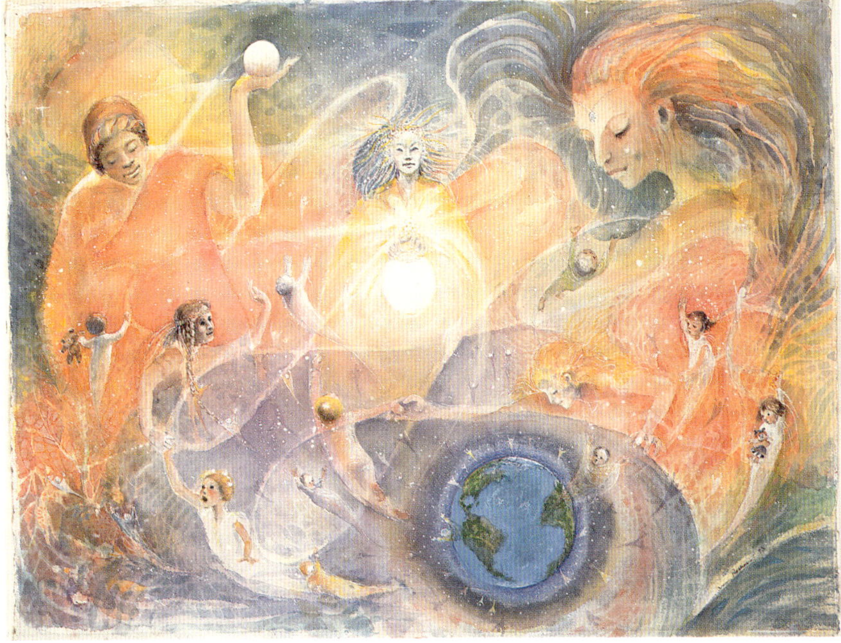

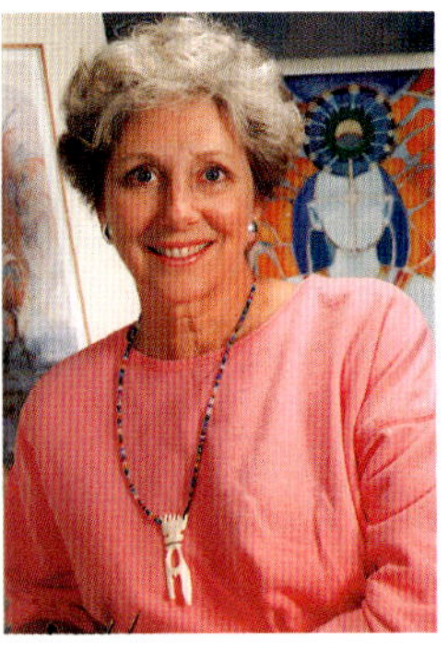

"I SEE THE SACRED ARTIST
AS THE VISION KEEPER ..."

— *ANN ROTHAN*

Painting Sacred Art has been a slow unfolding inner experience since 1968. For years I kept paintings I called "visual meditations" hidden. There was a sense that if anyone saw them they would see my soul, which would then be open to scrutiny. Since my spirituality is deeply personal, this caused a major conflict. My transition came when others, sincerely moved by the art, saw a "portal of entry" for *their* meditation. As people began commissioning me to paint their "visual meditations," a strong desire to complete a body of work about spirituality, using veils of color, movement and symbolism began.

I see the Sacred Artist as the vision keeper, preparing the planet for what will be a deep spiritual awakening. "AS ABOVE, SO BELOW." To bring the higher consciousness into the earthly plane through symbols, color, form and subject is the work of the Sacred Artists.

Ann Rothan
17420 Plainview
Bend, OR 97701
Tel: (541) 389-0798

Top: "Merging Spirits," 32" x 24" watercolor, 1994
Bottom: "Let Love Flow," 20" x 26" watercolor, 1995
Opposite page: "Winter Hunting Ground," 24" x 32" watercolor, 1995

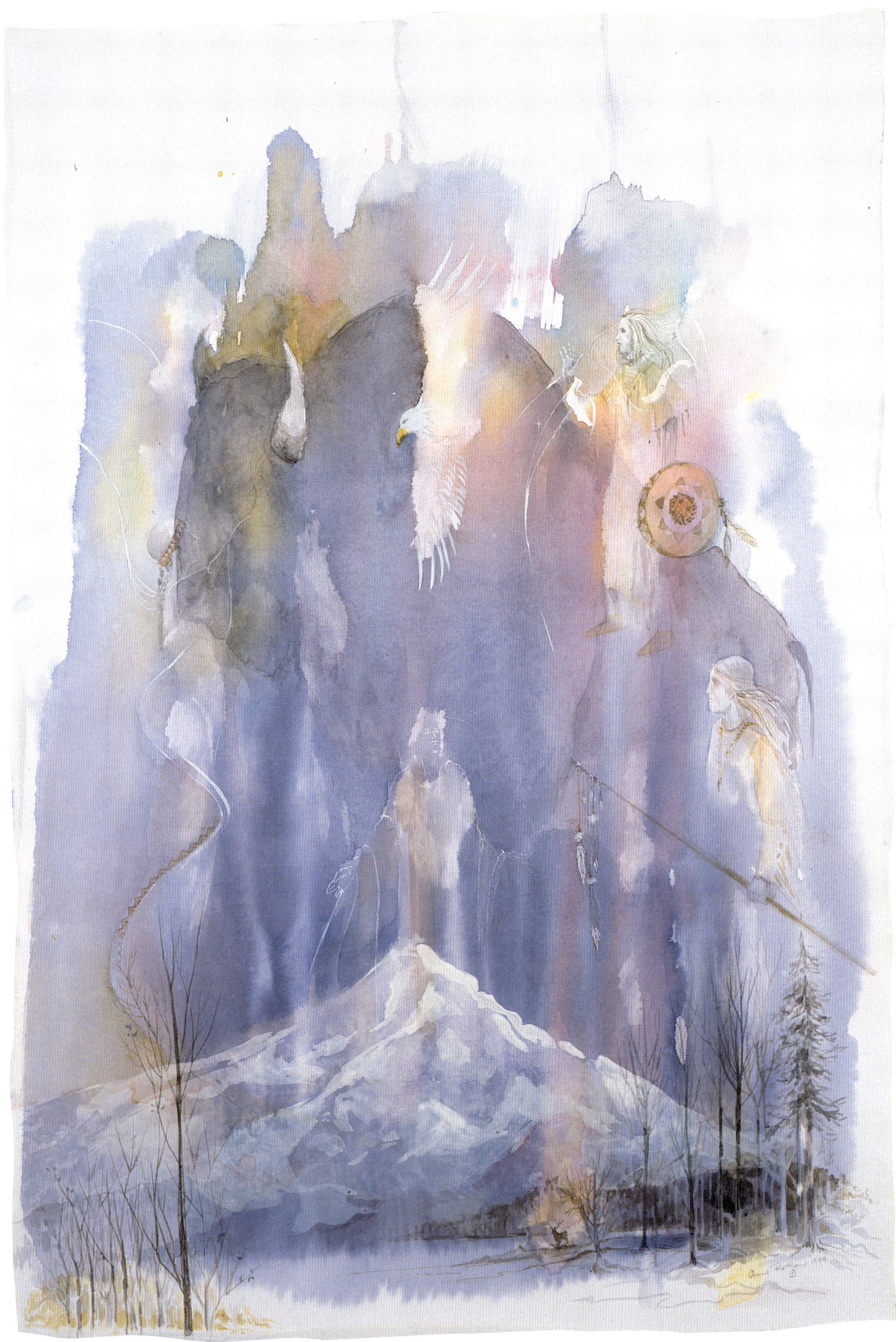

"CREATIVITY FOR ME IS WORSHIP, AND TO BE IN A WORSHIPFUL CONSCIOUSNESS IS A WAY OF DIVINE BEING."

— ALI MINER

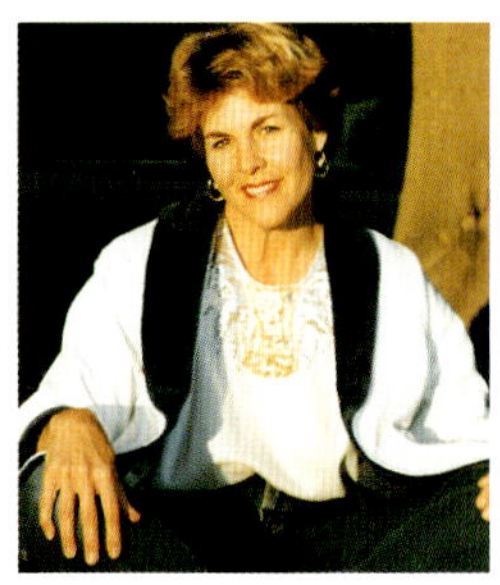

ALI MINER

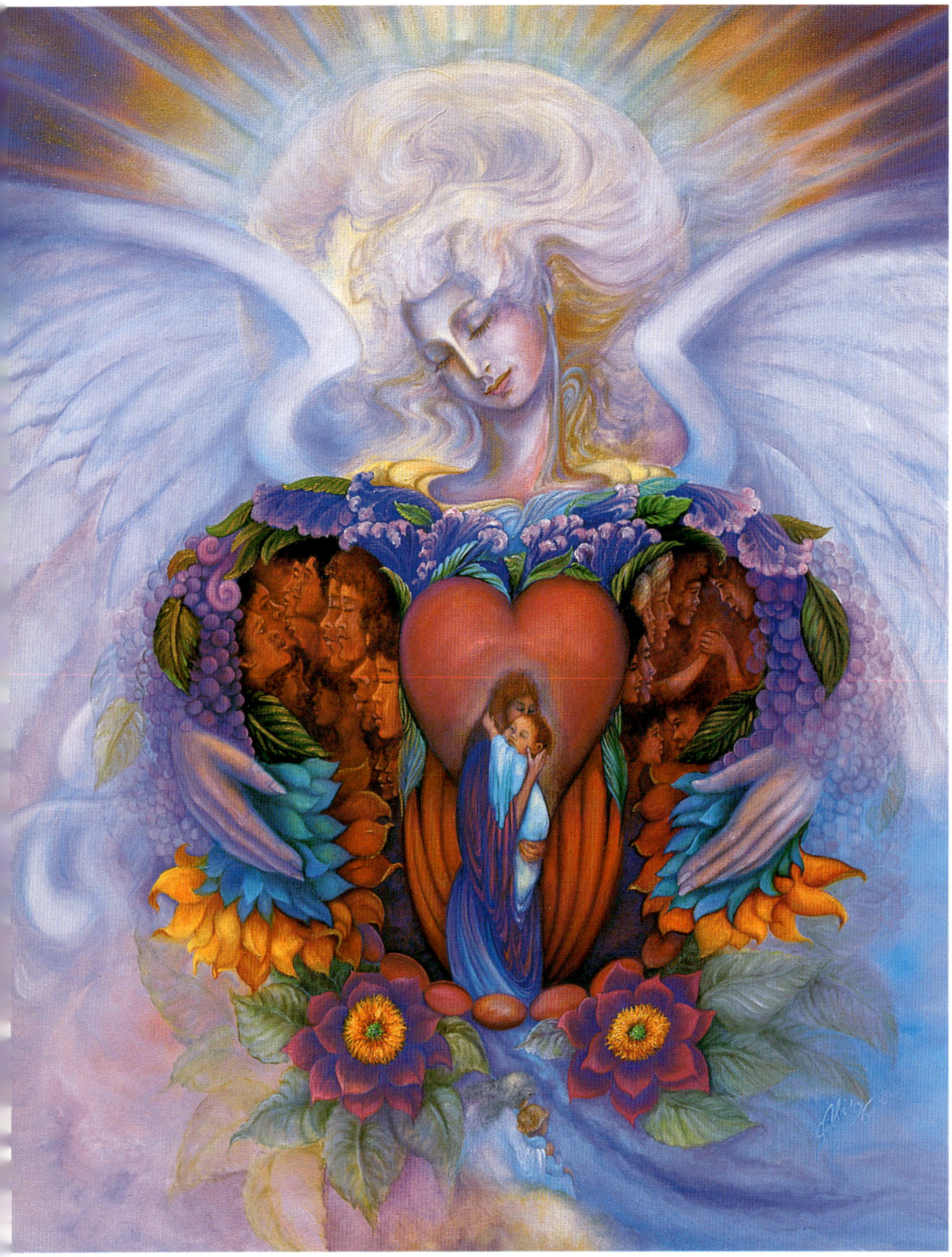

"Angel of Motherhood," 20" x 30," oil on canvas, 1996

*W*hy do I paint? Perhaps because it was all I really felt I could do. At first. It certainly was all I really wanted to do! Now, after some 35 plus years and billions of hours I realize I've always been trying to recreate the world and mold it into something I can live in! It has been my quest, my means of expression, my search for self. It is my true spirituality, my form of worship. It is who I am and how I see. Before I knew these things, I was vulnerable! Now that I have come to know these things, I am empowered! I quote a phrase that says more than I can invent, and I thank its author for having written it. Every time I read it I am humbled, thankful and my heart reminds me who and why I am. Written for French Post-impressionist, Louis Labro-Font, 1881-1952, a man of simplicity, lover of nature and all creation, whose art was his life, it speaks for the beauty found in so many artists ... and I hope, for me as well.

"le petit homme doux au visage précocement ridé, majestueusement seul sur sa colline heureuse, porte en lui-meme le trésor le plus beau et répète tout en caressant affectueusement ses toiles: "Mon Dieu, je Vous remercie de m'avoir permis de peindre ..."

"The gentle little man with his face precociously lined with wrinkles, magnificently alone on his happy hill, carries in himself the most beautiful treasure and repeats while fondly patting his paintings, "My God, I thank Thee for having permitted me to paint ..."

— *Marcel E. Grancher*

Ali Miner
1166 Chaparral Road
Pebble Beach, CA 93953
Tel: (408) 641-0845
Fax: (408) 641-0349

Opposite page: "Angel of the Rain Forest," 32" x 40" oil on canvas, 1991

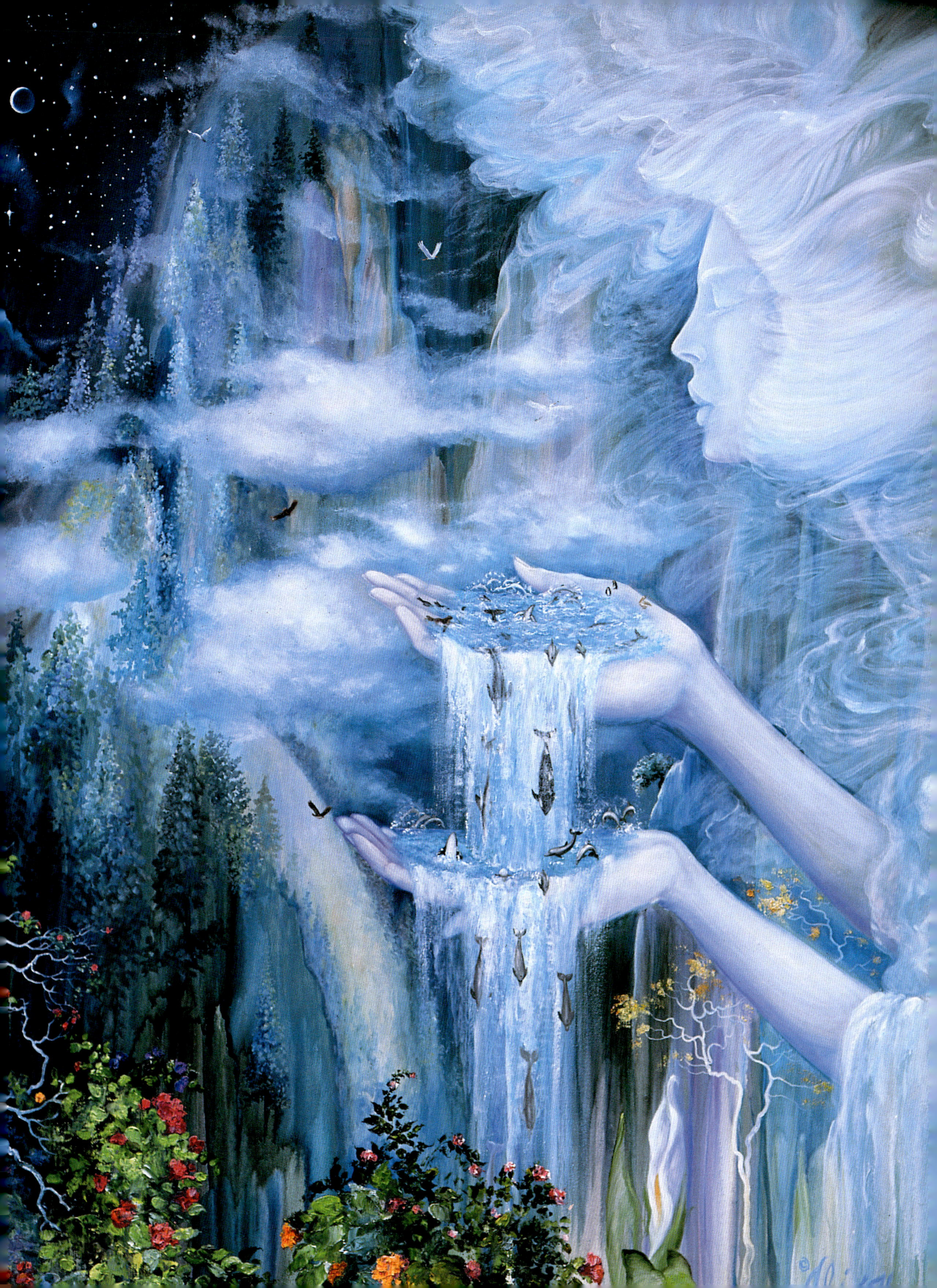

LAURA WALKER

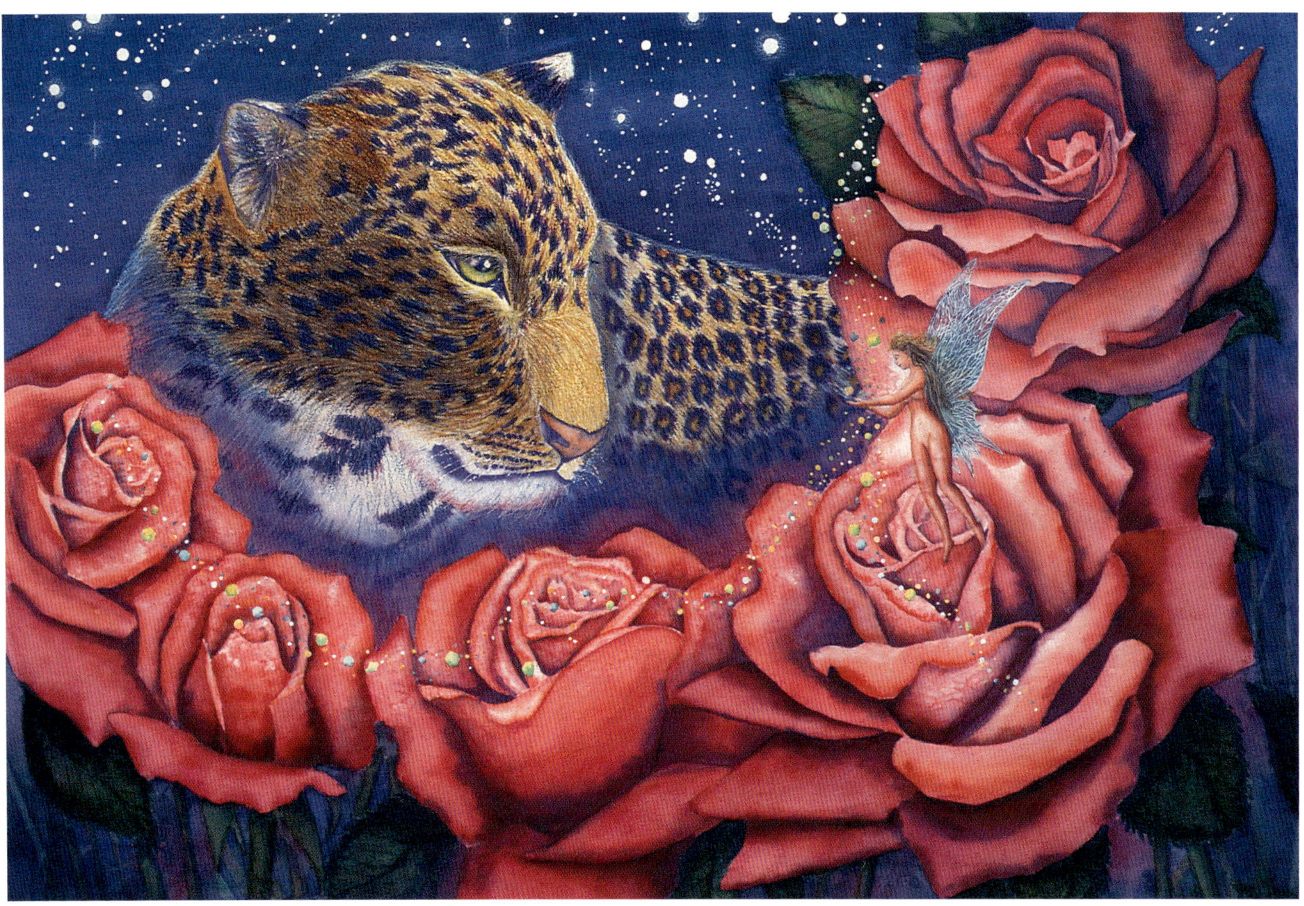

"Marriage of the Soul," 22" X 32" watercolor, 1995

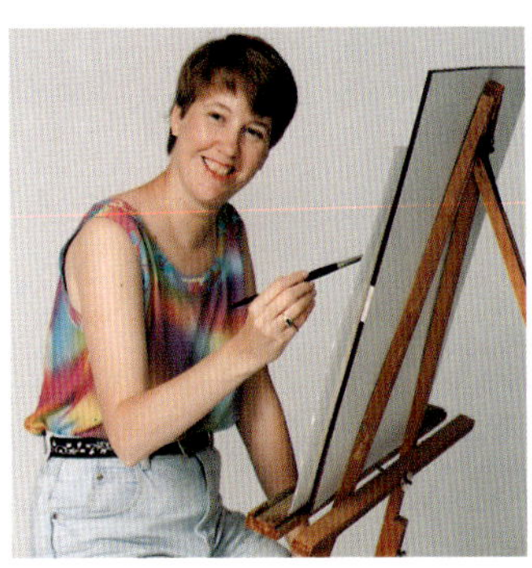

"I WANT TO PORTRAY A DEEP APPRECIATION FOR THE LIFE THAT SURROUNDS US."
— *LAURA WALKER*

My ideas usually come from dreams or visions before my eyes during the night — like a colored slide. Many times ideas grow from the original "slide" to form a continuity within my imagination. These ideas get transferred to watercolor paper or board. Although I have an idea of the meaning of the piece as I am painting it, the full meaning crystallizes at the completion. My work is developed through several layers/glazes of watercolor washes, and a great deal of attention is paid to positive and negative spaces.

The major artistic goal I have is to grow to my full potential as a painter; to develop continually my raw technical skills and marry it with my imagination so that I may perfectly express the dreams and visions I experience; and to continually share my artistic expressions with others so that I may communicate to people on various levels spiritually, about nature and life's magic, consciously and subconsciously. I want my fantasy/visionary paintings to send a message of hope, of belief in the miracle of life, and that dreams, magical thoughts can be expressed and transformed into a realistic pursuit and a positive environment where anything is possible and love is ever present; that happiness lies in our continued respect for creation, for all living things — seen and unseen. I want to portray a deep appreciation for the life that surrounds us. I want viewers to be so taken with the beauty and colors of my images that they feel renewed and inspired in a positive, energetic or peaceful way.

Laura Walker Fine Art
112 West Street
Wrentham, MA 02093
Tel/Fax: (508) 384-3298

LAURA WALKER

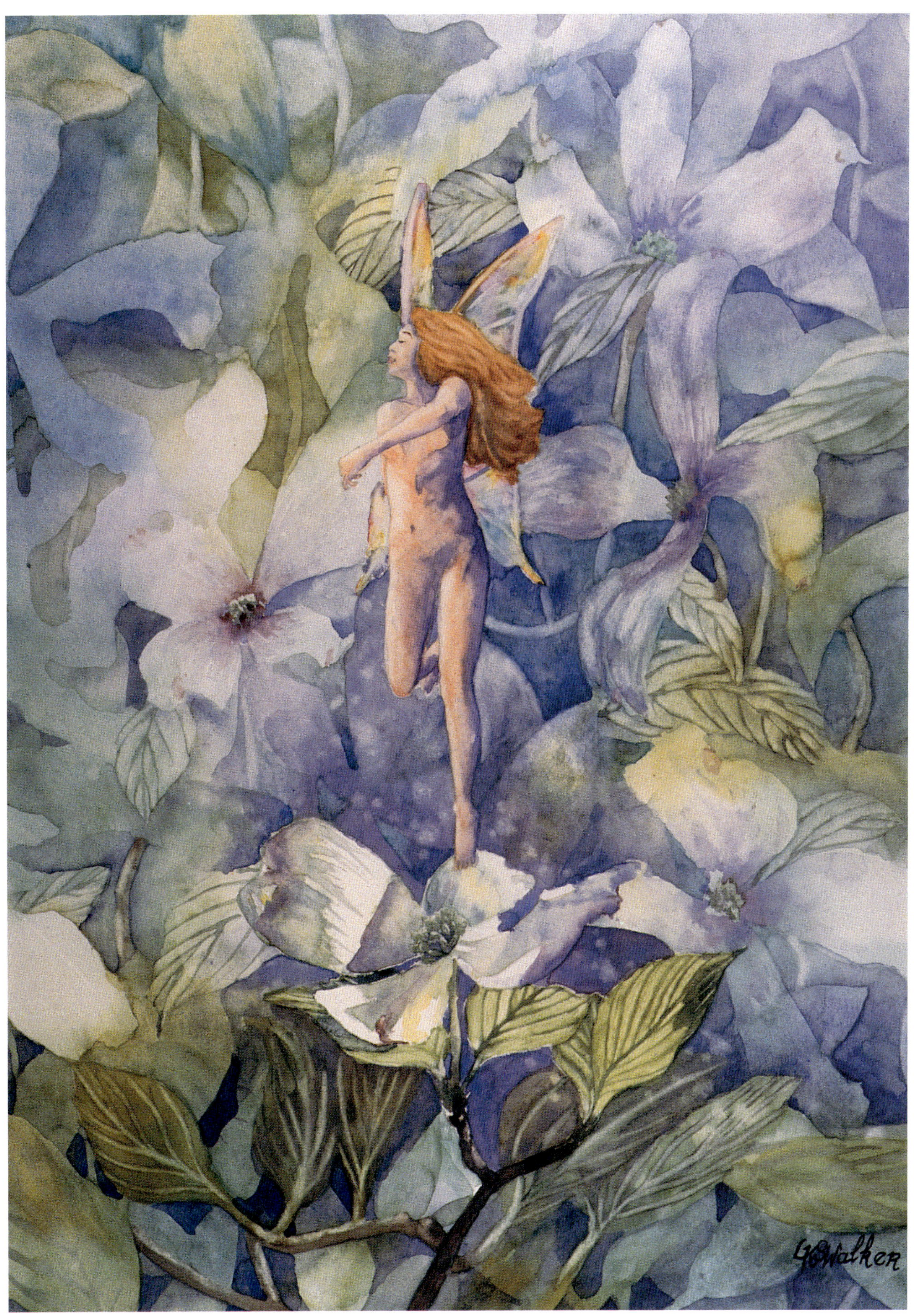

"Dogwood Fantasy," 15" x 20" watercolor, 1995

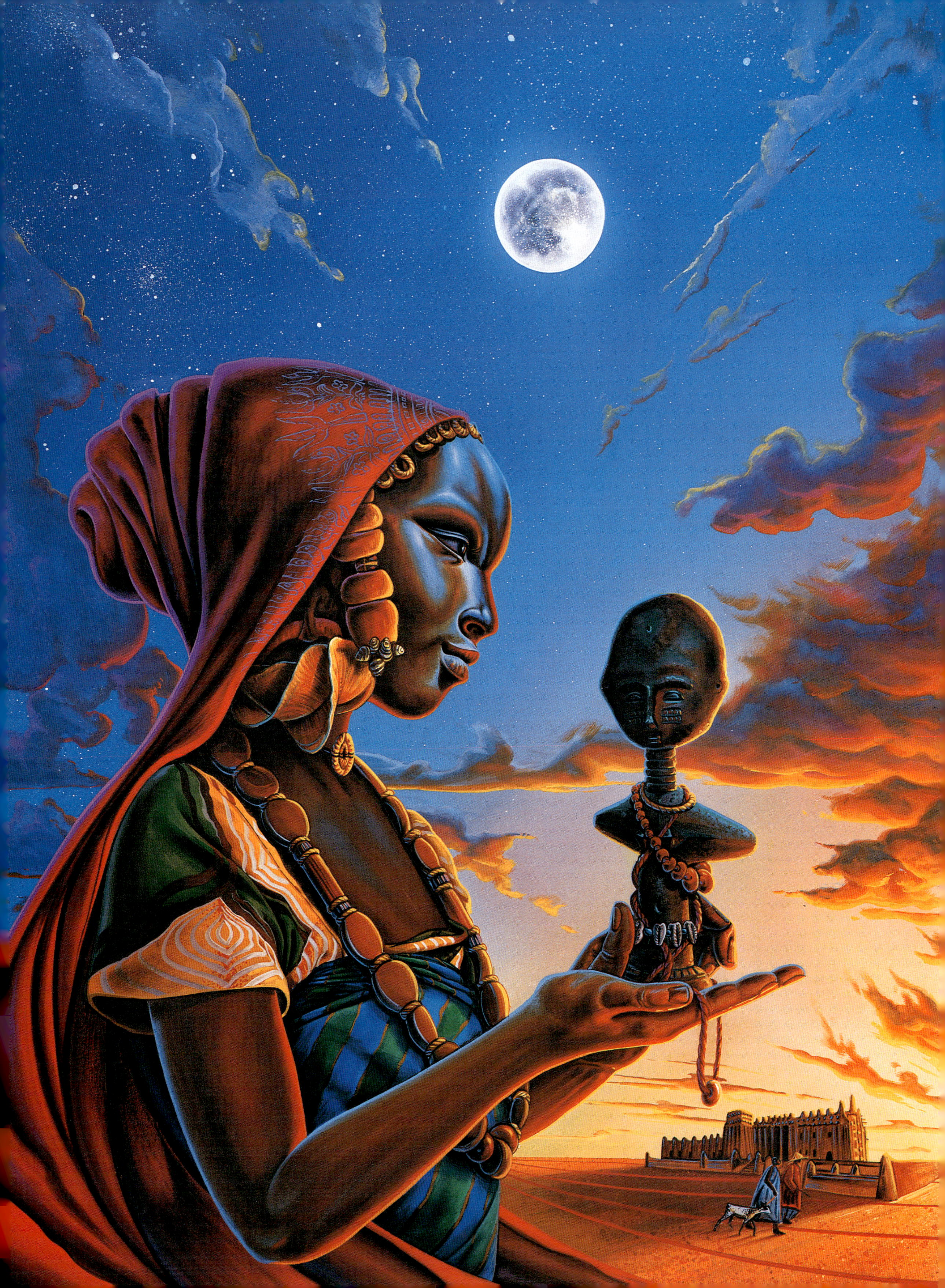

THIERRY CHATELAIN

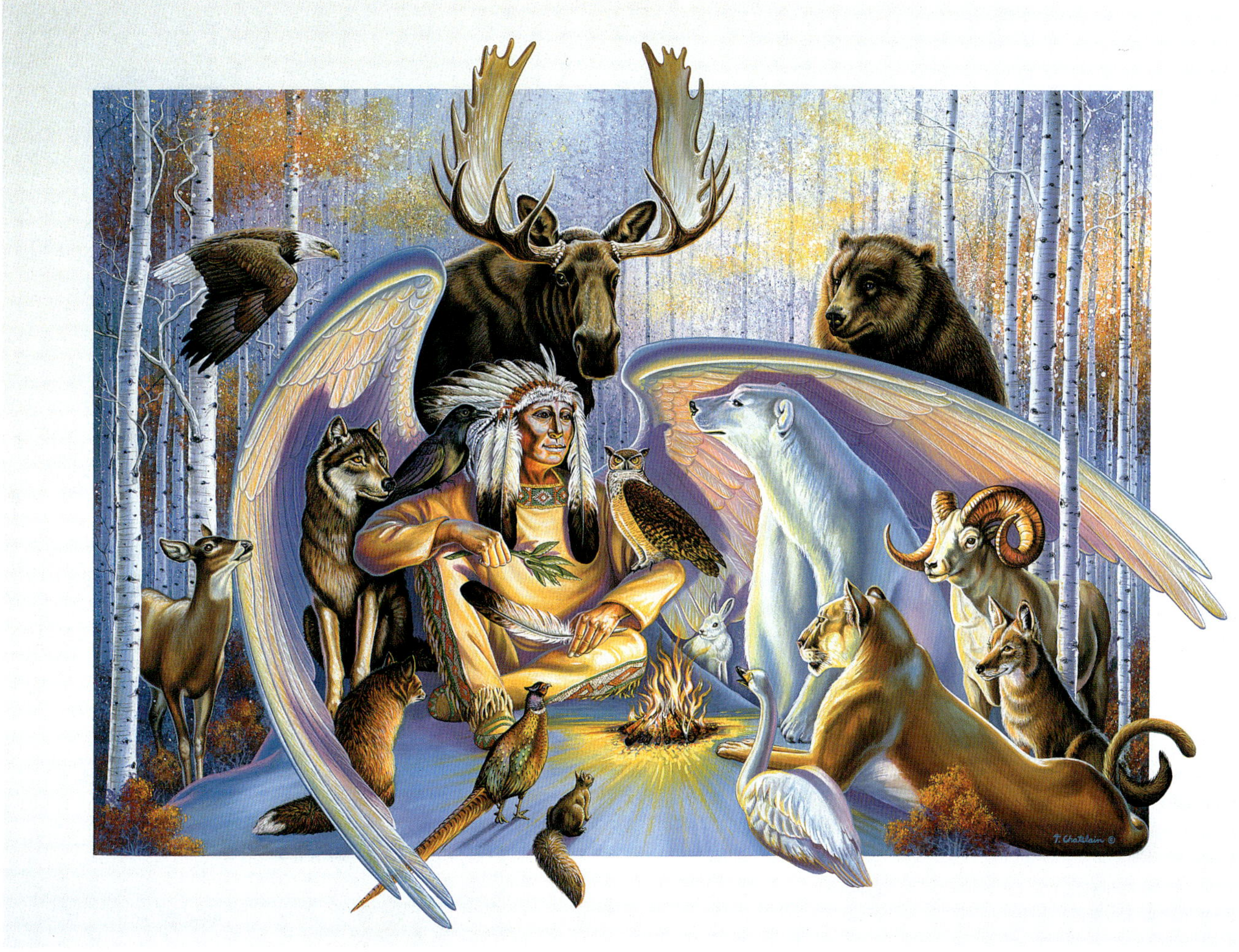

"Aspen Angel," 30" x 40" gouache medium on paper, 1996

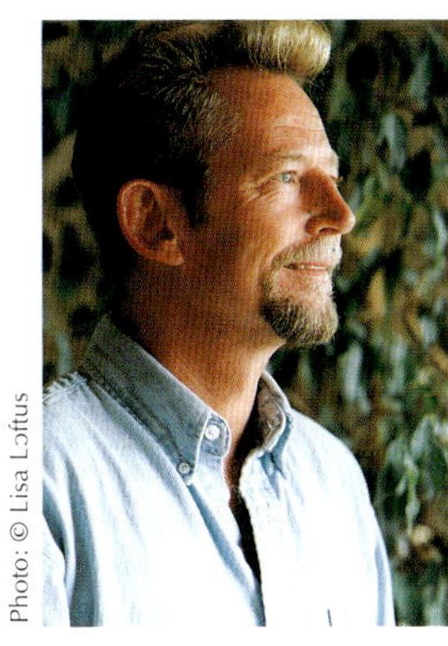

Photo: © Lisa Loftus

"PAINTING IS A MAGICAL MYSTICAL EXPERIENCE THAT FLOWS THROUGH ME AND TRANSCENDS TECHNIQUE."

— THIERRY CHATELAIN

When I was twelve, my mother gave me a book on Salvador Dali and it changed my life, even though I had been painting since the age of six. My father fed my fascination for the Egyptians, Mayans, and Native Americans, which even today, I find infinitely more interesting and relevant to my spirit than modern culture.

Painting is a magical mystical experience that flows through me and transcends technique. To bring imagination to life; to breathe color into intuitive thought and brush it upon the paper is a great privilege. It is such a natural experience for me that I often feel as if I am being praised for breathing. I am truly grateful.

The luminous quality that characterizes my work is created from many layers of gouache on paper. I was born in Casablanca, traveled a great deal and learned three languages by the age of four. I also studied art in Paris as a teenager, regaining my French heritage. This upbringing laid the groundwork for my ability to access the global native culture and spiritual force that resonates so profoundly throughout our world today.

Thierry Chatelain
4136B Falcon Street
San Diego, CA 92103
Tel: (619) 297-4642
Fax: (619) 297-0686

Opposite page: "Ebony Moon," 30" x 24" gouache medium on paper

"ART TENDS TO REFLECT THE CULTURE IN WHICH IT IS CREATED ... PERHAPS WE ARE SEEING A SPIRITUAL AWAKENING."
— *BEN HOWATT*

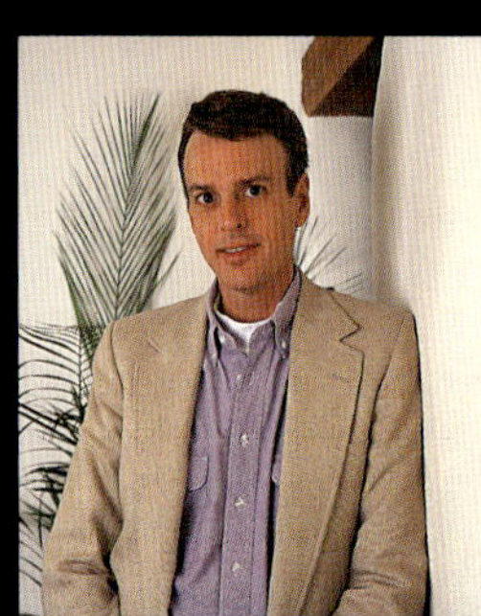

BEN HOWATT

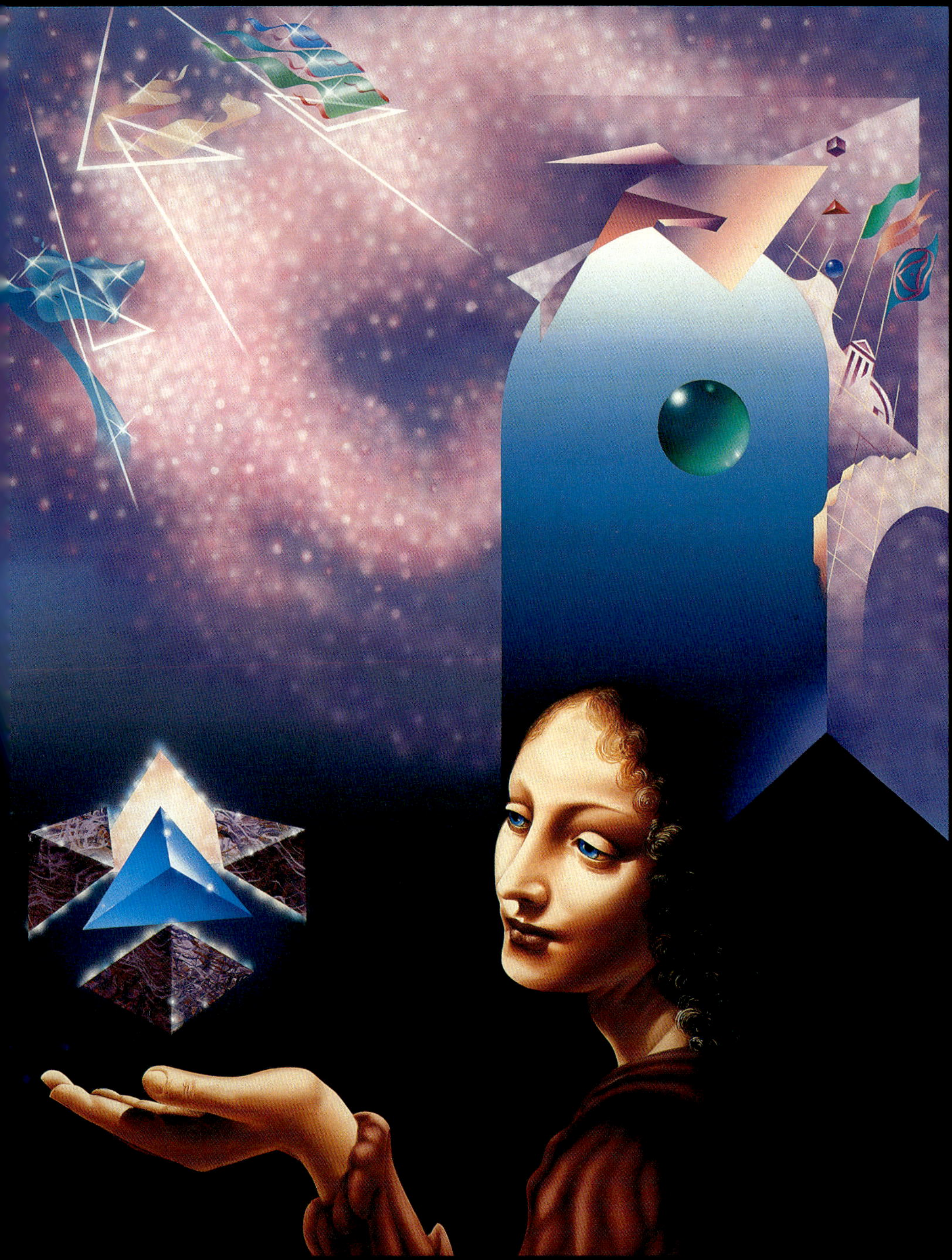

Until recently my images came solely from inner vision; not from replicating objects from the outside world. I would meditate on an idea, usually of a spiritual nature, and then listen for how that idea might be expressed in a visual way. Images will appear; abstract, structural images; and I will enlarge upon them. The paintings are largely complete in my mind's eye before I ever touch the canvas.

Crop circles, stylized Hieroglyphics and the geometric symbols of the Celts, the Navajo and agrarian cultures dependent on the "abstract" forces of nature and spirits fascinate me. At first I worked only in the strict purity of geometric forms. Now I have broadened to include more organic forms, even portraiture. The pursuit now is to explore the relationship between the inner worlds of the mental, emotional and spiritual states; to explore man's evolutionary accent between animal and God-man.

The images are not meant to be a succinct language communicating concrete information. But rather keys which will trigger ideas, curiosity and, perhaps, insight in the viewer. They are often descriptions of states of consciousness, symbolic and metaphoric. One visual theme which runs through the work is the use of the sphere, which is often found floating inside an arch. The sphere is a universal symbol of Wholeness. When placed in the arch it is intended to allude to the seat of Soul inside a cranium with the activities of the physical, astral, causal and mental bodies encasing it. Many of the works point to the fact that the spiritual heavens are within one's body.

"Angel of the Rocks," 48" x 36" oil over acrylic on canvas, 1990

Ben Howatt Studios
1230 N. June Street, #208
Hollywood, CA 90038-1379
Tel: (213) 463-5540

HARMONY WIND HARPS

R. SUNDHARA BARRABLE

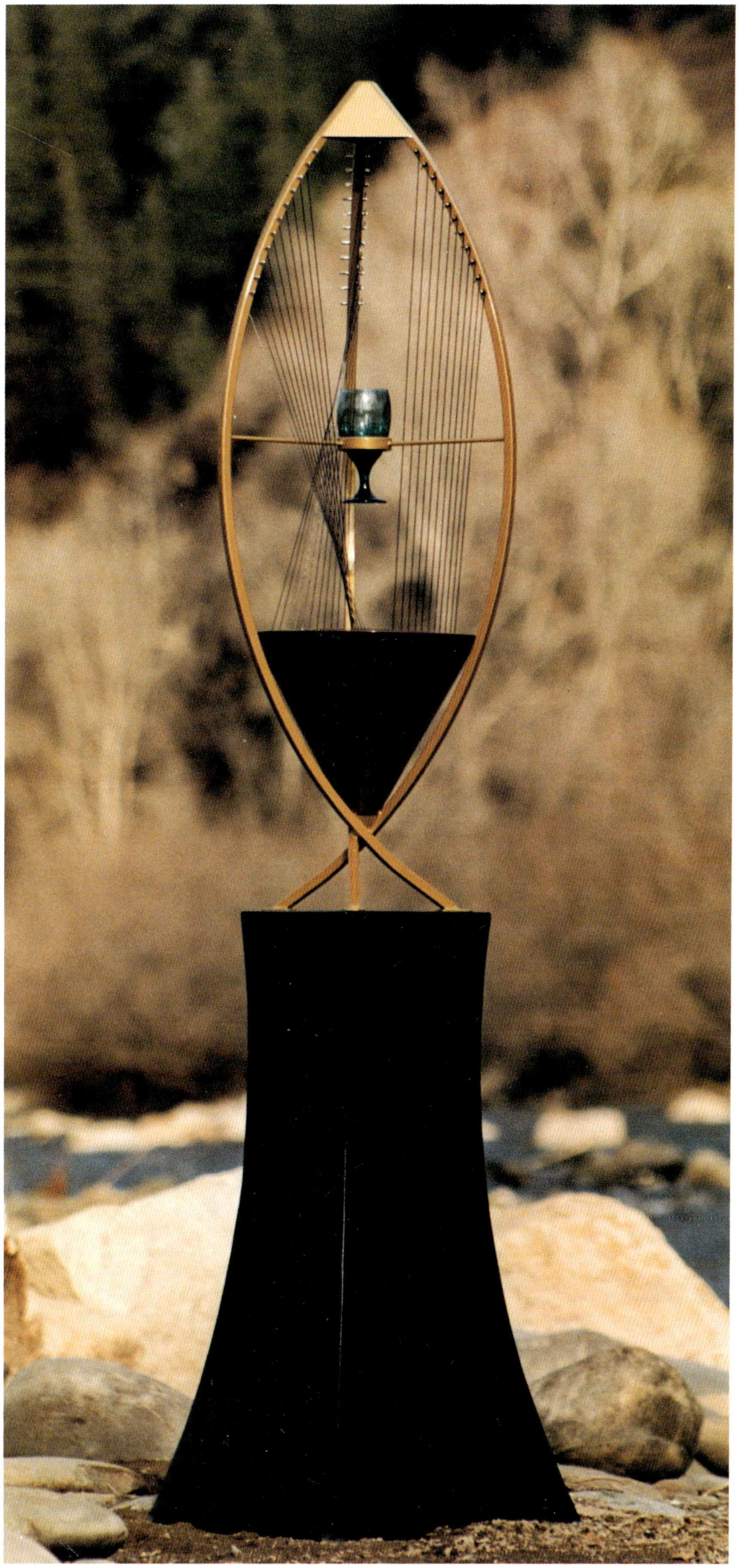

"Song of the Grail," Overall height 7′ - 6″ titanium, stainless steel and nylon
©1996 Harmony Wind Harps

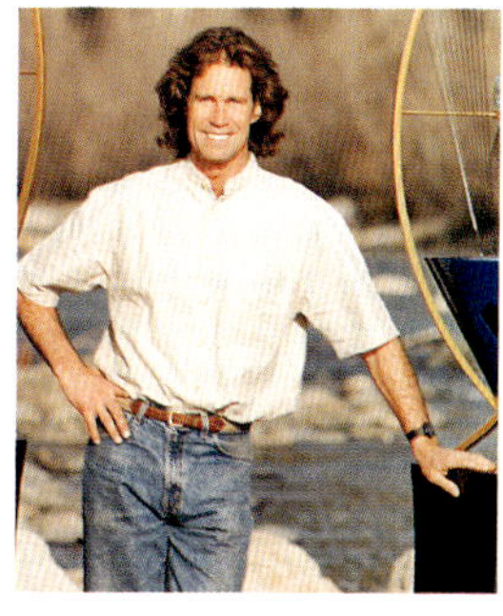

"WHEN THE WIND BLOWS
THROUGH THE STRINGS,
THE WIND HARPS GENERATE
HARMONIC OVERTONES ..."

— R. SUNDHARA BARRABLE

The major influence on my work is my love of sound and music. As a folk harp builder and player for many years, my life has always been filled with music.

I consider myself an artist who integrates both science and art, creating multidimensional sculpture which brings together the metaphysics of design and quantum physics of sound. My Acoustic Sculptures are cast and fabricated out of bronze, titanium, silver and gold using the principles of sacred geometry, creating forms of symmetry which duplicate the basic building blocks of the Universe.

When the wind blows through the strings, the Wind Harps generate harmonic overtones which have the same "centering" quality and ability to align energies as listening to Tibetan monks chant, playing crystal bowls or sitting in a circle chanting OM.

I am sincerely dedicated to creating sacred sound spaces which have the transformational power to unite the participant with all the elements of nature through the omnipresent power of harmonic sound.

Harmony Wind Harps
R. Sundhara Barrable
P.O. Box 3039
Pagosa Springs, CO 81147-3039
Tel/Fax: (970) 264-2962

C BANGS

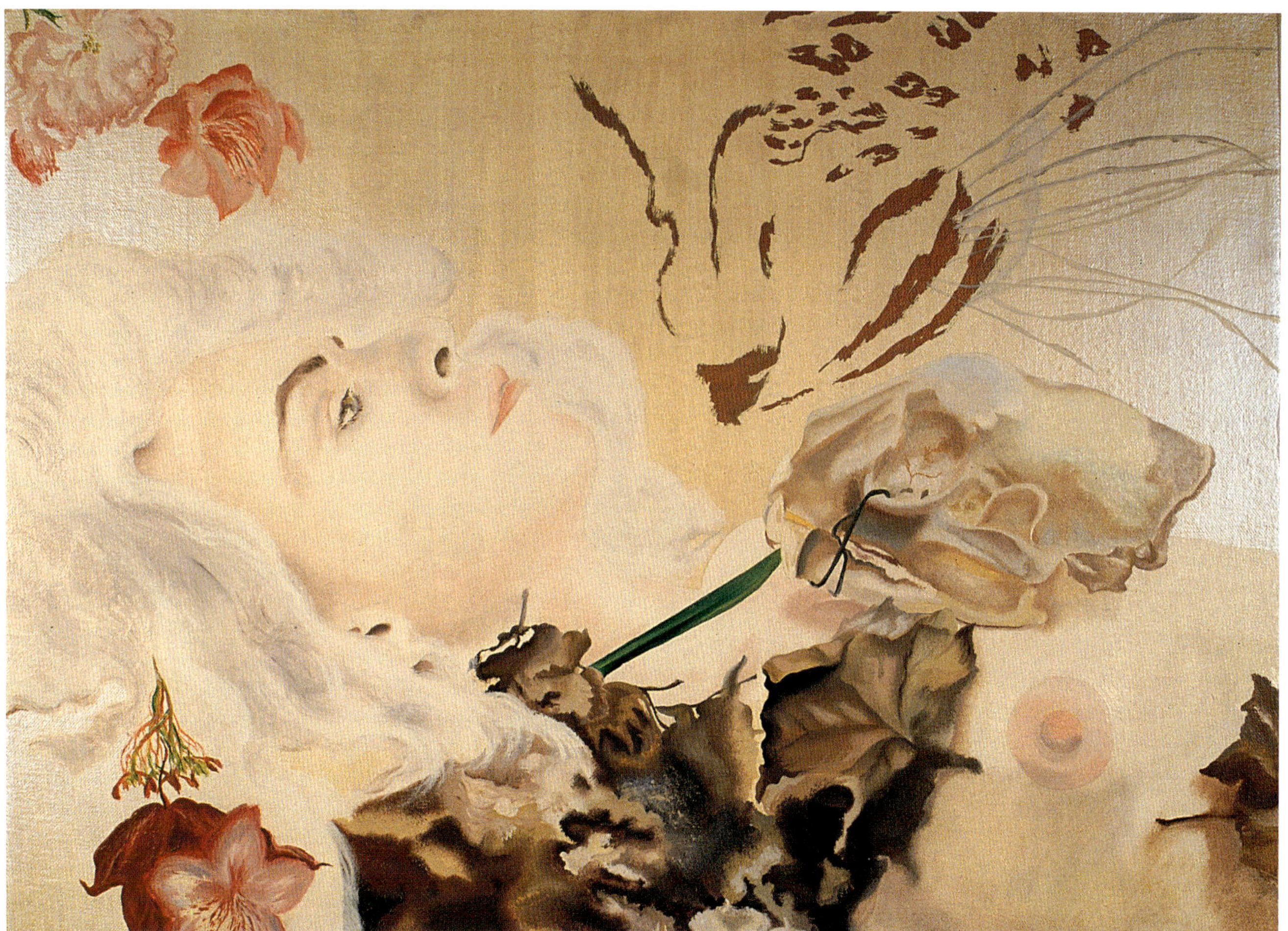

"Dream of Çatal Hüyük," 16" x 20" oil on canvas, 1992

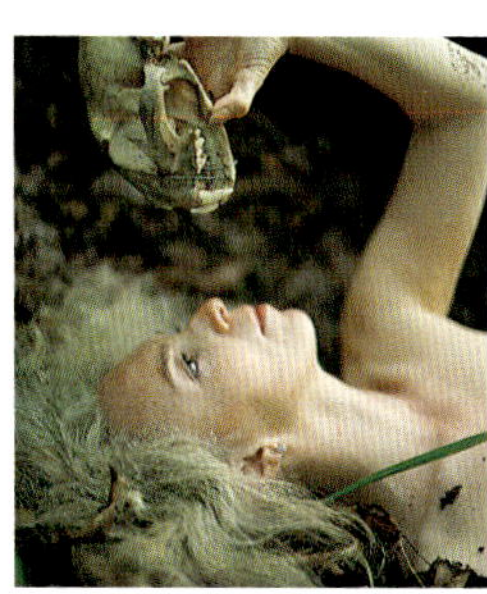

"... ON A QUANTUM LEVEL, THE MOST BASIC LEVEL, WE ARE ALL INTERCONNECTED TO EVERYTHING."

— C BANGS

My artistic investigation concentrates on the spiritual/ecological as represented by the modern archetype of the Earth Goddess Gaia (the ancient Greek word for the Earth). Gaia is the term used by contemporary ecologists to denote the Earth, life, and the system of interactions of life and the planetary environment. The Green Man, a male archetype of oneness with Earth is originally also an ancient Greek archetype.

My works include equations and quantum diagrams which function as design elements around or on the figures and are rendered as "sacred writing." The premise of quantum consciousness is that on a quantum level, the most basic level, we are all interconnected to everything.

My work includes personal symbols and images of friends and family. Starting with the personal enables me to investigate my feelings about death and rebirth and to explore how the Earth's ecology relates to our own bodies.

Dream of Çatal Hüyük is a self portrait with a leopard skull. In Çatal Hüyük, a Neolithic settlement that thrived from 7000 to 5000 BC in southern Anatolia, the leopard was the sacred animal of the Goddess. The leopard symbolizes all endangered species and the renewal of our ecological awareness of the Earth.

C Bangs
417 Greene Avenue
Brooklyn, NY 11216
Tel/Fax: (718) 638-7586

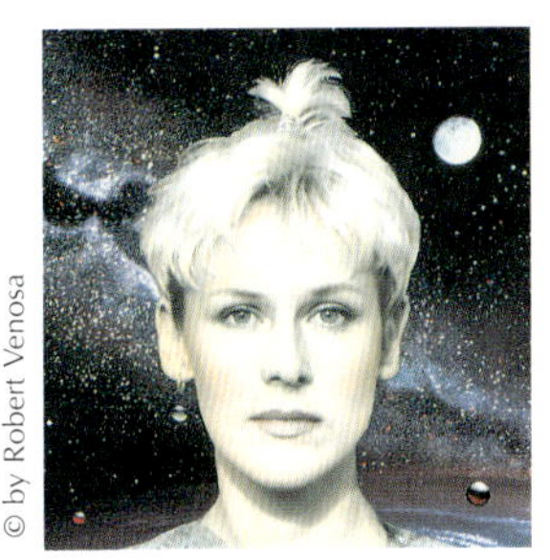

© by Robert Venosa

"MY CANVASSES SPEAK
THE LANGUAGE OF MY DREAMS."
—*MARTINA HOFFMANN*

MARTINA HOFFMANN

My inner visions are the guide and inspiration for my paintings. The medium allows me to exteriorize and manifest these visions. Only when once materialized on the canvas do I get the chance to understand what my inner eye sees. It is very much like deciphering a code or learning an unknown language. The discovery of the universe is an endless process, and the worlds beyond ours hold unlimited beauty and wonder for me.

The process of exteriorization is very 'stream of consciousness.' I try not to focus on the contents of the painting while at work. Thoughts, emotions and symbols will come in this 'meditative' state, but I won't judge nor select them until one of them will ring so true that I have no choice but to include its essence translated into form into the painting.

Initially I see myself as a tool and a translator. I am not the one who decides what the finished painting will look like. Rather, I let the painting tell me what it wants and needs to be.

I feel fortunate to receive and paint these visions for those who might not have the gift of 'seeing.' We are all here to share our blessings with each other in our quest for a deeper understanding of life and its great mysteries.

Martina Hoffmann
1430 High Street
Boulder, CO 80304
Phone/Fax: (303) 440-8905
email: venosa@csd.net

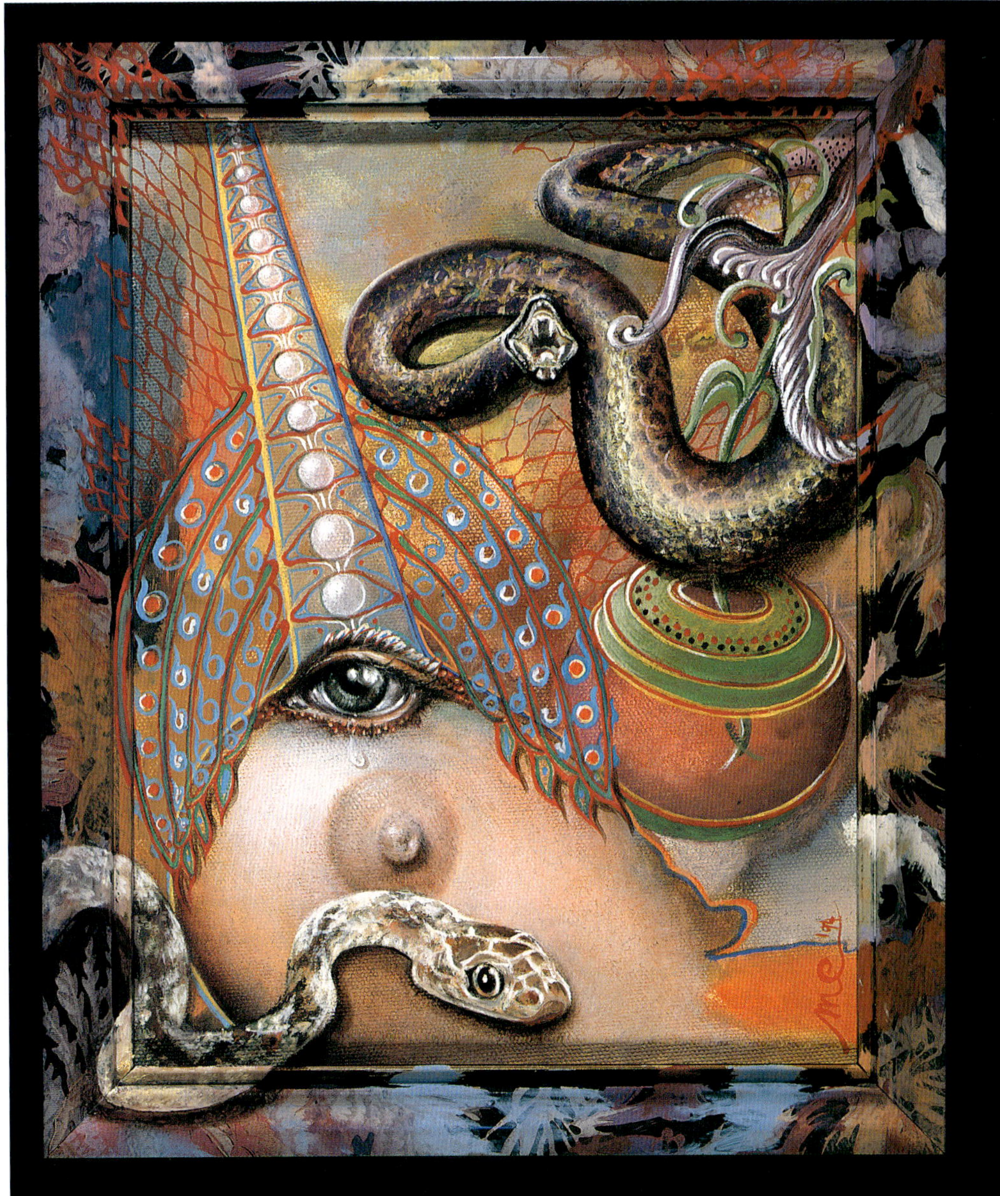

"DMT - Oracle," 11-1/6" x 11-1/6" oil on canvas, 1994

MARY CARROLL NELSON

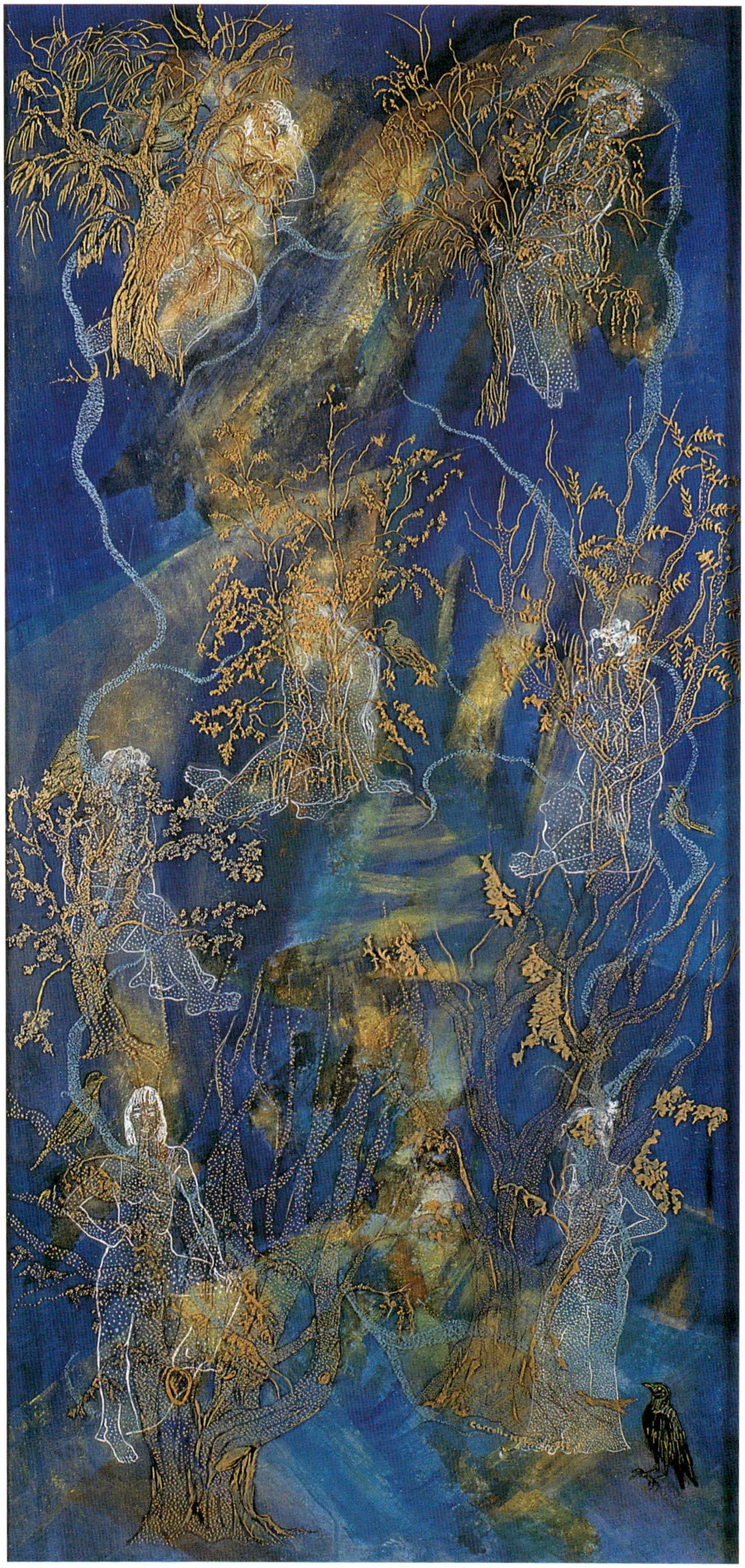

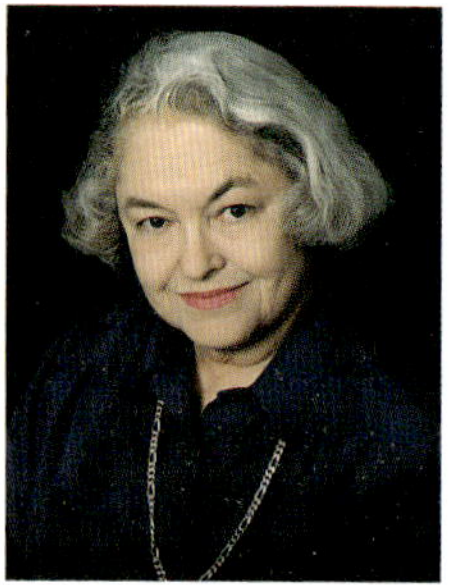

"MY IDEAL AS AN ARTIST IS TO EXPRESS THE PERCEPTION THAT WE ARE MULTI-DIMENSIONAL ETERNAL BEINGS."

A powerful emotional stimulus, beginning with the death of my father in 1982 and the subsequent decline of my mother's health, prompted me to spend several years developing symbolic images for spiritual concepts related to time, transformation, universal connectedness, and the cycle of life, death and rebirth. I continue to explore these themes in wall and table shrines.

By stippling with a pen or painting with a brush, I apply transparent and luminous inks to sheet plastic. Additions of gold leaf, mylar, natural stones, glitter and electric lighting are metaphorical connections between the tangible and the ineffable. I think of light playing through the plastic as the penetration of ordinary reality by the numinous dimension.

Since the late 1970s, I have used the word "layerists" to describe artists who create layered art as an expression of their worldview in which events, thoughts, material reality, space and time flow together In a seamless web. I founded the Society of Layerists In Multi-Media, in 1982, to serve as a national network. SLMM's exhibitions, publications and symposia manifest a holistic aesthetic.

Mary Carroll Nelson
1408 Georgia, NE
Albuquerque, NM 87110
Tel: (505) 268-1100

"Pleiadean Dimensions," 48" x 24" mixed media, plexi on masonite

MARCIA DIANE

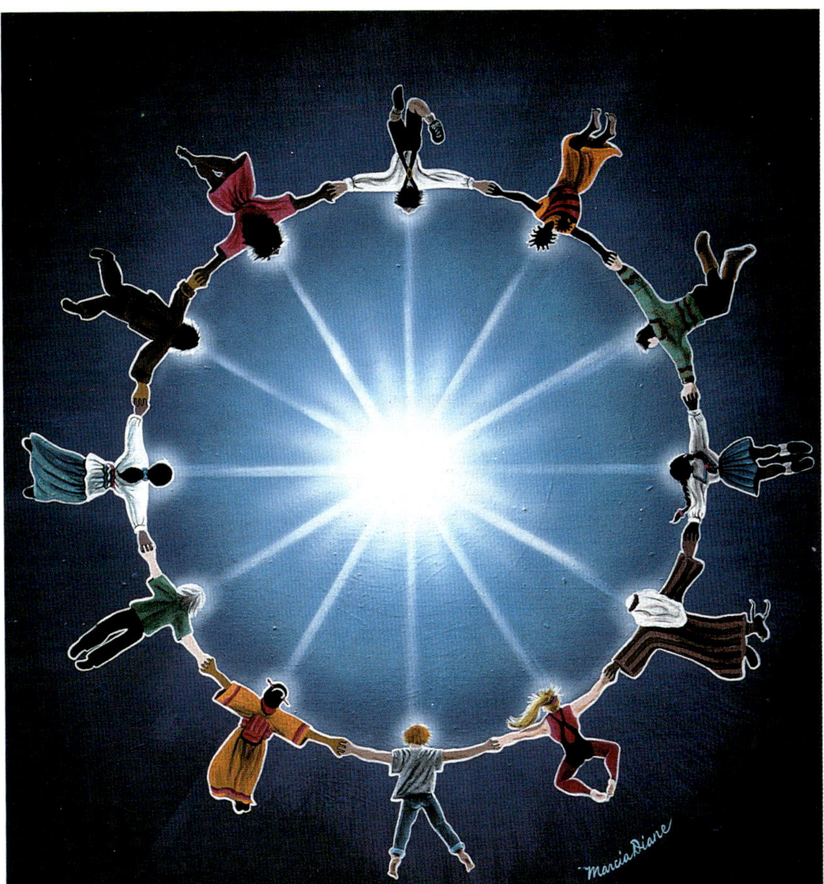

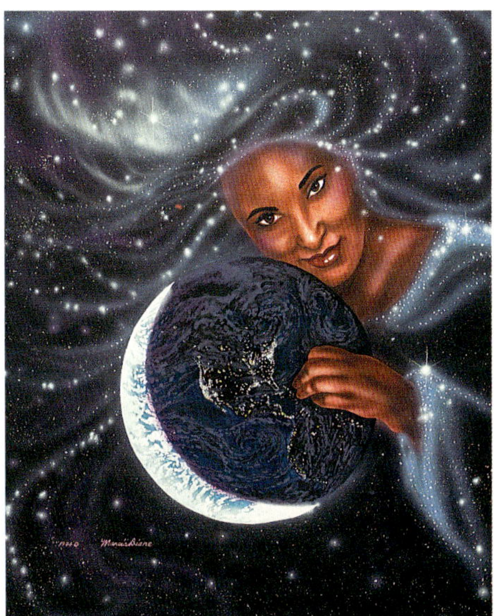

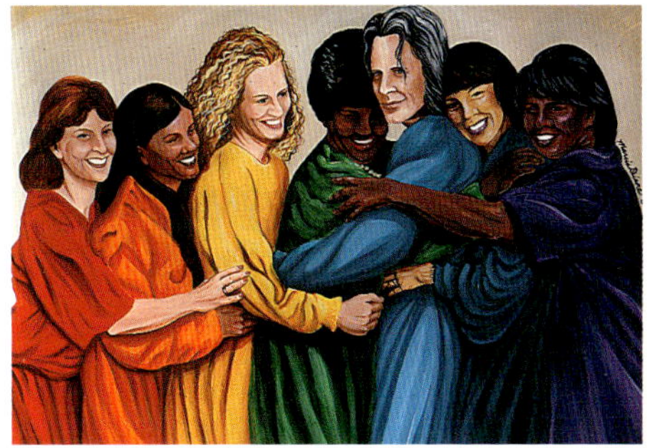

Top: "The Wheel," 30" x 30" acrylic on canvas, 1995 Top Right: "Earth Goddess," 24" x 30" acrylic on canvas, 1994
Bottom Right: "Rainbow Warriors," 23" x 29" acrylic on rag paper, 1993

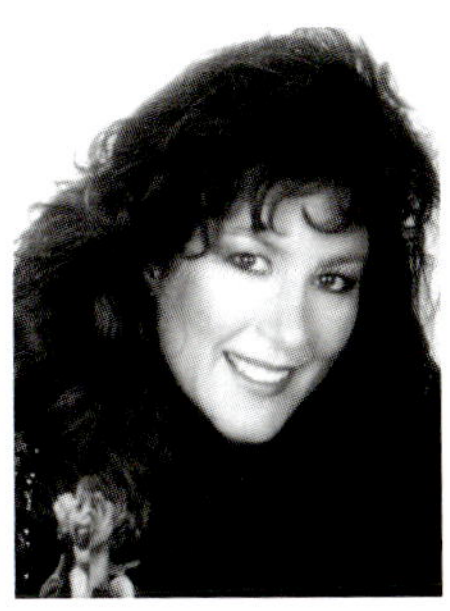

"IT IS TIME TO RECOGNIZE THE SPIRITUAL HEART OF OUR LIVES."
— *MARCIA DIANE*

My paintings honor Souls in communion — with friends, self and Divine Spirit — celebrating differences, similarities, mutual desire for peace and connection. By opening our hearts, discovery of and devotion to our unique paths, we create fulfillment.

Personal and collective awakening is happening today Experiencing spiritual light and sound, I discovered my true identity — Soul. Thus began my quest to live in full consciousness.

To balance imposing worldly powers, we must develop ourselves to our fullest potential. Our survival depends upon love of ourselves, of each other. Richard Moss MD invites us to radical aliveness: "It is time to recognize the spiritual heart of our lives. It is time to own the naturalness and universality of this without dogma and creation of new ways to separate ourselves."

Portraying our ideals visually can counter negative conditioning and empower us to take steps toward personal, relational, and global healing. Open further to your aliveness by actively participating with a spiritual painting. Relax, listen, imagine, experience. Allow limiting patterns to dissipate, new waves of life energy to permeate your being. Take a mini-vacation to observe and appreciate your own Sacred Journey.

Marcia Diane Studios
P.O. Box 3882
Chandler, AZ 85224-3882
Tel/Fax: (602) 821-0639

"I USE JOY AND LOVE TO GENERATE THE DIVINE CREATIVE ENERGY WHICH I BELIEVE IS GOD..."
— *JEAN FEAK FAHEY*

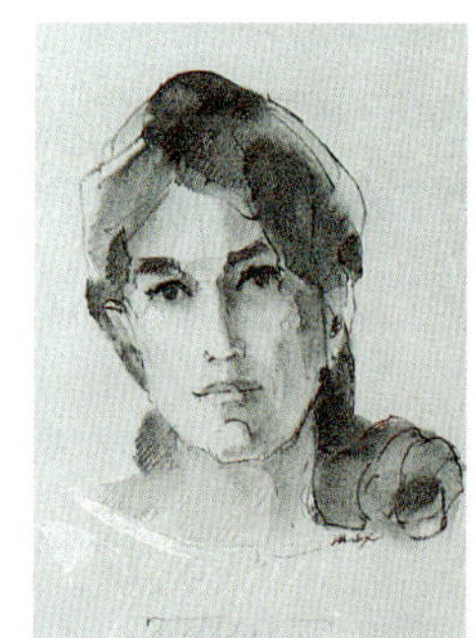

JEAN FEAK FAHEY

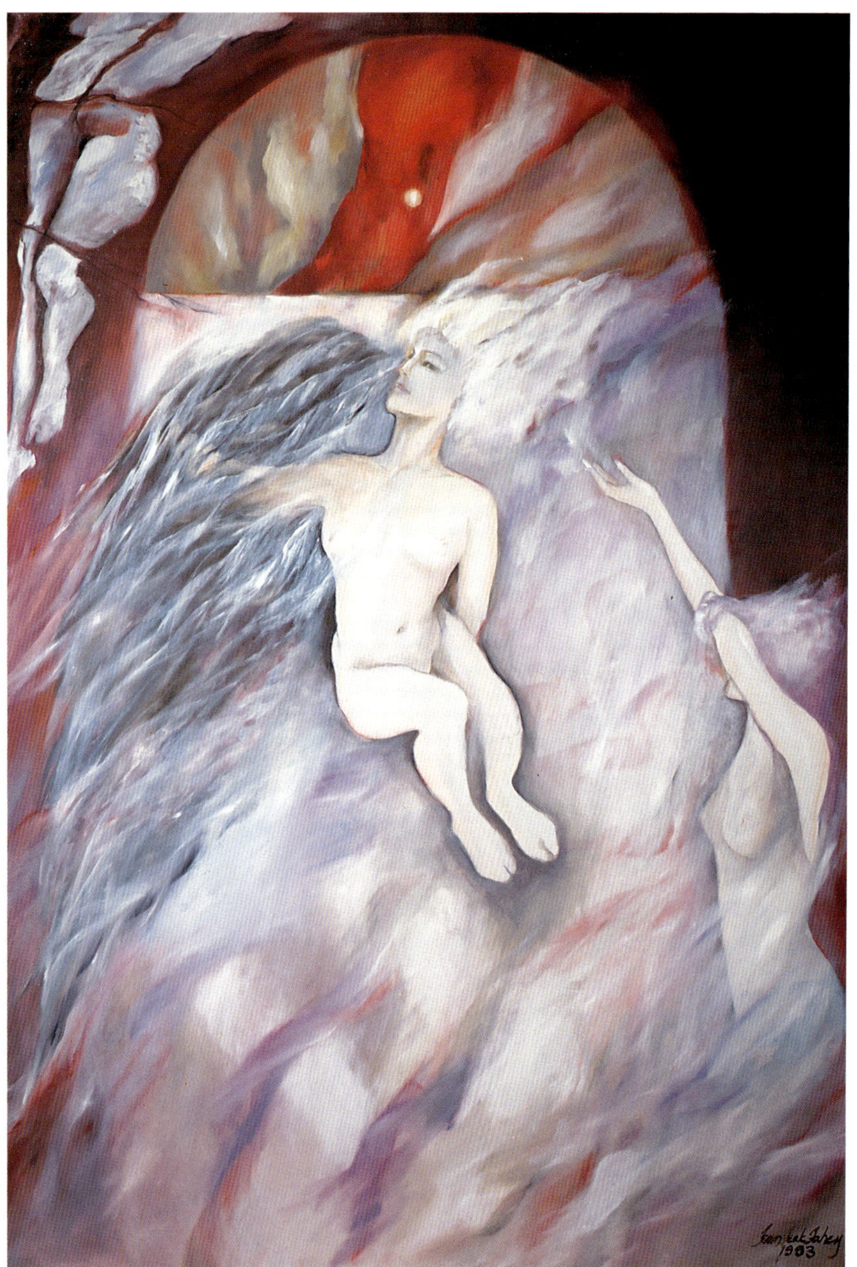

Above: "Antigone Ascending," 6′ x 8′ oil on canvas, 1995
Opposite page: "Eurydice: After the End," 6′ x 8′ oil on canvas, 1994

Tragedian Greek Mythology always held great fascination for me as have spirits, angels, saints and other mystifying guides. Although my work was abstract for many years, gradually an evolution of figurative matter took place and inevitably turned to Mythology. The need to express what was in my spirit overcame all judgement and confines of art as I had always known it. Eventually my subject matter became alive for me, and gradually I realized the tragedies I was painting brought about the identical tragedies in my own life, perhaps the "matter follows thought" theory.

To save myself and the concept of what I was doing, I spent several years practicing Yoga and studying Eastern philosophies. The concept of living in the now and the peace of Tao became integrated into my life. I use joy and love to generate the Divine Creative Energy which I believe is God in everything I do now.

I began to fantasize triumphant endings to these tragedies such as Orpheus' Eurydice rising like a phoenix after her final descent into Hades. She rose to become a glorious archetype and great inspiration for all to follow. Same with Antigone, the illegitimate and doomed daughter of Oedipus and his mother, Jocasta. To me, her doom became her great strength and power — becoming the foundation of her character. Since I have undergone this change of intent, the position and expressions of all figures are in the state of Tao. While about them the earth, wind, sea, and fire rage frighteningly, the figures remain in a state of peace and enlightenment.

Life for me has also changed. The situations and people that were murky and terrifying, one by one have mysteriously disappeared from my life. My new series "Back to Water" signifies the divine cleansing that takes place as we see the beautiful blue-white flow coming over us and, with it, bringing a new resurrection each day.

Jean Feak Fahey
4447 Kahala Avenue
Honolulu, HI 96816
Tel: (808) 735-4187
Fax: (808) 733-0808

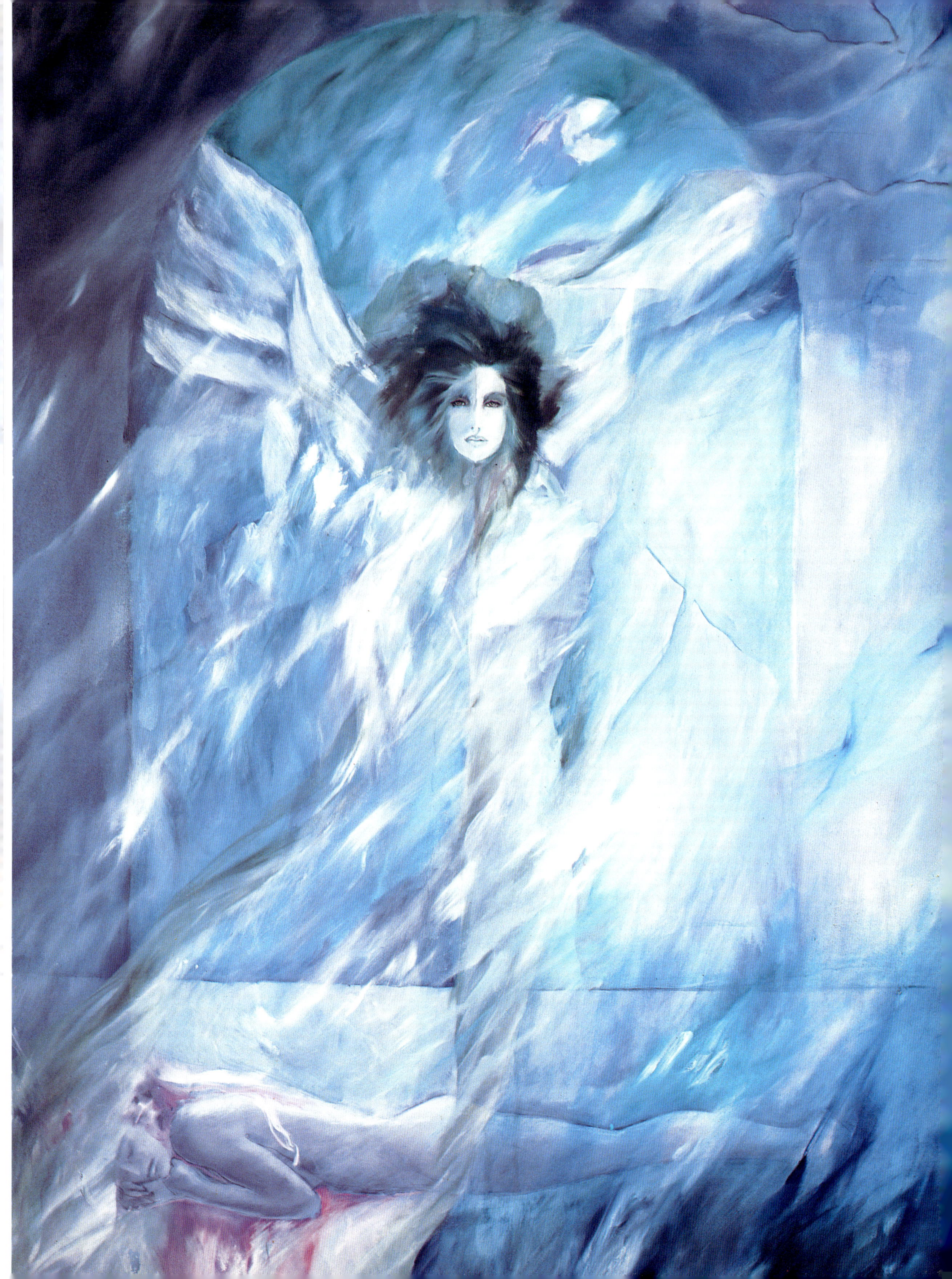

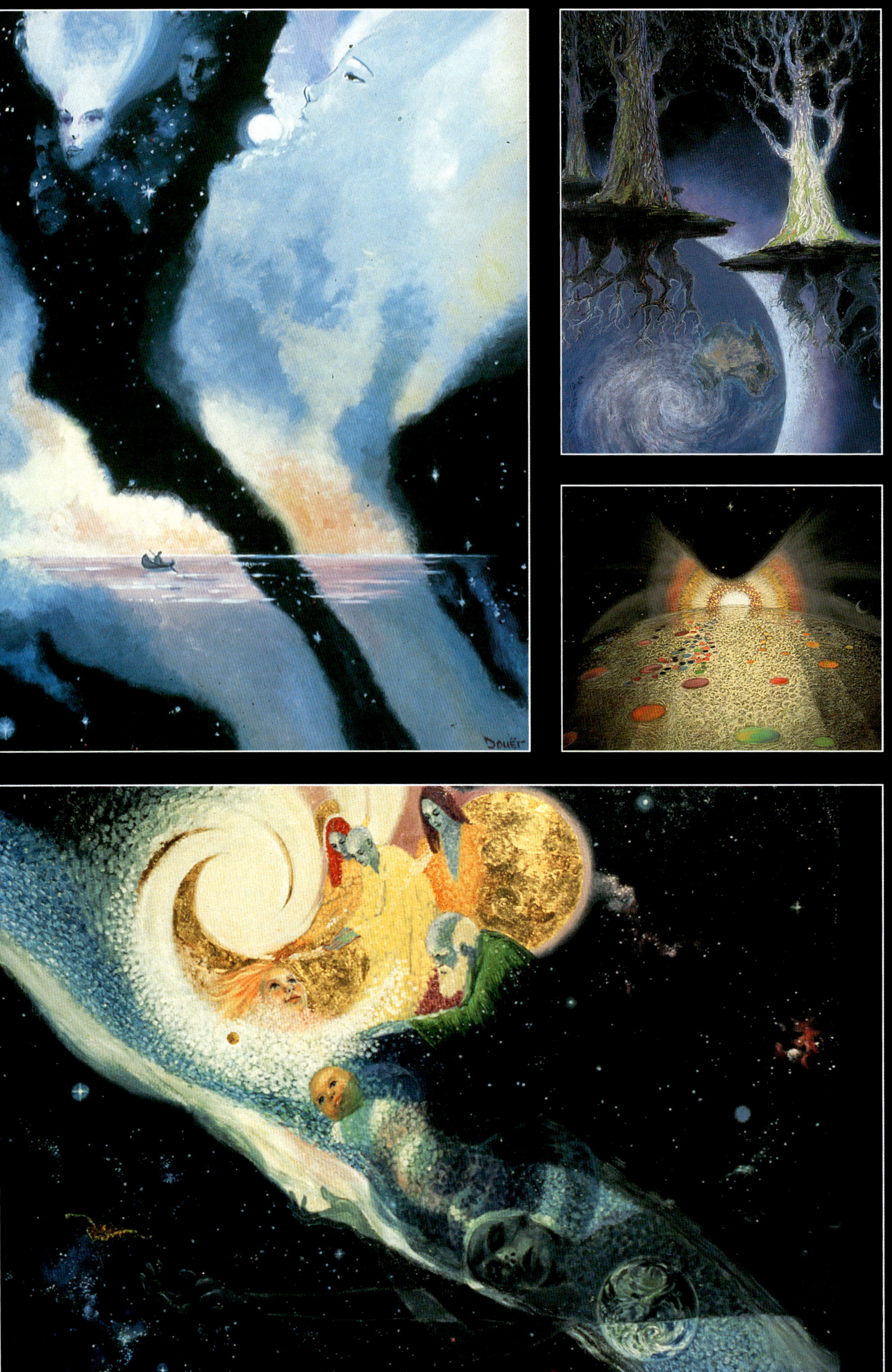
DOUËT

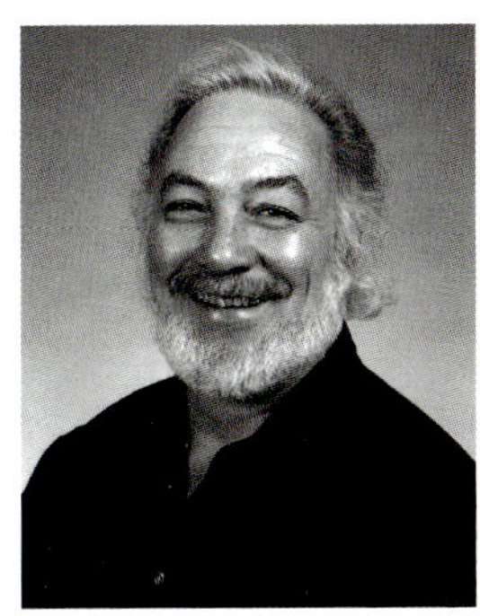

ARTHUR DOUËT

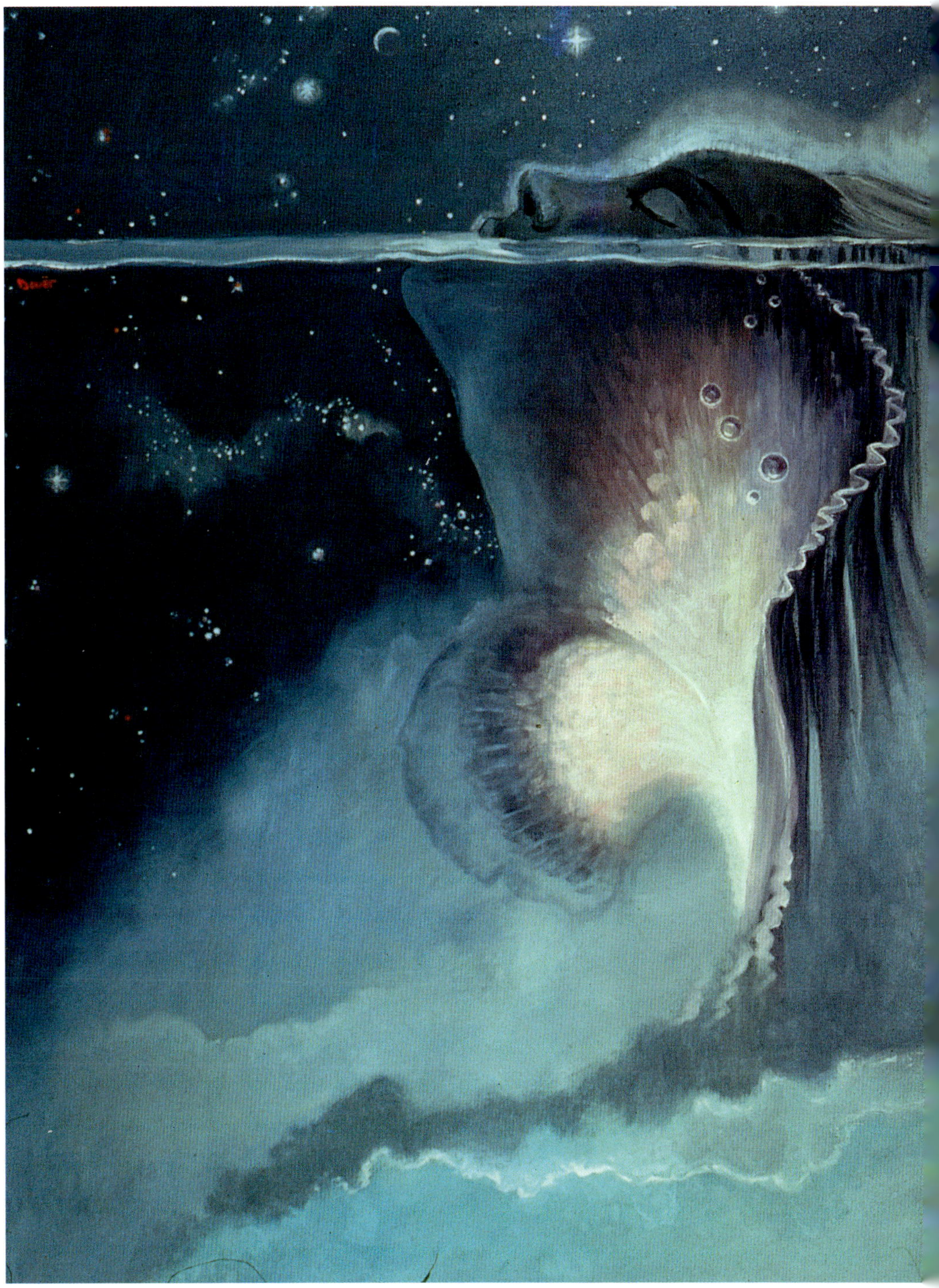

"The life within the rose is
more than the rose It shows you."
— from the poem "The Rose"
by Arthur Douët

Imagine yourself floating like a leaf on water and that you can see far above and below. In a flash of wonder you ponder the height and depth of the great Life that contains and sustains all things in this holy instant. Angels, like dolphins, surf on this Ocean of Oneness that we all share in timeless Being. If you can allow yourself to quiet the "chitter-chatter" of the mind and rise above the limited and the mundane you will touch the Core of Being and resonate with the profound vastness of all that is. Dissatisfied with mere effects or appearances, I attune myself to Essence to allow the expression of the Sacred Breath through my hands. The inspiration received brings meaning with message conveyed through symbols and colour. They are like notes of music crystallized — a language to reflect the harmonics of Consciousness. In gazing, we rediscover the song they sing.

Agents for Douët
Robert and Anna Lee Payne
Inner Space Scapes
13805 Wooded Creek #100
Dallas, TX 75244
Tel: (214) 243-3456
edistw@computek.net

Opposite page clockwise from upper left: "Omnipresence," 36" x 40" oil on canvas, "Trees - Our Silent Guardians," 19" x 26" pastel, "Angel Of Unity," 19" x 26" pastel, "Life After Life," 64" x 40" oil on canvas

Above: "Inner Light," 5' x 4' oil

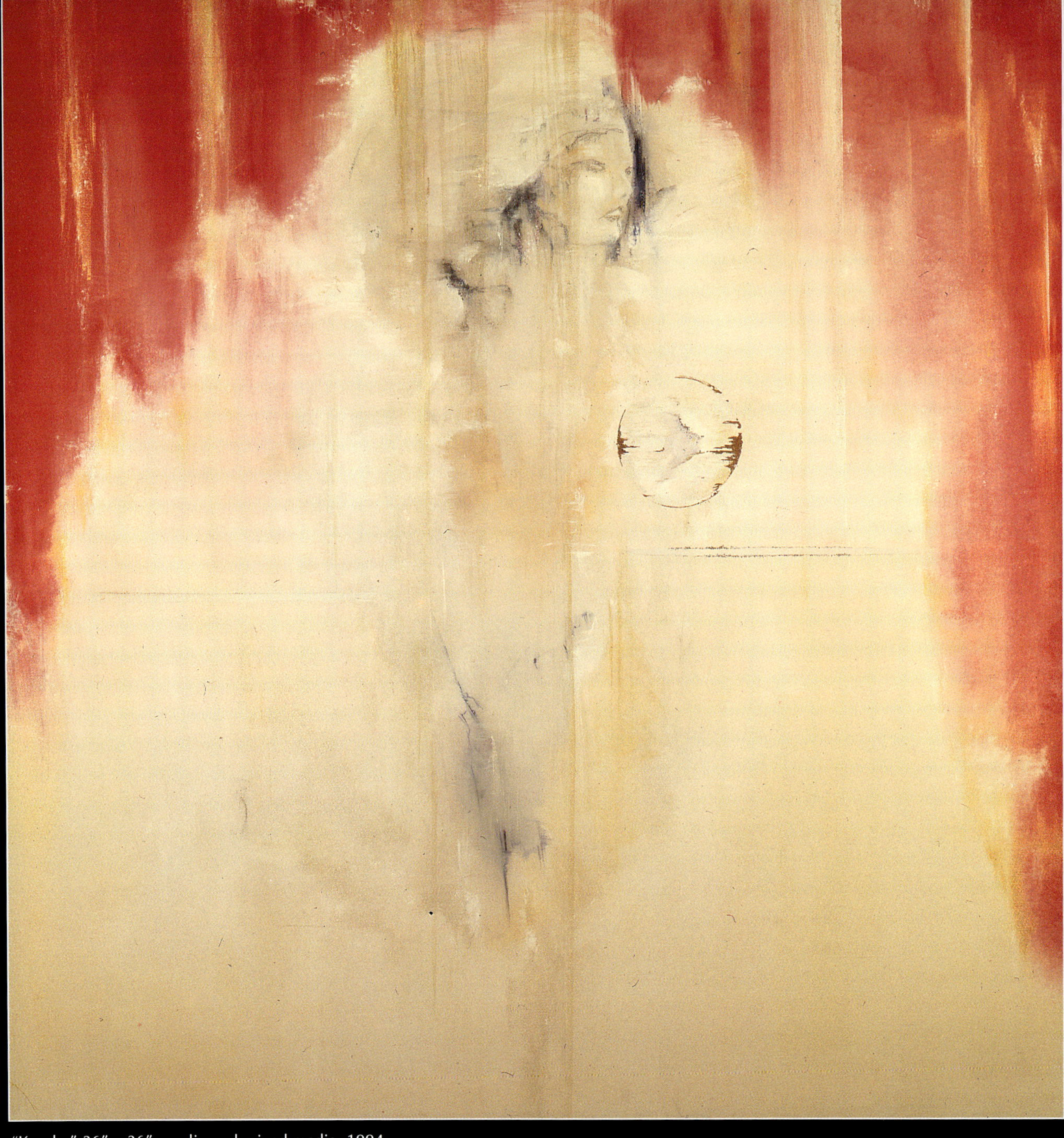

“Kunda,” 36″ x 36″ acrylic and mixed media, 1994

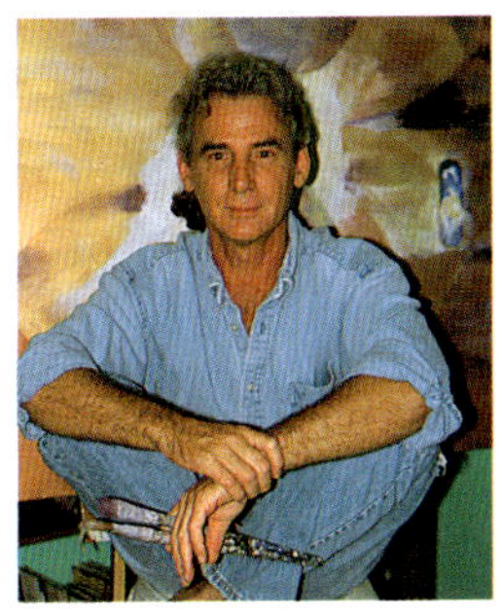

GARY MARKOWITZ

"THE PAINTINGS ARE PIECES FROM OTHER TIMES, OTHER PLACES. ALL PART OF A REMEMBERING."

— *GARY MARKOWITZ*

In 1991, I began to experience tremendous rushes of energy and Light. In one brilliant, golden second my vision of reality changed to include a multidimensional point of view and new understanding. A doorway of light appeared, the Akashic records were opened and time and space disappeared. I was surrounded in gold and white light, in the midst of a golden sun. I experienced total love, joy and a remembering. I knew I had been here many times before. I knew we were not alone, there was God, and that we are all one.

My work is a sharing of these experiences and the act of creating is part of my continuing quest for understanding. Painting is one way I connect again with myself — my higher self — that spark of golden light that lies within. My paintings are a reminder of our divine nature.

My art is about other dimensions and realities coming together with ours — angelic realms, the Central Sun, dimensions of light. It is about accessing our distant memories and remembering our origin and our selves.

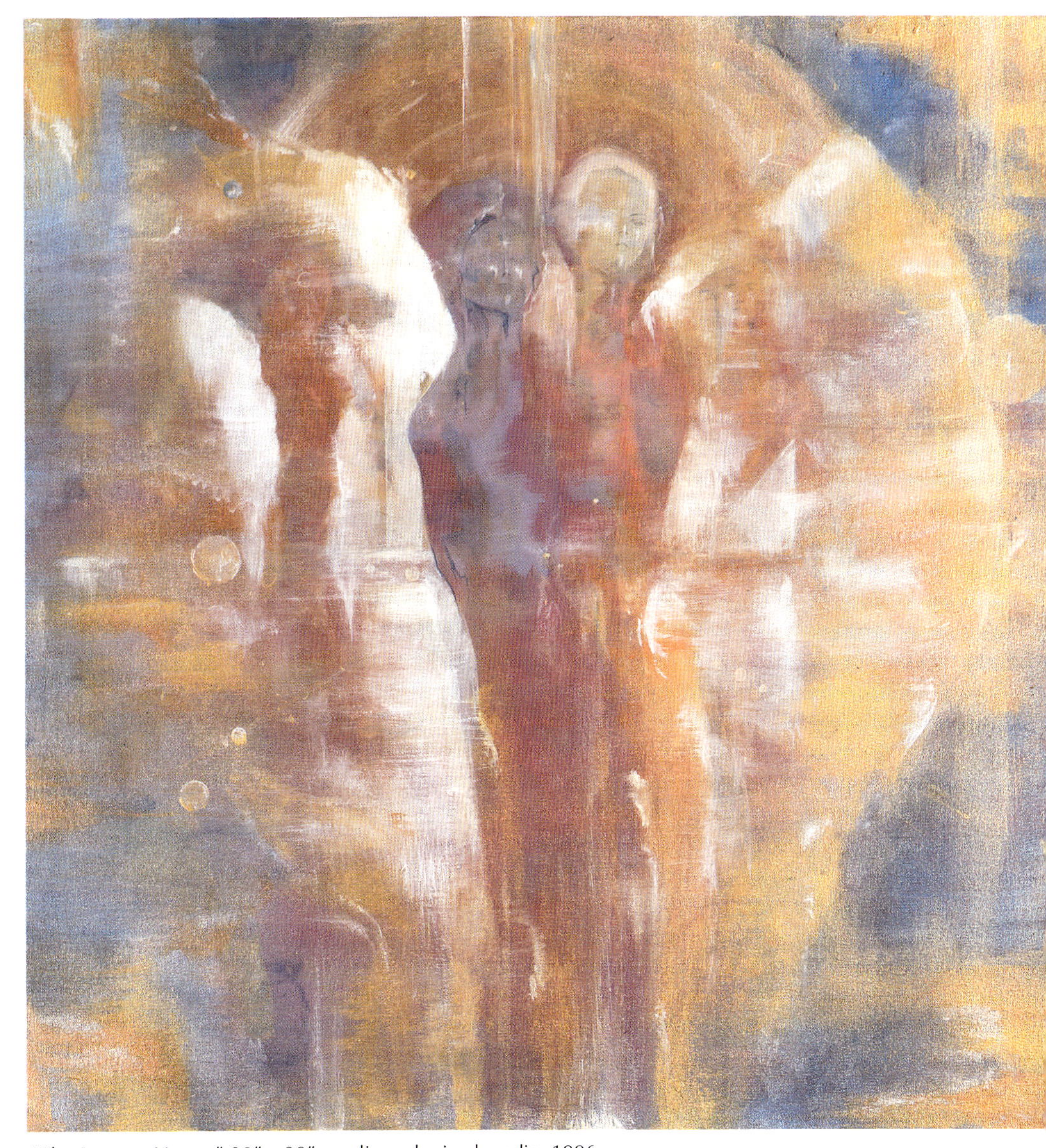

"The Journey Home," 30" x 30" acrylic and mixed media, 1996

Gary Markowitz
P.O. Box 1250
Paia, HI 96779
Tel: 808 579-9737
Fax: 808 579-9387

LISA GORDON

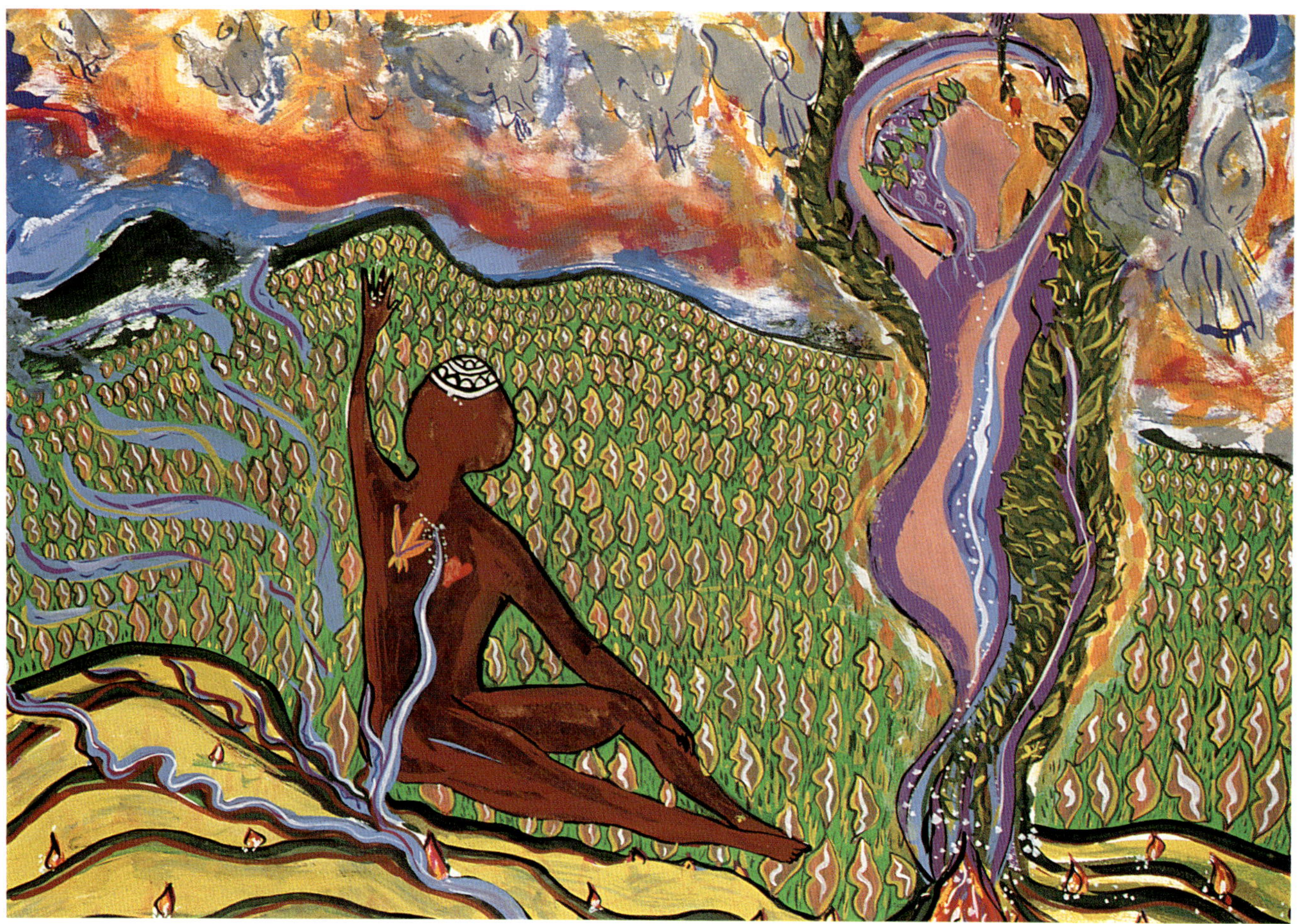

"Farewell to Sukkot," limited edition lithograph, 1996

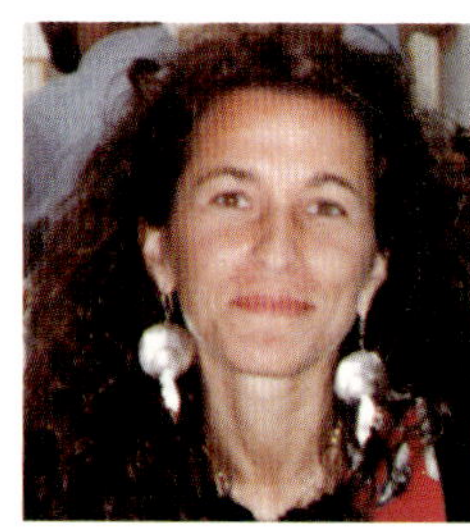

"... PAINTING ALLOWS ME TO EXPLORE AND INTEGRATE MY EXPERIENCE AND KNOWLEDGE ... THAT DEEPENS MY RELATIONSHIP TO G-D."

— *LISA GORDON*

The art of painting is a form of creative expression and personal prayer. The textural accounts of my Jewish ancestry are the source of my inspiration — the port of entry through which color and form merge with ancient ritual. Painting allows me to explore and integrate my experience and knowledge in a way that deepens my relationship to G-d and to the collective.

"Farewell to Sukkot" — the earth lies dormant, then slowly replenishes for the harvest festival. The valley is filled with willow leaves singing praise to G-d. On the last day of Sukkot the angels depart while the prayer "Farewell to Sukkot" is recited to escort our honored guest.

"Shavuot" is the holiday that commemorates the receiving of the Torah at Mount Sinai. The mandala represents the continuous process of refining consciousness in order to sanctify and elevate the world.

Lisa Gordon
LiebArt
520 North Avenida Presidio
Walnut, CA 91784
Tel: (518) 458-9619

Opposite page: "Shavuot,"
32" x 40" gouache on paper, 1995

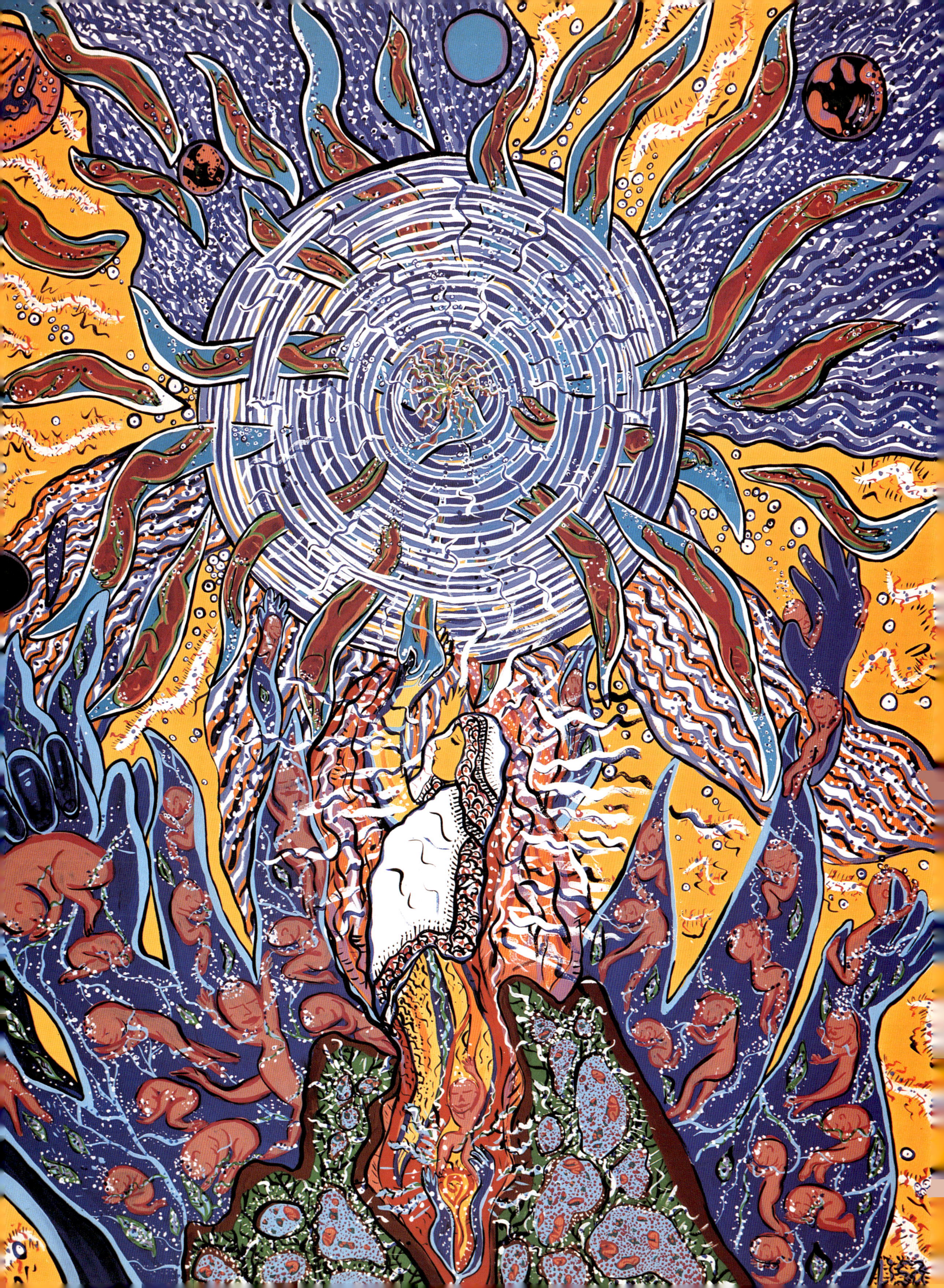

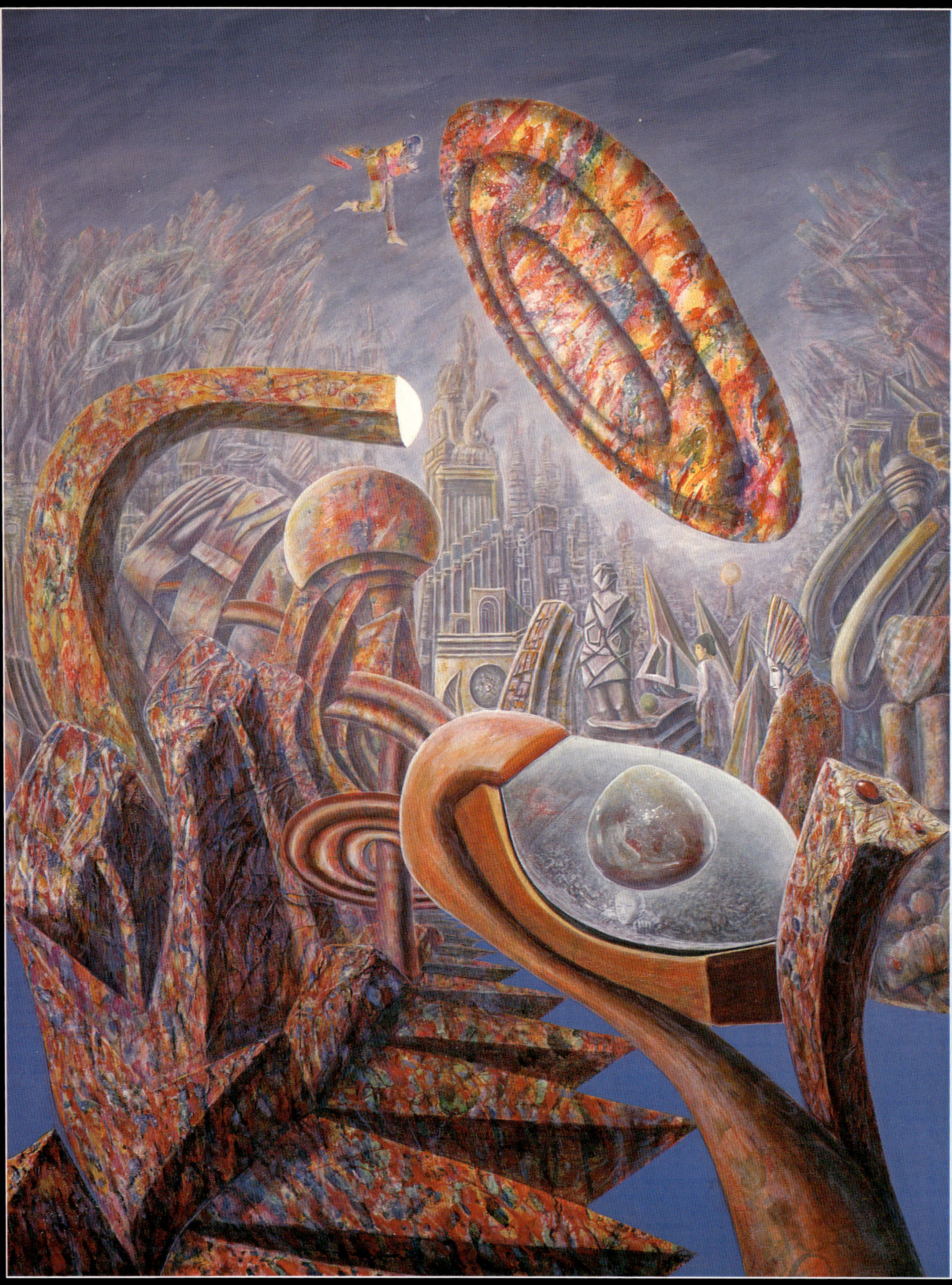

"Zero Gravity One," 48" x 60" oil, 1988

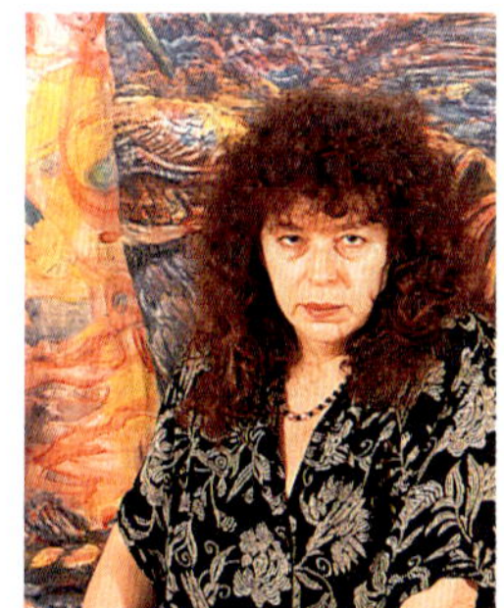

"LIFE IS INVENTIVE — CREATING MIMICS LIFE AND CREATES LIFE."
— *OLGA SPIEGEL*

OLGA SPIEGEL

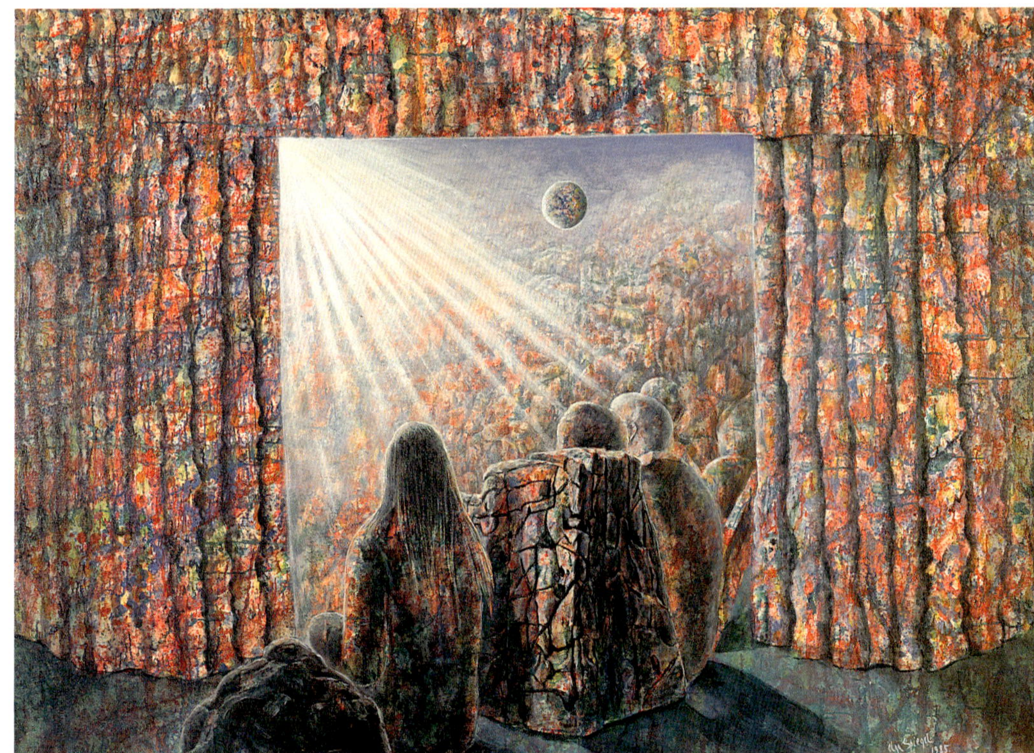

"Watching the Light," 86" x 62" oil, 1985. Collection of Randy Liebermann

Inspiration exists when the soul finds joy in the infinite. A spiritual traveler journeys through experiences. I am preoccupied with associations about nature in its multitude of forms, the Universe telling the story of life, an evolutionary unfolding of the mind. Improvisation is a tool to probe space and bring back images and concepts manifested through color, form and three dimensional illusions. Out of abstract layers of organic formation a more descriptive and symbolic imagery emerges.

Life is inventive — creating mimics life and creates life. My paintings focus on an inner process, an alchemical art of transmuting the higher self's messages to be deciphered through images and symbols, through improvisation; intuition is permitted to soar freely.

Paintings are poetic apparitions where the world is the kindling, consuming fire for the soul. I paint images as if they exist in front of my eyes, dreaming up forms and entire environments, a mysterious dreamland where shapes have no name and space has no reason, liberated from everyday imprinting, floating in a realm of pure imagination. Petrification and decomposure of matter is part of the pictorial search, a penetration on the cellular level extracting a meaning that infuses all things.

Nurtured by psychedelic art, European fantastic realism, surrealism and science fiction, for me, color plays a strong role, creating a scenario of elemental configurations.

With "Watching The Light," a stage is viewed from the public's perspective, the characters with their backs to the audience, looking at a beam of light and facing an inner landscape, alien, imbued with mystery — it's like the being looking at his beingness, his presence in a temporal place.

Looking at ourselves, looking at the light yet grounded on the stage of life, in perpetual evolution ... growth birth expansion evolution unfolding, voyage in search of past and future.

Light equals life. To speak in a universal tongue of futuristic dreams and furtive inklings of possible outcomes and multileveled civilizations bequeaths a promise of new life which inhabits the future, seeing the freedom beyond the stage.

Olga Spiegel
60 Lispenard Street
New York, NY 10013
Tel: (212) 925-0511

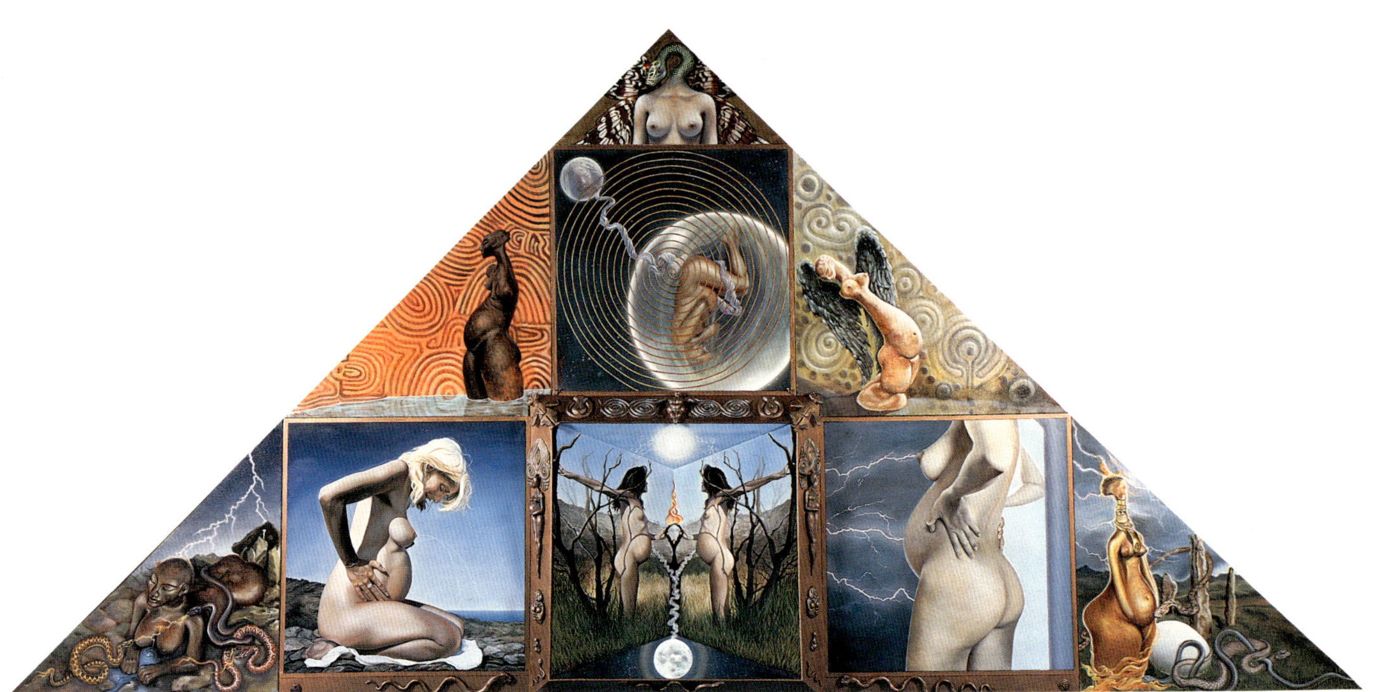

"The Goddess Triangle," 10′ x 20′ multi-media installation; oil, clay and sound by Martina Hoffmann, 1995

ACKNOWLEDGMENTS

This book was made possible by the generosity and contributions of each artist featured in this first volume of *One Source — Sacred Journeys.* The creating of this book has truly been a cooperative effort of all the artists involved. They have been gracious and open in sharing their art, stories and insights.

Ernst Fuchs, Ramon Kubicek, K. Martin-Kuri, Mary Carroll Nelson, Zannah and Nancy E. Levin all helped to write the forward and essays.

Philip M. Rubinov-Jacobson was a great help in bringing a vision into form by sharing his enthusiasm, insights, knowledge, writing and time.

A special mahalo to Aanjelae Rhoads, my partner in creating this book, for her vision, love and dedication.